After obtaining a de
having teaching expe
school, C. W. Valentine became a Foundation Scholar
of Downing College, Cambridge, and obtained first
class honours in Philosophy and in Psychology.

While a lecturer in St Andrews University he obtained the degree of Doctor in Philosophy of that University, for researches in psychology, and later was Professor of Education at the University of Birmingham from 1919 to 1946.

He was President of the British Psychological Society and President of the Psychology Section of the British Association for the Advancement of Science. He was the first editor of the *British Journal of Educational Psychology*, and held that office for twenty-five years. The *Journal* now goes to over forty countries throughout the world.

He wrote several books, including one on *The Psychology of Early Childhood* which was at once acclaimed as an authoritative work. The author also had long experience in the diagnosis and treatment of 'problem' children and dealt further with those aspects in his book *Parents and Children*. Another volume, *Psychology and its Bearing on Education*, has passed through many large editions, and his books have appeared in foreign editions. He died in 1964.

THE NORMAL CHILD

AND SOME OF
HIS ABNORMALITIES

———

A General Introduction to
the Psychology of Childhood
C. W. VALENTINE

———

PENGUIN BOOKS

Penguin Books Ltd, Harmondsworth, Middlesex, England
Penguin Books Inc., 7110 Ambassador Road, Baltimore, Maryland 21207, U.S.A.
Penguin Books Australia Ltd, Ringwood, Victoria, Australia

—

First published 1956
Reprinted 1957, 1960, 1962, 1963, 1964, 1966, 1967, 1968, 1970

—

—

Made and printed in Great Britain
by Cox & Wyman Ltd,
London, Reading and Fakenham
Set in Monotype Baskerville

CONTENTS

EDITORIAL FOREWORD   9

PREFACE   11

1. WHO (OR WHAT) IS 'NORMAL'?   13

The meaning of normality. The neurotic and unconscious influences. Dissociated influences in childhood. 'Normal' in the sense of 'average' or 'unselected'.

2. SOME APPARENT ABNORMALITIES IN ORDINARY CHILDREN   23

Obsessions. Nail-biting. The supposed relations of nervous habits or temperamental difficulties to breast-feeding. Marked emotional symptoms in very young children. The work of Gesell in the U.S.A. An inquiry as to emotional symptoms in infants. The passing of infantile emotional disturbances with increasing age. The frequency of undesirable behaviour in children as reported by parents. The frequency of maladjustment or neuroticism in children. Biographical and cross-section studies of children. Order of topics.

3. THE BASIC IMPULSE OF PLAY   47

The meaning of play. Maturation. Early social play. Make-believe play in the first two years. Supposed symbolic and fantasy interpretation of early play. Imaginary companions. Other play in later infancy. Some reports and interpretations of play. Dramatic play with dolls. Play in later childhood. The play of gifted children.

4. SELF-ASSERTION, ANGER, AND AGGRESSION   67

The beginnings of self-assertion. Assertiveness, competition, and individual differences. The rebellious period. Adler and the goal of dominating others. Assertiveness and the inferiority complex. The moral significance of aggression.

5

Contents

5. SYMPATHY AND THE IMPULSE TO HELP   80
Responsive laughter. Sympathy with distress. The impulse to help or protect. The frequency of sympathetic responses in infancy. Examples of sympathetic behaviour. Individual differences. The effects of experience and training.

6. BASIC AFFECTION, AND EARLY ATTITUDES TO PARENTS   94
Affection shown by babies to other babies. Early affection may be disinterested. The frequency of disinterested affection. Age of maturing of disinterested affection. Kissing as a learned sign of affection. Affection towards parents. The supposed Oedipus complex.

7. THE DEVELOPMENT OF SEX AND SEX INTERESTS IN CHILDHOOD   110
Curiosity about sex. The 'castration complex'. Erections and anticipatory development. Manipulation of the genitals.

8. INNATE AND ACQUIRED FEARS   123
The value of fear. The first innate fears. Fear of pain. Fear of the very strange and uncanny. Fear of the sea. Maturation and the fear of animals. Experiments with fear. Fear of the dark. Group studies of fears in infancy and middle childhood. School and home worries.

9. MOTIVATION AND ENVIRONMENTAL INFLUENCES   141
Learning and conditioning. The limitations of environmental influences. Prejudice against the idea of innate individual differences. Some illustrations of innate differences Some questions of innate differences on which there is substantial agreement. The trend of opinion on motivation. Generally recognized innate tendencies. Individual differences in innate tendencies. General emotionality and the intensity of drives. The unification of individual impulses in the whole personality.

Contents

10. IMITATION AND SUGGESTIBILITY 156

The main environmental influences. The role of imitation. Early examples of primary imitation. The scope of primary imitation. Suggestion and suggestibility. Suggestibility in infancy. Prestige and suggestibility. Influence of suggestion on conduct. Contra-suggestibility.

11. SOCIAL DEVELOPMENT AT SCHOOL 167

The pre-school child. Characteristic social behaviour in school for the years 2 : 0 to 5 : 0. The child in the infant school or first grade. The influence of the nursery school on early years in the primary school. Late entry to school. Reports on immediate effects of entrance to the primary school. Some types of teachers. Children's attitudes to teachers. The child and his fellow-pupils. Group play. Clubs and gangs. Sex grouping. Friendships and popularity. Sociometric studies. Limitations of group influences. The relation between popularity and personality traits.

12. MORAL BEHAVIOUR AND CHILDREN'S IDEALS 197

Moral habits. Objective tests of honesty and cheating. The heroes and ideals of children. Adventurous characters. Is there no advance in moral behaviour in middle childhood? Tests of character among gifted children. Individual and sex differences in character among gifted children. The growth of general ideas of right and wrong. First general concepts of right and wrong. The transition at adolescence. Children's ideas as to punishment. The effectiveness of different forms of punishment. The National Foundation research on rewards and punishments. Opinions as to rewards.

Contents

13. GENERAL INTELLIGENCE — NORMAL, SUB-
NORMAL, AND SUPER-NORMAL   222
*Popular misconceptions as to intelligence tests. General
intelligence and general ability. Non-verbal tests. The
correlation of orders or scores. The correlation of different
tests of abilities. The evidence of a general ability. Individual differences in general ability. Mental age. Intelligence quotient. The need of more than one testing. Group
and individual tests. The constancy of the intelligence quotient at different ages. Estimates of intelligence before
the age of 5. The maturing of innate general ability by
adolescence. The influence of general ability on school
work.*

14. SPECIAL ABILITIES AND INTERESTS   247
*The influence of interests. The influence of specific factors.
Independence of general and special abilities. Imagery —
visual and auditory. Musical abilities. Drawing. Verbal ability. The innate basis of specific verbal ability.
Vocabularies at various ages. Verbalism and fluency.
Number ability and mathematics. Mathematical geniuses. Practical ability. Interests in the school. Interests
outside school.*

15. THE ADOLESCENT CHILD   271
*The age of puberty. The attitude to the opposite sex.
Masturbation. Emotional experiences and fluctuations.
Other characteristics of adolescence. Are neurotic
symptoms normal in adolescents?*

BIBLIOGRAPHY   279

INDEX   284

'PSYCHOLOGY,' it has been said, and tediously repeated, 'merely reports what everyone knows in words that no one understands.' This is one of the oldest, and one of the least unkind, of the jibes directed at this science. Latterly the trend has been rather more offensive. It is not infrequently suggested that what psychology reports is just preposterous nonsense veiled by unintelligible jargon. No stick, it would seem, is too crooked for beating the wretched psychologist.

It is therefore a source of exceptional satisfaction to be able to introduce in this series of psychological Pelicans the work of an elder statesman of British Psychology in reference to whom any such jibe would be unthinkable. Emeritus Professor C. W. Valentine in the course of his distinguished career has contributed to the advance of psychology in works which range from the pure laboratory science to such peripheral studies as psychological aesthetics. His largest contribution has been to the psychology of childhood. He has written on things about which every parent and every teacher wants, or ought to want, to know; and he has written in words which no one can fail to understand.

This book has been written for this series expressly to answer a question of great concern to parents and teachers today: *Is this child 'normal' or shall I take him to the clinic?* Parents are worried by variations in rates of development. 'My child is nearly two, and still he does not talk! What *shall* I do?' They are worried if the child sucks his thumb. What on earth shall they do? They are worried, and so are the teachers, by the problems of discipline. They are unsettled, rightly or wrongly – partly rightly *and* partly wrongly – by the impressive impact upon methods of child-rearing in Western civilization of the doctrines of Sigmund Freud. They need reassurance and they need sensible guidance. William McDougall says somewhere that every psychologist ought to keep a dog. By parity of reasoning, it would surely be a good thing if every child psychologist himself had children. The author of this book meets this requirement. He writes not only as a psychologist but also as a parent. He has checked innumerable theories against careful observations of his own children, and against intimate records of his colleagues and friends. He is himself a teacher and has trained many teachers. So he understands the parents' and the teachers' point of view. He has studied Freud; but he has also studied children.

C. A. MACE

Preface

IN writing this book I have tried to keep several things in mind:

(1) To make it readable by an intelligent person who knew nothing about psychology except what he had picked up in the Press, which is often very misleading.

(2) To stress individual differences as normal and to show that many things thought by some (psychiatrists especially) to be signs of serious abnormality are not so.

(3) To make it comprehensive enough to be useful to teachers, training-college students, and Child Guidance Clinic and social workers or students, as a first introductory book on child psychology.

(4) To make it solid enough, and dealing sufficiently with procedure, to appeal to scholars in other subjects who want to know something about child psychology.

My warm thanks are due to Sir Cyril Burt, who has so generously read through the typescript and made many helpful comments, and to the general editor of this series, Professor C. A. Mace, for his final supervision of the book. I am also indebted to my son Hugh for help with the proofs.

C. W. VALENTINE

The White House, Wythall, near Birmingham
May 1955

CHAPTER I

Who (or what) is 'Normal'?

The meaning of normality. Any reader of this book is likely to have noticed in recent years many references, in newspapers and popular journals, to young delinquents, problem children, neurotics, and criminals with strange obsessions; and often these reports will have been accompanied by the remarks of some psychologist or psychiatrist (medical psychologist) stating that this or that type of conduct or emotional outburst was 'abnormal'. Hence the term 'abnormal' is usually taken to mean something extremely undesirable and unhealthy. The frequency of such reports in the press has also had the result that, in the eye of the general public, there has grown up an illusion that psychology is mainly concerned with the abnormal – a view which has been encouraged by the great interest roused by the work of Freud.

In this book we shall often have to refer to abnormalities in the child which imply something seriously wrong; but we shall be still more concerned with conduct or traits which may look strange but are only abnormal in the sense of unusual or differing greatly from the average.

The word 'norm' means a rule, standard, or average. In reference to measurable things, like the height or weight of, say, 10-year-old children, or even of their performance on some test of intelligence, the standard of normality is not difficult to determine. We have only to measure a large and representative sample of children of a given age in height or in any ability and we can calculate the average and regard the mass of children round that as 'normal'. Here 'normality' is a statistical concept: it is a question of frequency and averages. It should afford no great difficulty even for the layman to grasp this usage, though I have seen a letter in the daily press deploring the fact that the 'great majority' of children in this country are below normal intelligence. This is of course an absurdity, though the majority of children in a given slum area may be below the average or normal intelligence of the whole country.

Curiously enough, though the term 'normal' is often applied to intelligence, the term 'abnormal' is not. The term 'subnormal' is often used, and 'super-normal' sometimes. The fact that we can make so much more accurate estimates of intelligence than we can of emotional states or of social behaviour has led to the use of a grading scale. We find that there are no sudden jumps in the scores for intelligence tests, but gradual transitions: so much so that we can, with a fair degree of accuracy, separate children into about a dozen divisions in a scale of intelligence, which we might label idiot, imbecile, low-grade mental defective, high-grade mental defective, very dull, dull, average, slightly superior, very superior (or highly intelligent), brilliant, and perhaps genius. (For the frequency of the occurrences of different intelligence quotients in the population as a whole, see the table, p. 237.)

When, however, we come to problems of normal or abnormal behaviour, or of degrees of internal emotional disharmony, the correct or precise application of this term 'normality' is much harder, and finer grading is harder still.

We have to distinguish first between normal in the sense of average, and normal in the sense of not undesirable or unhealthy. Thus we might try to define the degree to which a normal individual at a given age may be expected to be attracted by the opposite sex. If this were concerned only with the variation in the 'strength' of the impulse we could describe the facts in such terms as 'highly sexed', 'under-sexed', etc., which would be equivalent to super-normal and sub-normal. But sex attraction varies in many other ways. If it is directed to a member of the same sex we regard this condition of 'homosexuality' as abnormal, in kind and not merely in degree. So too if sexual attraction is expressed, not in its usual form of tender behaviour, but in the infliction of pain on the loved object, we then describe such 'sadism' as an abnormality.

Again, as will be illustrated in detail later, what is abnormal at one age may be normal at another. Thus nail-biting, as we shall see, is rather more normal than abnormal about the ages of 9 to 12; but it is abnormal in adults; thumb-sucking and bed-wetting would be abnormal in an adolescent, but normal in both senses of the word in the mere infant.

To judge the normality of the whole personality is far from easy. A well-known British psychiatrist, giving evidence before a Royal Commission on punishment, was asked about the advisability of carrying out the death sentence when the prisoner showed 'some abnormality'. He replied, 'A good many people consider that normality is a myth, and personally I am not sure that it is not'; and he added: 'I cannot define a normal person.' One of the wisest of our British psychiatrists wrote: '. . . apart from definite mental disorder, the limits of mental abnormality are indefinable' [30].* He and a non-medical psychologist made a careful study of a thousand people in all walks of life – workers, clerks, students – all doing their ordinary work. They estimated that about 60 per cent showed some sign of mental ill-health or neurotic symptom – irrational fears or anxieties, obsessive thoughts or compulsive actions, and so on. On this reckoning, it is more normal in the statistical sense to be slightly neurotic than not! The fact is that there are many forms of highly *specific* abnormalities – or shall we say eccentricities? – one or other of which may appear in most people who, *on the whole*, appear normal. This, we shall find, seems to be true also of children.

* In this book a number given in square brackets refers to the book or article listed under that number in the Bibliography at the end of the book (p. 279).

15

Several other estimates by medical psychologists suggest that probably about one-quarter of the population reveal at least some neurotic symptom which would usually be called 'abnormal'. Incidentally, then, unless married people are better than the average, we should have between one-quarter and one-half of our families with one parent at least mildly neurotic. At first sight this seems a grave fact, as some forms of neurosis in a parent appear to be one factor in the production of some problem children. For example, I have known several cases of the following type. A mother who desired intensely that her coming baby should be a boy (or girl) and found herself disappointed, then allowed this so to spoil her affection for the child that she (or he) suffered gravely. We may fairly label such a mother as abnormal. In the case of one girl brought to me, I finally traced her emotional disturbance to her cold treatment by a neurotic mother, who had wished for a boy; but the father said that he dare not tell the mother as it would break up the home.

Two psychologists, indeed, who dealt with nearly 500 problem children, estimated that 41 per cent of the mothers were neurotic [7]. However, there are no doubt some forms of neurosis from which a parent can suffer without it affecting the relation with the child, so that some 'abnormal' parents may have quite 'normal' children.

Of course, in investigations of the type just described the numerical results depend on the varying interpretations the psychologists concerned may give to the terms 'mental ill-health' and 'neurotic'.

The neurotic and unconscious influences. Here it may be well to interpolate a note on the meaning of this term 'neurotic' as we shall have to use it occasionally in reference to children later. As to neurotics I can only give a brief description here, as we are concerned in this book with the normal child, and must only discuss the neurotic (or even the 'maladjusted', which is by no means the same) to bring out the contrast.

Nor can the topic be adequately treated without a much fuller exposition of the psychology of unconscious influences on thought, feeling, and action, for which the reader must be referred elsewhere [20, 39, 51, 88, 102, 104]. We can say briefly, however, that it is now generally agreed that a 'neurosis' is an emotional disturbance of a peculiar kind. Though 'neuron' means a nerve cell, the common phrase 'It's my nerves' is very misleading. A neurosis is the result of an emotional conflict within the individual. This may lead to repression and to irrational conduct, or to expressive symptoms, e.g. stammering or extreme outbursts of anger for apparently trivial reasons.

In one youth, for example, who stammered at certain words and could not overcome it by continued effort, I quickly found a clue when the first word at which he stammered when talking to me was the name of the house he lived in. From one of his parents I found that the home was a very unhappy one for him, and this was probably the source of the trouble (though he was unaware of it). This may fairly be called a neurotic symptom, though one would hardly call the youth neurotic as a whole.

The literature of neurosis is crowded with examples of excessive irrational fears, of exaggerated and even quite illusory ideas as to bodily illness, of violent antagonism to a certain type of individual (even when the particular individual has done the patient no harm), of constant states of anxiety when there is nothing in consciousness about which to be anxious, and so on – and these cases, by patient analysis, can very often be traced to earlier experiences which have been so repressed that they have been quite forgotten and yet continue to affect the social efficiency and happiness of the patient and to influence his behaviour under certain conditions.

As my first example of such unconscious influences I give the record of a case that has become almost a classic in the literature, and was dealt with by the late Dr W. H. R. Rivers, one of my own former teachers at Cambridge [88].

It is the case of a young medical officer who even before the war had a horror of closed-in spaces such as tunnels and small rooms. He would not travel by the tube railway. He suffered intense distress when on entering a dug-out he was given a spade and told it was for use in case he was buried alive. His sleep was greatly disturbed, and his health became so bad that he was invalided home. He had terrifying dreams from which he would awake, sweating profusely, and thinking he was dying. At this stage he came under the care of Dr Rivers. The patient was asked to try to remember any memories which came into his mind while thinking over the dreams. Shortly afterwards, as he lay in bed thinking over a dream, there came into his mind an incident which seemed to have happened when he was about 4 years of age, and which had so greatly affected him at the time that it now seemed to the patient almost impossible that it could ever have been forgotten. He recalled that as a little boy he and his friends used to visit an old man in a house near his own, and to take him odd articles discarded at home, in return for which they received a copper or two. On one occasion he went alone down the long, dark passage leading to the old man's home, and on turning back found that the door at the opening of the passage had banged to and he was unable to escape. Just then a dog in the passage began to bark savagely and the little child was terrified, and continued so until he was released. After another dream the patient woke up to find himself repeating 'McCann, McCann'. It occurred to him, suddenly, that this was the name of the old man. Inquiry of the parents of the patient revealed the fact that an old rag-and-bone man had lived in such a house as the patient remembered, and that his name was McCann.

The result of this recovery of memory, with the explanation of his abnormal fears of closed-in spaces, had a great effect on the patient. A few days afterwards he lost his fear of closed-in spaces, and he afterwards travelled in tube railways and tunnels without discomfort. Indeed, he was so confident of himself at once that he wished Dr Rivers to lock him up in some subterranean chamber of the hospital as a proof of his cure.

It is worth adding that this young medical officer had before the war been treated by a psycho-analyst along strictly Freudian lines, a search being made for some sexual origin of the claustrophobia, naturally without success. It had then proved impossible to get this early experience with the dog brought into consciousness.

In many such cases the laying bare of the original source of the trouble leads to immediate or almost immediate relief. True, one psychologist has recently collected evidence which suggests that the majority of cases cured by such psycho-analytic procedure would have eventually cured themselves without treatment [36]. Even if this were finally substantiated, however, I would suggest that one important thing is the time factor; it is surely of great value if the patient can be saved a year or even a few months of his trouble without waiting for spontaneous recovery.

Dissociated influences in childhood. The sceptical reader must be referred elsewhere for further evidence of the unconscious influence of experiences repressed to the extent of complete forgetting. They are much more evident in adults, who can also be relied on better to give accurate accounts of what they can and cannot recall than can children. In children, indeed, it seems probable that any repression, which is not entirely harmless, is more likely to lead merely to what we may call 'dissociation'. I may illustrate this first by the case of an adult with whom I dealt. A young woman, nearly 30 years of age, consulted me about recurring feelings of intense anxiety and fear. When she experienced these she had no idea what she was afraid of, but the emotion was intense. Inquiry and analysis revealed that she had been, as a girl, entirely ignorant about matters of sex development, and when menstruation began she was terrified. She thought she had some serious disease, but was too frightened to tell anyone and so endured this anxiety for a long time. Now, of course, before she came to me, she had long been fully aware of the naturalness of menstruation. But when she had learned the true facts about menstruation, in some mysterious way the fear at times recurred, and with some repression enough to keep out of the conscious mind the original cause of the fears. They were, in fact, when she came to me not fully forgotten, but the link between cause and effect had been broken. After this original cause had been revealed to her, she never again had a period of that intense meaningless fear; at least she had not had a recurrence when I saw her some half-dozen years later.

Now such 'dissociation' (without repression to the extent of entirely forgetting) seems to occur in the milder forms of neurosis and, I am inclined to think, may be especially characteristic of childhood. Thus I should agree with Burt's view that in childhood 'The distinction between conscious and unconscious is harder to draw. Children . . . are never quite so conscious, nor yet so completely unconscious, of their deeper motives and desires as adults often seem to be' [20].

Let me now give an example to illustrate how behaviour of a neurotic type can reveal itself in a child. A boy referred to me was very difficult at home and bullied his younger brother there. At the residential school he was quite pleasant to him but indulged in much excessive self-display. I found out that, in early years, he had been separated from his parents for some months in hospital and later feared he was being displaced by the baby brother in the affections of his mother. So far as there was a repressed fear resulting in excessive assertiveness and irrational behaviour, one may say it was a neurotic response. Indeed, even if the boy had not repressed from consciousness the thought of his earlier displacement in his mother's affections, and if there was only dissociation of that awareness, on the one hand, from his violent impulses on the other, still the behaviour might be regarded as of a neurotic type. In many cases, however, bullying and boasting assertiveness may be due merely, or largely, to excessively strong innate tendencies of assertiveness and aggression, in which case one would speak of 'maladjustment' rather than 'neuroticism'.

We shall see later that we may expect to find great individual differences in the strength of such innate tendencies; and the extremes may lead to trouble even where there is no repression or dissociation, and so nothing genuinely neurotic as we have defined it; maladjustment would be a better description. Yet excessively strong tendencies to assertiveness and aggression and extremely intense and frequent emotions of anger or fear may lead to conditions in which a neurosis is likely to be developed.

'Normal' in the sense of 'average' or 'unselected'. In psychological textbooks and in reports of researches as to children frequent use of the term 'normal' will be found in the sense of 'average' or 'unselected'. That would, of course, exclude children who had been removed from an ordinary school because of very low intelligence and placed in a special school; it would also exclude the children referred to a Child Guidance Clinic because of extremely bad behaviour or neurotic symptoms. It is with children in the unselected groups that this book is primarily to deal, though of course even within the large unselected groups in the ordinary schools we are likely to find a few children who will soon be 'selected' for special behaviour problems, and others who ought to be but have not yet been detected. It should be noted that the grammar schools contain children specially selected for good intelligence and good progress in school work. In some degree, therefore, they are, as a group, supernormal, though some grammar-school teachers would be surprised or even amused to hear it!

At all ranges of intelligence, among children not 'selected' (because of specially bad behaviour or of nervous habits or neurotic traits) for Child Guidance treatment, we shall meet with examples of the type of children already referred to, who possess to a most unusual degree some temperamental trait, apparently largely innate, e.g. in one child sympathy, in another aggressiveness. In the statistical sense both of these would be 'abnormal', but, while most clinical psychologists would apply the term 'abnormal' to the excessively aggressive child, they would not as a rule apply it to the highly sympathetic one – another illustration of the fact that the term 'abnormal' usually carries with it something derogatory, as well as implying something unusual.

CHAPTER 2

Some Apparent Abnormalities in Ordinary Children

THE only reliable way to decide what is normal (in the sense of usual or average) and what abnormal (in the sense of very unusual) in the development of the child is to study large groups of *unselected* children. That is equally important if we wish to show what traits or forms of behaviour are signs of present or future abnormality in the sense of highly undesirable. It is not satisfactory to study only those referred to Child Guidance Clinics as difficult children, nor is it satisfactory to inquire merely into the early history of children who have turned out badly. I wish to emphasize the importance of this study of unselected children *before their later development is known*, because there is a great danger of starting with your known delinquent or neurotic, and then inquiring into his temperamental traits and behaviour when he was a little child. No doubt we are often compelled to follow this latter method, and valuable information may sometimes be obtained in this way; but it is fatally easy for an investigator who already knows in what way an adult or adolescent is abnormal to surmise that there were certain corresponding weaknesses or symptoms during infancy that fit in with his own preconceived theory, and to get these recalled and perhaps exaggerated by parents, largely through the unintentional suggestion of the inquirer.

Furthermore, unless we have studies of unselected children, some traits found in certain problem children may be wrongly taken as signs of future maladjustment in others. I may illustrate this by an example.

Obsessions. I once heard a leading authority on Child Guidance work state that he had found one girl with a strange obsession. She felt that she must count the windows of every room she went into. The psychiatrist took this as evidence that she was abnormal or neurotic. Now I could remember that as a boy I had had some curious obsessions. For example, if I accidentally knocked my right elbow I was not comfortable until I knocked the left elbow! I had also noticed a number of such obsessions in children whom I did not think abnormal; so I felt very sceptical about the psychiatrist's conclusion as to the girl who counted the windows. Indeed, when I mentioned it at the family breakfast table my elder girl, aged about 12, said, 'That's nothing; whenever I see a Greek Key pattern I have to try to trace one with my tongue'! That daughter volunteered for service abroad in the A.T.S. and managed to rise to the rank of Junior Commander, so she hardly proved a neurotic. Later I made an inquiry among three large classes of university students, about 300 graduates in all. About 90 per cent reported that they had experienced such obsessive compulsions at one time or another; yet practically all of these students were sufficiently stable to carry on satisfactorily the difficult work of school-teaching practice under the critical eyes of tutors. Several other children I have known intimately were considerably troubled by such compulsions in later childhood (e.g. repeatedly shutting and re-shutting a door), yet they grew up to be thoroughly well balanced in temperament and character.

Again, in a recent book a medical psychologist gives the impression that, because *some* neurotic children had been reported as excessively conscientious at an early age, therefore any over-conscientious child is 'really presenting signs of mental illness'. Yet Freud himself uttered a warning against such illogical reversals. He wrote : 'Signs of childhood neuroses can be detected in *all* adult neurotics . . . *but by no means all children who show these signs become neurotic in later life.*' The seizing on over-conscientiousness as a sign of neurotic tendencies is another example of the danger mentioned at the beginning of this chapter, of inquiring into the infancy of children already known to be problem children or neurotics and noting what seem like peculiarities in them, and then assuming that such peculiarities can always be taken as an indication that the child is or will become a problem child.

Nail-biting. Some extensive records on nail-biting provide us with another remarkable example of the danger of assuming that a so-called 'nervous' habit is a sign of general abnormality. One will often find nail-biting listed as a notable characteristic of problem children, especially of the 'nervous', anxious, or depressed type. In a book on Child Psychiatry by a group of psychiatrists one of the supposed experts writes that: 'The child who, as an infant, felt deprived and insecure, having been frustrated in its strong suckling interest, is liable to develop compensatory habits as it grows up – thumb-sucking, nail-biting, excessive sweet-eating, for example.' In another recent report a psychiatrist included nail-biting under 'Neurotic Symptoms'.

Yet an American psychologist who gathered reports of unselected children in school found that, among children of about 15 years of age, nearly one-third still bit their nails, and over one-third had done so previously. In other words, two-thirds of all pupils in representative high schools either were or had been nail-biters. So it was really more normal to be a nail-biter at some age than not. This seems a very high percentage, but the findings were supported and amplified by two other investigators [79] who obtained observations on 4,587 school pupils in Chicago, ages 5 to 18. In the youngest group nail-biting was not common, but of 346 boys of ages 8, 9, 10, and 11 about two-thirds were nail-biters. For girls of the same ages the percentage was slightly less. Of all the nail-biters nearly half bit their nails severely and on all fingers; only one-quarter were classed as biting 'mildly'.

These American figures were so striking that I thought it well to make an inquiry among English children, also unselected. A preliminary inquiry in a rural mixed primary and secondary school (ages 5 to 15) showed an average of about 45 per cent as finger-nail biters for all the 272 children, the peak being in two classes, ages 11 to 13, when it reached about 57 per cent. Of nearly 100 children, ages 11 to 16, about 34 per cent bit their nails 'severely', as I should call it, i.e. right down to the quick. (In this Church of England school one teacher had given her class of 9-year-olds a talk about Lent and told them she was going to give up sweets. When later she examined one little boy's nails, she said, 'Oh, Johnny, you still bite them badly, don't you?' 'Yes, Miss,' he replied, 'but I'm giving it up for Lent.')

Inquiries in a mixed junior school gave similar results.

In a girls' grammar school in a small town in the north of England, even at the age of 12 there were 56 per cent nail-biters.

Much larger figures were provided for me by my friend and former student Major L. B. Birch, who had begun an inquiry chiefly in or near a large town in the north of England. This covered 2,350 children in schools of all types. For all ages combined (nearly all between 5 and 16) the figures were: boys, 54 per cent nail-biters at that time; girls, 46 per cent. The percentages for the various ages were fairly steady from 8 to 14. There was a slight peak for 295 boys at 12, when 62 per cent were nail-biters, and for 122 girls at 11, when 51 per cent were nail-biters. Again, of these boys of 12, 40 per cent bit their nails *severely*, and 32 per cent of the girls of 11 did so [9A].

In this city and district at least there was no evidence that nail-biting increased at 10, the age when many children were specially preparing for the entrance examination to the grammar schools.

Nail-biting is no doubt a very deplorable habit, and we may admit that in some cases it may be a symptom of excessive tension. One investigator in a clinic found that friction in the family was more frequent among seventy-five problem children who bit their nails than it was among seventy-five other problem children who did not bite their nails. But so far as these American and English school children were concerned it clearly could not be taken in itself as a sign of abnormality in the sense of diverging markedly from the average. As to the supposed sexual significance of nail-biting or thumb-sucking I shall have something to say in a later chapter.

The supposed relation of nervous habits or temperamental difficulties to breast-feeding. As already indicated, some psycho-analysts regard nail-biting and thumb-sucking as due to frustration in suckling, the deprivation of breast-feeding, or too sudden weaning. Here again it is so easy to find *some* problem children who have been bottle-fed and connect their behaviour with some supposed frustration; but the only scientific thing to do is to take a large group of unselected children and collect the facts about them. One such inquiry deserves reporting here. It was made about 162 children of ages 5 : 0 and 6 : 0 in middle-class American families, all 'unbroken' homes. Of these children it was found that sixty had been exclusively breast-fed and forty-three exclusively bottle-fed. Very thorough methods were followed to get good estimates as to such children: viz. (1) interviews with the mother by a skilled investigator; (2) tests of personality by a trained clinician during the first year of school; (3) assessments by teachers of the children's emotional adjustment, etc.

The results of this inquiry are on the whole decidedly against the view that absence of breast-feeding and sudden weaning are harmful to the children or lead to more frequent nervous habits such as nail-biting, stuttering, or finger-sucking even as late as 5:0 or 6:0. The authors [91] are moderate in their conclusions and applied rigid methods of statistical calculation to determine what difference, if any, occurred so frequently that the odds were overwhelmingly against the difference being due to mere chance. But practically no such differences were found; and indeed, so far as the figures go, there was rather a bigger proportion of breast-fed babies than of bottle-fed who indulged at 5:0 or 6:0 in nail-biting; and a bigger proportion of the gradually weaned than the suddenly weaned were nail-biters and stutterers. The results were similar for emotional adjustment as judged by the teachers.

In a similar inquiry among eighty children aged 2 to 7 it was found that the amount of thumb-sucking was not related either to the age of weaning or to the manner – sudden or gradual. Yet another investigator supported this finding, but did find that thumb-sucking in infants from 4 to 6 years of age was less frequent in those who had been provided with dummy teats. This is readily understandable, as the habit of sucking would become attached specifically to the dummy, which would later on tend to be sometimes not at hand, and so the habit would be broken. My mother told me, I regret to report, that I continued to suck a dummy until I was over 2. Then one day in a train I threw it out of the window. My mother then pointed out it was gone for ever – and she said I never asked for it again.

I may add that the two last inquiries, one made in the U.S.A. and the other in Sweden, agree in reporting that about 40 per cent of the infants between 2:0 and 7:0 indulged in thumb-sucking.

Marked emotional symptoms in very young children. Many parents and even teachers seem to be unduly concerned or annoyed by the extreme emotional behaviour, aggressiveness, or 'nervousness' even in very little children, or by their extreme restlessness, lethargy or laziness, 'nervous habits', and so on. I have known some well-educated parents to be greatly relieved when told that it was the usual thing for a child to pass through a very naughty and often rebellious period between the years of about 2 to 5, and indeed that there is some evidence that it is rather a good than a bad sign, giving

28

promise of a persistence and a firmness of character at adolescence.

While the reaction from Victorian ideas of strict discipline towards more freedom for the child has gone too far in many quarters, there are still many parents and teachers who expect too quickly in children an adjustment to adult standards. The gem of my examples of this is the actual report of a nursery-school teacher on a little boy of 3 years to the effect that he was 'lacking in leadership'! But for the moment let us consider not merely good or bad behaviour, but the more intimate personal emotional adjustments, the lack of which may be revealed in fears, extreme shyness, general anxiety, nervous habits, and so on.

To illustrate the *possibility* of such extreme emotional behaviour and symptoms revealing themselves in little children who afterwards develop successfully, I venture first to give brief notes on three of my own children. As I shall give many more examples from records on my own children later in this book I want to emphasize at once that we cannot, of course, regard a few examples as evidence of general tendencies. For that we must have records of many children representative of all types and social conditions, etc. But personal examples may serve as illustrations of types of behaviour, and indeed they can at least show that it is *possible* for certain disturbing traits revealed at, say, 2 years of age, to be consistent with satisfactory development later.

Here then I give, as to three of my children, records of emotional outbursts which were certainly disturbing at the time:*

1. There were fairly frequent violent tempers shown by one of our boys at about the age of 1 : 6 to 2 : 6. Sometimes he would roll on the ground screaming with apparent rage merely through the frustration of what seemed a trivial wish.

---

* Here, and throughout this book a recognised convention is followed for expressing age; thus 1:6 stands for one year and six months.

This behaviour, however, proved consistent with development into an exceptionally equable temperament in young manhood.

2. Hysterical night fears (seeing 'horrid' faces, etc) were experienced by one of our little girls at about 5 : 0. They were very troublesome over a considerable period. These night fears proved consistent, not only with a marked stability of emotion later but with an unusual absence of fears of all kinds – darkness, animals, rough seas, burglars, and with a passion for aeroplane flying. She was, indeed, the A.T.S. officer already referred to. Yet I find that the director of a Child Guidance Clinic declares that night fears are the sign of a 'nervous' child!

3. An outburst of violent temper in our other little girl, Y, noted at about 2 : 6, in which she struck a maid with a knife and afterwards boasted, 'I did bleed her!' Yet this girl grew up to be extremely sympathetic to pain in other people and in animals.

To these cases I may add another of a person well known to me. She reports that she had marked night fears about the age of 7 or 8 and was in particular terrified by the sight of the moon. Yet at 19 years she was a nurse in a mental hospital, sometimes being responsible alone for guarding a room with dangerous patients in it; and she was so confident and successful as to be promoted to be a Sister at a very early age, and later a Matron.

Now let us turn to the reports of observations as to typical emotional behaviour on large groups of unselected infants, ages 2 to 6. As a first sample I may mention that in one American investigation among over 300 children of 'pre-school age', about whom the mothers did not think they needed any psychological help or advice, it was found that over 90 per cent presented one or more of the following symptoms: temper tantrums, food refusal, enuresis, lack of bowel control, breath-holding or mouthing, finger-sucking, manipulation of genitals, vomiting. Temper tantrums were found in about half. The normality of such behaviour in early years is more reliably established, as we shall now see, by other investigators.

The work of Gesell in the U.S.A. The great pioneer work of Dr Arnold Gesell and his collaborators in the U.S.A. has substantially added to our knowledge of average normal children, especially during the first five years of life. Here, for example, are some descriptions of typical traits of unselected, presumably normal, children drawn from middle-class houses:

At 2 years: There is little give-and-take in play, but much physical snatch-and-grab, and kicking and pulling hair.

The typical 4-year-old: Quarrelsome; boasts and threatens [41].

The typical 6-year-old: Highly emotional. There is a marked disequilibrium between the child and others. Lack of integration. Tends to go to extremes; oscillates. He may say 'I love you' at one minute and shout 'I hate you' the next. He reacts with his whole action-system. He does not only smile – he fairly dances with joy. He cries copiously when unhappy, kicks and shakes with his grief [43].

Gesell's numbers (fifty children in each age group) were not, I think, sufficient to justify some of his generalizations about marked fluctuations from year to year. But we can accept his report as to the main characteristic behaviour and temperament traits of these groups of fifty children at the ages of 2, 4, and 6. Taken in conjunction with other records I shall give and others for which I have not space, we have sufficient evidence at least to say that difficult behaviour, extreme temper, undue fears and anxiety, etc., are very common at these early ages in groups of unselected children who might reasonably be labelled average or normal. At least they were not selected for study *because* they were troublesome; and the fact that they came from middle-class rather than economically poorer homes accentuates if anything the significance of their unstable behaviour.

It is, however, regrettable that in some of the work of

Gesell's collaborators precise statistical statements are not made. We may mention one extensive report based on the careful study of 210 children of the age of $3\frac{1}{2}$, drawn chiefly from upper-middle-class homes, and with intelligence as a group above the average. Unfortunately the investigators give no numerical estimates of the frequency of the various traits noted or their degree. This lessens the value of their general summary that: 'This is an age of many and intense tensional outlets. Not only stuttering but eye-blinking, nail-biting, thumb-sucking, nose-picking, rubbing of genitals, chewing at garment or sheet, excessive salivation, spitting, tics, and simple compulsive patterns occur. The frequent whining which occurs at this age may also be considered a tensional outlet.'

Yet even such general reports have their value in their bearing on some studies of children living under abnormal conditions. Thus the following is worth considering with the reports of harmful insecurity experienced by little children separated for a time from their parents. Even of these 210 children in ordinary homes it is reported that: 'The child seems to feel extremely insecure emotionally. Parents often feel that the child is "insecure". The child seems to be much concerned about the parents' attitude towards him. He asks his parents frequently, "Do you love me?" He does not allow the parent to laugh at him; the child's feelings are easily hurt, particularly when he is excluded by contemporaries in play. Night-time requests for lights on and doors open frequently begin at this age, and nightmares are sometimes reported.'

An inquiry as to emotional symptoms in infants. More precise figures are given in another investigation made in England, and this is perhaps the inquiry of the greatest interest for our present purpose. It was made on 239 children (ages 2 to 7) in Leicester in nursery classes and infant schools.

The survey was concerned with emotional symptoms of a type which *might* be thought abnormal under certain conditions; but no attempt was made to label them normal or abnormal, healthy or neurotic. Furthermore, when reports were made on such traits as restlessness or excessive shyness, due regard was paid to the fact that extremes in such matters are more likely to be found in such very young children than in older.

Nineteen teachers volunteered to make special notes, on record forms, of children in their classes for a month under the instruction and supervision of the psychologist, Mrs Jean D. Cummings [31]. They included the following:

Incidence of Emotional Symptoms (Grouped)	*Percentage Frequency*
Excitability, restlessness	28·9
Day-dreaming, lack of concentration, laziness	28·9
Generalized anxiety, timidity or shyness	23·0
Specific fears	22·2
Poor bladder control, frequency of micturition	21·3
Nervous habits, including nail-biting	18·0
Cruelty, aggression	15·1
Speech difficulties	14·2
Lack of appetite, food faddiness	11·3
Babyish behaviour, frequent crying	11·3
Lying, stealing	10·1
Tendency to constipation, headache, stomach-ache	9·2
Obstinacy, disobedience	8·8
Bedtime problems	7·1
Undesirable sex habits	6·3
Easily and frequently tired	4·6
Obsessions	4·2
Hysterical outbursts	4·2

It was found that practically every child revealed two or more of these emotional symptoms, the average being over three for each child. Paradoxically, then, it would seem quite normal in the statistical sense for a child at this early period to be apparently maladjusted and, as some would say (in another sense), abnormal.

Some of the more striking results found by Mrs Cummings were as follows:

1. Boys show significantly more symptoms than girls. Boys are shown to be more aggressive, cruel, and obstinate than girls, and also to be more lacking in concentration. Girls tend to be more fearful of animals and more fearful generally.

2. Comfort habits (thumb-sucking, sucking bricks, etc.) tend to decrease with age, but there may be a regression at 5 (figures only suggestive).

3. Parents could in thirty-five cases be roughly classified into two groups: the neglectful or frequently absent parents and the over-anxious or spoiling parents. There was a significant difference in the types of symptoms shown by the children of the two groups. Over-protected children showed more 'nervous' symptoms than neglected children. Neglected children, on the other hand, were more anti-social in that they were more frequently described as aggressive, cruel, and addicted to lying.

The passing of infantile emotional disturbances with increasing age.
Later on Dr Cummings was able to make follow-up studies of 145 of her children previously observed, and reports were made six months after the original reports, and again eighteen months later [32]. Dr Cummings herself discussed each case with the teachers concerned, to keep the standards the same as far as possible; but of course precision in such cases is extremely difficult.

The following were the most interesting results discovered:

1. Over a period of eighteen months there was a gradual fading out of symptoms of emotional disturbances for the majority of children; seventy-eight children showed improvement. Of these twenty-four were 'very greatly improved'; thirty-six showed no improvement, three of them some deterioration or the appearance of additional symptoms.

2. There was a difference, which statistically was highly significant (the odds being nearly 100 to 1 against the difference being due to chance), between the improvement of the children under 5 and those of 5 to 7 inclusive. Of the children of 5 and over, only 18 per cent showed improvement after six months, and 53 per cent showed improvement after eighteen months. Younger children attending nursery classes seem, therefore, to have more chance of recovering from emotional difficulties than do older children showing the same difficulties. It is not certain whether this would be true of pre-school children generally, since one cannot be certain that nursery-class children are truly representative.

3. Speech difficulties disappear only slowly.

4. Day-dreaming, or lack of concentration, seemed to be very resistant to change.

5. Among children showing anti-social behaviour (aggression, stealing, cruelty) there was a very great improvement in the younger children after eighteen months.

6. Specific fears (of animals, other children, etc.) seemed transitory.

It should be emphasized that the children below 5 were in nursery classes, and therefore in the school all day, with more individual attention. I should also add that, though the children were described as 'unselected', those in the Infant School were taken from the 'B' stream classes as being nearer the average in intelligence. The whole group included eleven who seemed to be seriously disturbed, i.e. genuine problem children, and only four of these showed improvement at the end of the eighteen months. One other general point is worth noting: in some cases one symptom disappeared only to be replaced by a different one.

I quote the description of two cases of particular interest. P, a boy of 6 at the time of the first recording, was described as excitable, aggressive towards the other children, fidgety and lazy in class, and very difficult at home, where his mother said she 'could do nothing with him'. His mother worried unduly about him because of a history of bronchitis and pneumonia, and P apparently played on this obvious anxiety. He was very food-faddy and lacking in appetite. He would show off a great deal, but was nevertheless popular because of his abundant energy. He suffered from disturbed sleep at home, but the nature of the disturbance was not known to the teacher. The teacher described him as 'lovable, but needing firm handling'.

After six months he was still very excitable, still suffered from sleep disturbances, and was still rather aggressive towards the other children, though a little improved in this respect. After eighteen months, at $7\frac{1}{2}$ years, sleep disturbances had apparently cleared up; he was now very popular and not at all aggressive. He had made good progress in school work. Altogether, he seemed to have improved considerably. Yet his excitability remained very noticeable and he was very much the showman, described by the teacher as often 'silly and self-conscious'.

My own interpretation would be that he was probably innately highly emotional – a point which will be discussed in a later chapter.

K was a girl of 4:1, a child who had had a very bad beginning at school. For a full month she cried every day and all day except when asleep after dinner. She would be interested in a toy for a few minutes, then wander to the window to look for her mother and start crying again. Her mother was in the habit of leaving K alone in bed in the afternoon and going out, never putting her to bed (to sleep) until 10 p.m. at the earliest. K was described as very nervous and tired, always wanting to be picked up and nursed, crying and asking for her mummy perpetually. The mother was evidently antagonistic to the school to some extent and made such remarks as 'You don't like school, do you, K?'

There is no record of K at the end of six months (the teacher was away at this time), but after eighteen months (at 5:7) she was very well settled in school, able to concentrate in her play and thoroughly happy. Yet her mother apparently still left her alone in the house and there was no obvious change in the home situation. It must be taken into account that in this case the school provided a very much needed security – companionship, free play (K played end-lessly with dolls when finally she did start to play), and a teacher who was at great pains to encourage her and give her confidence. Much of the therapeutic practice of a clinic was, Dr Cummings considered, in this case provided by the teacher and the school.

Summing up the results of Dr Cummings' inquiry we may say that all these children of ages 2 to 7 revealed some symp-toms disturbing and undesirable in the minds of the teachers concerned. On the average they showed more than three of the symptoms each; none is reported as showing only one, so that we cannot say that, for a child in this age group, to reveal a few of these symptoms is unusual or 'abnormal'. In-deed, a child who did not show one would be 'abnormal' in the statistical sense of the term. We have to admit, however, that such emotional symptoms might be less frequent in some homes with different training or in some schools with different atmospheres. On the other hand, in some other schools and homes the symptoms might be even more fre-quent. The fact, however, that so many of the symptoms passed away as the children grew from 3 or 4 to 5 or 6 years of age is encouraging.

One other point must be mentioned about these results: the 239 children would probably include a few who could properly be labelled neurotic or, better, maladjusted to a sufficient degree to need more special treatment in a Child Guidance Clinic. Indeed, Dr Cummings herself, as we have seen, found eleven children whom she described as seriously disturbed, only four of whom showed definite improvement at the later time of recording, and one of those had been receiving treatment at a clinic. There may have been a few others who were future problem children who helped to send up the average. But substantially the records may be taken as fairly representative for children of these ages and from these types of schools.

The frequency of undesirable behaviour in children as reported by parents. Dr Cummings' inquiry was concerned only with children up to the age of 7 and with emotional symptoms as reported by teachers. Accordingly it is well to supplement it with a valuable inquiry made in the U.S.A., in which reports were made by parents and the age range of the children was from 3 to 18 [71].

A questionnaire giving descriptions of fifty-six different types of 'undesirable behaviour' was sent to parents, who were asked to report which of them were shown by their own children. The replies were anonymous so that parents could reply freely. Most of the parents were reached through parent-teacher associations or child-study clubs, so that in a sense the parents were a selected group, though they included very varied social ranks.

Two hundred and seventy-five families co-operated in the study, giving records of 338 children. Two-thirds of the replies came from urban centres. The fathers of the children were engaged in eighty-five different occupations. The reports used in the study represent children from 3 to 18 years of age, 80 per cent of whom were under 12 years of age. Almost exactly half were boys. About 23 per cent of the children were only children; about 37 per cent had one brother or sister; and about 40 per cent had two or more. Practically no difference from the averages were found in the reports on only children.

In view of the obvious importance of the age of the child in judging behaviour I give first some selected figures for the various age groups. (Unfortunately the author does not state the numbers in each group, except that there were only 65 children over 12.)

Note the big drop in temper tantrums after the period 3 to 5, and in bed-wetting also after the period 3 to 5, when it appeared in nearly one-fifth of the children. At 7 : 0

to 10:0 it only appears in 2·6 per cent, so can certainly be taken as abnormal at that age; so can the thumb-sucking of the 2 per cent in the 14 to 18 group.

Percentage of children showing the forms of behaviour which were much more frequent at certain ages than at others

Behaviour	Age group, in years				
	3–5	*5–7*	*7–10*	*11–14*	*14–18*
Disobedience	46·6	52·6	39·8	33·3	28·0
Temper tantrums	24·4	10·5	9·7	5·6	4·0
Shy, uncommunicative	0·0	7·9	7·1	20·4	20·0
Thumb-sucking	20·0	10·5	13·3	5·6	2·0
Bed-wetting	17·8	9·2	2·6	1·8	0·0
Many fears	11·1	14·5	23·0	7·4	10·0
Over-conscientiousness	4·4	15·8	18·6	37·8	14·0

We have to bear in mind that the above records are only of what these parents considered undesirable behaviour, and of course their standards would vary. But the general reliability of their reports and soundness of their attitudes are strongly suggested by some of the figures given. For example, note the large number of children reported at 11 to 14 (and even adjoining ages) as being over-conscientious – a trait which thoughtless parents, who only considered their own comfort, would surely think most desirable!

In view of several other investigations, the report of temper tantrums in only 24 per cent of the children of 3 to 5 also suggests that these parents made due allowance for these little children and only reported rather extreme tantrums. That suggests that the 4 per cent who showed such tantrums at 14 to 18 are really abnormal, though we have to bear in mind that the parents reporting on the later ages would not all be among those reporting on the earlier ages.

The only other very high figures not given in the table above were 'resisting bedtime', 43·6 per cent at 11 to 14; 'whining', 30 per cent at 5 to 7, and 24 per cent at 3 to 5 and even at 7 to 10; 'many fears', nearly 40 per cent at 7 to 10, 'specific nervous habits', about 24 per cent at 11 to 14. As we give a special chapter to adolescence later, the most frequent items are worth noting for 14 to 15, viz. 'very shy : too restrained', 20 per cent; 'over-self-confident', about 14 per cent.

The great majority of the children – 80 per cent – were reported as showing from one to ten forms of undesirable behaviour, but some showed twenty or more of the items. A 'small number' were considered to have none. Perhaps these few paragons of all the virtues had mothers who were very lenient in their judgements. As already stated, we cannot get away from the fact that all these reports depend on the standard of conduct set in the minds of the parents, though some of the items deal with plain matters of fact, e.g. bed-wetting, thumb-sucking, and fears.

What we can safely conclude is that among this large sample of American mothers all or nearly all find a number of forms of undesirable behaviour in their children, and some of these forms are reported of a substantial proportion (from a third to a half) of all the children, in spite of the large age range.

I append below a brief list of some of the methods adopted by these parents for dealing with the misdemeanours.

Parents' methods of dealing with misdemeanours

	Per cent
Reason at length with child	41·3
Scold; tell child emphatically what he must do	12·0
Ignore completely; let child choose his own course	11·3
Make child feel ashamed of his behaviour	10·9
Reward, praise, promise extra favours	9·0
Make special effort to cultivate companionship with the child	9·0

Unfortunately the report does not give separately the treatments adopted for the different ages; massing all the children together, the report shows that by far the commonest method adopted was 'reasoning at length with the child' (41 per cent). Then come the other methods listed above, adopted in 9 per cent or more of the cases. 'Spanking' was mentioned by only 5·7 per cent of the parents.

The frequency of maladjustment or neuroticism in children. Among the American children referred to in the preceding section a few might be seriously maladjusted or neurotic; among Dr Cummings' infants, as we saw, it appeared that eleven, or between 4 and 5 per cent, were 'seriously disturbed'. This fits in closely with previous estimates as to the frequency of seriously maladjusted children among the normal school population. Here we have no better guide than Sir Cyril Burt, who made such extensive studies of many hundreds of school children in London. He estimated that of the general school population about 4 per cent of the children showed neurotic symptoms so marked as to need immediate special treatment, and a further 13 per cent showed symptoms sufficiently severe to warrant further investigation. Other investigations in England and the U.S.A. suggest that the definitely neurotic children of school age are about 5 per cent. A more recent estimate by Burt as to the frequency of maladjustment (rather than neurosis) gives, for London, 10 per cent as cases of *mild* maladjustment, such as might be adequately dealt with by the teacher or social worker or family doctor; and about 2 per cent cases of severe maladjustment (or 3 per cent if delinquents are included) which need the attention of a specially qualified psychologist [22].

If we take the estimate of 3 per cent for serious maladjustment, and another, say, 10 per cent as doubtfuls, that would mean that on the average teachers of classes of forty children or over would have one or two seriously maladjusted (possibly neurotic) children in the class, and another four as doubtfuls – which is bad enough.

Nevertheless, in the records we have already quoted of

unselected children, e.g. as to nail-biting or the various emotional disturbances reported by Dr Cummings, or of the undesirable behaviour reported by the American parents, we still have very big groups of children showing emotional disturbances, or nail-biting or other undesirable nervous habits or behaviour, even if we first deduct 5 per cent or even 10 per cent as possible neurotics or maladjusted, so that these various weaknesses are normal in the sense of usual or frequent.

It seems, then, that, though the number of children who are seriously maladjusted or 'neurotic' is very small, the great majority reveal at some time some symptoms which, if carried to extremes or continued beyond very early years, might be considered by some psychologists as signs of serious maladjustment or even neurosis, but which are so frequent, and yet usually so transitory, as to be 'normal' in the sense of usual and nothing much to worry about.

This needs emphasizing again because some child psychologists of considerable reputation, especially psychoanalysts (followers of Freud) have tended to exaggerate the importance of such emotional symptoms. Thus the late Dr Susan Isaacs claimed that: 'Few people would deny the term "neurotic" to the phobias and night-terrors, to nail-biting and excessive masturbation in young children'; and she adds: 'I find it hard to recall, from twenty years' study, more than a handful of children known intimately who have not at least minor and transitory signs of neurotic conflict at one point or other of their early development' [58].

Now, Dr Susan Isaacs won a reputation for the practical handling of young children, as well as for her books on the psychology of childhood; but her theoretical interpretation of child behaviour was, in my opinion, warped by her too ardent Freudianism, and she, like others I have mentioned, often read meanings into the actions of little children which were rather far-fetched and could be more readily explained on everyday common-sense grounds as we shall see in later chapters.

In any case, the list given by Mrs Isaacs of neurotic traits in children under 6 or 7 includes the following: difficulties in relation to authority, such as excessive defiance or stubbornness; failure to respond to training in cleanliness; thumb-sucking and nail-biting; difficulties with regard to food and feeding; aggressiveness, jealousy, shyness, destructiveness, stammering, sleeplessness, and unwillingness to be left alone. But, as we have seen, one or more of these appeared in every one of a large group of *unselected* children; and these symptoms usually disappeared, merely in the course of a year or two's normal development and training in school, in the majority of young children, especially those in nursery schools or in good homes. As to nail-biting, labelled definitely 'neurotic' by Dr Isaacs, we have seen that at some time or another it is indulged in by some 55 or 60 per cent of school children, even at the age of 9 or 10 and beyond. So for children as well as adults it is apparently more normal (in the sense of usual) to be somewhat neurotic than not in Dr Isaacs' interpretation of the term. In fact, of course, it points to the desirability of confining the term 'neurotic' to that very small minority of children whose conduct seems almost completely dominated by motives of which they seem unconscious or only half-conscious, including those extremely diffident children who seem in a constant state of intense anxiety about nothing apparent.

Before we close this chapter a word might be said about the importance of the age at which an extremely emotional, or 'nervous', supposedly neurotic symptom occurs. This relation to the age varies greatly in importance according to the different symptoms. Thus, as we have seen, nail-biting is actually more frequent at the age of 10 or 12 than it is at the age of 5; consequently there is no reason to be more perturbed about it in a child of 10 than in a child of 5. It is quite different, however, with, say, bed-wetting (enuresis). About 30 per cent of children achieve bladder control by the age of 18 months; about 70 per cent by 2 years, and the great majority by 3 : 0. Burt found that only about 3 per cent of children of school age revealed it during peace-time, though this increased to about 7 per cent among children evacuated from bombed areas. Enuresis, then, may be regarded as 'normal' for the child of 18 months, very common at 2 years; but after 3 years one would regard it as symptomatic, in many cases caused by anxiety; the increase of enuresis among evacuated children suggested that the anxiety due to removal from parents and homes was greater than that due to the bombs.

Broadly speaking, we may say that on the whole the uncontrolled expression of violent emotions and unprovoked aggressions get rarer as normal children grow older, and socially approved behaviour increases with experience and training. Under some special stress, however, a child may 'regress' to more infantile behaviour; for a time the child of 10 may act in a way typical of the average child of, say, 8 or 7. Now, any normal child may so regress for a time; indeed, many adults when extremely irritated or very angry may regress to conduct at the level of childhood or even infancy. But when a child of 10 constantly behaves in ways and exhibits emotional reactions typical of a child of 8 or 7, then we regard him as emotionally immature.

For the present we must be content with this very general and vague statement. We can only fill in the concrete details in the study of particular tendencies and emotions in later chapters.

Biographical and cross-section studies of children. Here let me interpolate that, while I shall often supply illustrations of types of play, imitation, emotional development, innate impulses, and so forth in the very early years from notes on my own children, ample confirmation of these various activities will be found in the valuable records of other psychologists who have made careful notes on the early development of their own children. Over a score of these now exist, including detailed records not only by British and American, but by French, German, Danish, and Japanese psychologists. I shall sometimes use their reports, but for precise references and much fuller discussion of all aspects of child development in the first 4 or 5 years of life I must refer the reader elsewhere [102]. These studies of individual children cannot, of course, be a basis for generalization. In particular we should bear in mind that the children of psychologists (as of all professional parents) are likely to be somewhat above the average in intelligence. As to my own five children, I shall give actual results of definite intelligence tests and their 'intelligence quotients' (see p. 236), which ranged from about 130 to 145. These must be allowed for in noting any ages in the process of intellectual development, and to some extent in social development.

In addition to all these individual biographical studies we have the many detailed studies of groups of children in nursery schools, or kindergartens and other schools, and the establishment of average standards of development, to which I shall often refer, as grounds for generalization and for determining what is normal at least in the sense of 'usual'.

We shall adopt both of these approaches, the biographical or longitudinal studies of children in their day-by-day development, and what we may call cross-section studies of large groups of children at given ages. Naturally the latter are more frequent and the only ones possible for most researchers. But something of great value is lost if the continuous studies of individual children over several years are ignored. It is regrettable that the birth rate in the families of eminent psychologists is so low! Certainly, I think that some of the fantastic interpretations of child behaviour by some psycho-analysts would not have been made if they had watched the daily progress of several infants of their own.

In discussing the findings of cross-section studies of large groups of children I shall sometimes refer in some detail to the methods of inquiry used, partly because small differences in method may have important effects on some results, and so account for differences in conclusions, and partly to exemplify some methods of research in child psychology.

Many books on psychology begin with a chapter on the scope and method of psychology; but that is usually a dull beginning for the general reader, and even for the professional student it is better to get his first impressions of method from actual researches, in which findings are studied at the same time.

I will only add here one general point: some of the groups of children on whom I shall give reports may be only small; but the massing of results by different investigators on small groups is likely to be more dependable for generalization, at least as to temperamental behaviour, than the results obtained by only one investigation on the same number of children in one big group, as it lessens the likelihood of the undue influence of one person's peculiarities or prejudices in his observation of children or in interpreting their behaviour.

Order of topics. In writing a book on psychology one of the hardest problems is to decide what topics to deal with first. The fact is that all aspects of mental life – temperament, motives, intelligence – are so intermingled that no one of them can be properly studied without reference to the others. In this book I have dealt in the early chapters chiefly with development and behaviour in the earliest years, coming later to middle childhood.

Also I have dealt first with impulses to action and with emotions, behaviour in the home, sex, etc., partly because these are so intimately connected with apparent abnormalities. In these early chapters I repeatedly stress the fact of individual differences: yet the most convincing evidence of such differences is found in studies and tests of intelligence. The reader who feels more attracted by the latter may quite well proceed at once to Chapter 13, on Intelligence, and then return to Chapter 3.

CHAPTER 3

The Basic Impulse of Play

FOR our first topic I have selected play chiefly because it reveals itself at the earliest ages and affects all other developments, but partly because the play of children has been a favourite source for some psychologists and especially psycho-analysts in inferring alleged abnormalities.

The meaning of play. First I must briefly state the interpretation to be put on the term play. I adopt the view that the very essence of play is that it is an activity carried out entirely for its own sake – for the mere enjoyment of the activity. No doubt most activities of this kind, in adults and even in children, are complicated by other motives. A man plays golf partly for the sake of his health; a child is fond of carpentering partly because he likes to have the boxes or boats that he can make. Nor does this view of play exclude other interpretations, such as that of Groos, that play is biologically valuable for children or young animals, as a preparation for more serious later activities of life. Indeed, Nature seems to begin the maturing not only of physical but of intellectual capacities, and of tendencies to act and feel, long before they are important for individual or group life; and so she provides the means for learning the modification of crude impulses. Even Herbert Spencer's view that play is an outlet for excess of energy is probably often true – witness the rowdy rushing about and aimless shouting of a class of schoolboys let out into the playground after a long quiet spell in the classroom.

In the first few weeks of a healthy baby's life, apart from

47

ordinary cries and gurgles and certain reflexes, nothing is so prominent as vigorous spontaneous movements, constantly occurring even when the baby is lying at rest; legs are kicking, arms waving; the head waving about to and fro, all apparently not reflexes, but produced by internal processes in the nervous system. From these spontaneous movements voluntary control of movements develops, and as soon as some movements can be managed even clumsily, we find the baby constantly practising them. Thus I noted of my boy B that at 0:2½ he learned the trick of getting his dress between his fists and then raising it up to his face, and I noted that he was constantly repeating this for considerable periods.

Similarly each new accomplishment seems often to be practised intensely for a time with obvious enjoyment; for example, at 0:5 B had just learned to strike the notes of the piano, as I held him on my knee, and I have a record that he struck it forty-nine times in three minutes with cries of joy. Not long afterwards I counted a continuous series of 100 such bangings, again with obvious delight.

The maturing of the capacity to grasp things results in constant playing with this new experience. All our five children would often grasp at their mother's dress or a paper she was reading when she was feeding them. This turning even from the breast simply to play has an obvious bearing on the supposed intense fixation of the 'libido' on the breast during the suckling period, which some psychoanalysts have emphasized.

Every mother is familiar with the delight with which babies will persist in continuously banging things or dropping them and watching them fall, whilst such activities are still novel to them. Gesell [42] reports that such throwing of objects to hear them fall is rare at 0:6, but frequent at 0:9. Perhaps the tendency to play at a new-found skill is shown most in the beginnings of babbling. Thus my little girl Y at 0:6 was noted as constantly practising for a week or more two new noises, a kind of lip-trilling and a sound rather like 'tch'. Several other psychological observers have noted this tendency to practise repeatedly newly acquired sounds.

There are numerous examples of repeated playing with a newly acquired skill, scattered through the records by psychologists on their own children. I will add merely two from the careful and detailed reports of Miss M. W. Shinn on her niece [93].

'During all this period (1:2 to 1:6) a noticeable trait was the child's interest in doing something novel with her body, apparently in mere curiosity and sense of power. In the sixty-first week she found that she could walk about with her head thrown back, looking at the ceiling, and practised it for a long time. In the sixty-fifth week she walked about in her father's slippers, lifting her encumbered feet skilfully. At 16 months old she hit upon the feat of walking backward, and practised it all day, much interested and amused. In the seventieth week her great joy when indoors was a shallow box, some 2½ inches high, on which she would stand, stepping on and off with endless pleasure.'

By the age of 6 months the co-operation of mother or father may enhance the delight of play. Thus I noted of my boy B: 'Greatly amused (day 165) at my repeatedly covering him with eiderdown which he knocked back each time with one motion of his arms. On day 182 this was done 100 times in quick succession until I tired.'

Possibly already here there was added some satisfaction of an incipient impulse to overcome others and in some delight in achievement. This latter there certainly seems to be in some forms of play common in the latter part of the first year; thus B at 0:6½. 'We noticed for the first time a new movement; he took a spoon by the handle and then gyrated his fist so that the spoon described a semi-circle in the air. He repeated this five or six times, watching it meanwhile.' Also 'Sometimes B would seem to set himself *difficult tasks*. Thus not long after learning to stand up he tried to stand up while holding his big ball in his mouth. There were repeated failures, the ball dropping, but again he would try until successful.'

Many such special activities the child may initiate himself. In some ordinary performances such as standing and walking he is usually aided in the first attempts and even initiated by the mother. But crawling must be largely self-initiated and merely dependent on the maturing of the nervous mechanisms and the impulses to set them going. So individual and independent is this that my boy A usually moved backwards in his first efforts before he could crawl forwards. With B even the act of standing was self-initiated. At o:8½ he tried to pull himself on to his feet when sitting in his little railed playground, grasping the upright rods firmly. He persisted in these efforts every day until two weeks later he stood for the first time straight up, clinging hard to the top rail.

In the practice of such actions we see the co-operation of the child's own activity with the slow maturing of the capacity. If, as in the case of the boy A, an illness stops the learning of some activity such as crawling or walking for some weeks, we may note a marvellous advance in the action, as soon as the child is fit again to try it. Here we have an example of the share of maturation in the progress made partly through playful exercise of new activities.

Maturation. We must pause for a moment in our description of play development to consider this important concept of maturation. This term refers to that aspect of growth and development which is due to the inherent ripening of the elements and organization of the nervous mechanisms (including the brain cells) concerned with any form of activity, as distinct from the organization or co-ordination which is due to learning through practice or training.

Some remarkable experiments have been performed in which like twins have been considered at an age when some activity such as climbing stairs is just beginning.

One notable experiment was performed by Gesell on identical twins aged 10 months [45]. Twin T was given daily training in climbing for a period of six weeks, beginning at the age of 46 weeks. Twin C was meanwhile deprived of all specific training in climbing. After four weeks of training (age 50 weeks) T climbed the staircase with avidity and without assistance. At 52 weeks she climbed the staircase in twenty-six seconds. Twin C, who had been prevented from trying any climbing, was now put to this test, and she at once climbed the staircase unaided in forty-five seconds, and after two weeks' practice climbed it in ten seconds; that is, two weeks' training of the more mature C resulted in a 'far superior climbing performance' than had the six weeks' training of T. Indeed C walked up the stairs when T continued to crawl.

Similar results were obtained with groups of children of 2:0 in cutting with scissors and buttoning, one week's training at a more mature age producing the same efficiency as twelve weeks' training earlier.

In the acquisition of language similar experiments were made with like twins. At 1:8 twin A was intensively trained in the acquisition of words for four weeks; twin B's training was begun five weeks after A's. Yet shortly afterwards at every stage of development B was slightly ahead of A.

Of course, we cannot entirely separate the maturation aspect of development from the environmental and learning aspects. The infant who has no stairs to climb will not learn to climb them in infancy. There is indeed evidence that, provided there are ample opportunities, some infants under 1 year may learn to swim by mere immersion in water without instruction. Rhythmic swimming movements have been noted in babies of under 1 month when they were immersed in water [78], but few parents would be disposed to try the experiment.

Early social play. Some forms of social play are common before the end of the first year. Gesell reports the game of peek-a-boo as played by between 50 per cent and 64 per cent of the children at 0:9. Social play is, of course, more likely to take place first with a loved mother or father, but it may soon extend to others if known and liked. Thus 'B at 0:10 threw sugar tongs on the floor. Miss L picked them up, and so on about fifty times, B laughing constantly.' Miss L was a visitor who had been some weeks in the house and spent much time with B.

In such elementary social play, however, it is usually an adult co-operating with the child in something which in itself delights him. When infants are together it is another matter. Sometimes, as we shall see in a later chapter, an infant of only 1 year old may show delight at the sight of another baby; but one careful investigator (Mary Shirley) in a study of twenty-five infants, found that when two babies (strangers) of 0:10 were put together in a play-pen they took little notice of one another, though they often disputed for possession of a toy [94]. Dr K. Bridges [11] also found that infants of 2:0, when newcomers in the nursery school, paid little attention to one another at first, but after a month or so there were the beginnings of social play. Another investigator in a study of over 100 children found that only 10 per cent of the 2-year-olds actively co-operated in play; and even among the Dionne Quins, though brought up together from birth, play was still largely individual at the age of 2:0 [10].

While delight in being played with by a known parent seems then to be the normal thing before the end of the first year, it is no abnormality if the child co-operates little with other infants before the age of 2:0.

Make-believe play in the first two years. Evidence of make-believe play as early as 1:6–2:0 is given by a number of the records by psychologists on their own children to which I have referred earlier. Thus a girl of 1:6 would feed her dolls with imaginary food and another of 1:4 would show furniture to the dolls. Our own little girl Y fed her dolls with imaginary food as early as 1:0 and at 1:11 poured imaginary tea into her doll's teacup and added imaginary sugar. Such dramatic play, according to Gesell, has considerable significance as a sign of mental development. He noted it in about 75 per cent of the children of 2:0.

An element of enjoyment in sheer nonsense appears in much of the dramatic play of the period 2:0–2:6. Thus, after a period of a few days in which I had been drawing some figures for B and teaching him to draw a triangle and a circle, I then drew a tiger for B and said that it was going to eat a little boy. B then drew a triangle and said mischievously *that* was going to eat the little boy! Earlier still, B would give me some imaginary object and then laugh. Again, the girl Y at 2:6, long before she went to school, when playing one day in the nursery, suddenly looked at the clock (which she could not understand) and said, 'Oh, dear, it is ten o'clock, I must go to school'.

In play at this period almost anything can apparently represent anything else. Thus in one game strips of paper stood for beans, and a pan in which they were cooked was placed on a fire represented by the blankets piled up. In view of the constant recurrence of such imaginative games and the delight in sheer tomfoolery, it is not necessary to suppose that when my younger girl at 2:7 pretended her knitting needles were knives and cut imaginary slices of meat from her sister's knee and handed them round to each of us, she had repressed cannibalistic tendencies! No doubt at this time some play is the expression of dawning instinctive tendencies, as when a little girl fondles her doll so lovingly or a boy plays at fighting. But much of the play seems like that of the carving of the sister's knee, sheer fun. Yet some interpretations of dramatic play are quite gratuitous, as we shall now see.

Supposed symbolic and fantasy interpretations of early play. In view of the fantastic interpretations put by certain psychoanalysts on some of the play of infants, let us consider one or two of these in the light of what we have seen already about early play, especially the delight in practising all sorts of new skills. In his book, *Beyond the Pleasure Principle*, Freud tells of a boy of 1:6 who used to throw his toys into the corner of the room with an 'expression of gratification'. 'One day', writes Freud, 'I made an observation that confirmed my view. The child had a wooden reel with a piece of string wound round it. It never occurred to him, for example, to drag this after him on the floor and so play horse and cart with it, but he kept throwing it with considerable skill, held by the string, over the side of his little draped cot, so that the reel disappeared into it, then said his significant "o-o-o" and drew the reel by the string out of the cot again, greeting its reappearance with a joyful "Da" (there). The meaning of the game was then not far to seek. It was connected with the child's remarkable cultural achievement – the forgoing of the satisfaction of an instinct – as the result of which he could let his mother go away without making any fuss. He made it right with himself, so to speak, by dramatizing the same disappearance and return with the objects he had at hand.'

To one who has watched the repetitive play of a few infants in the first year or two, such an explanation seems quite gratuitous. The little ape, by the way, which the Kelloggs brought up with their little boy [68], when she discovered the joy of dropping things from her high chair, became addicted to the habit. Must we assume she was symbolizing the disappearance of the mother, or human substitute?

In a later chapter we shall discuss some Freudian views about the relations between children and their parents, especially the supposed antagonism of the little boy of 3 or 4 to his father (or of a girl towards her mother). But it is appropriate to refer here to the child's frequent playing at representing someone, especially a parent. Now such representative play has been interpreted by psycho-analysts as indicating a boy's wish to replace his father in his mother's affections, or a girl's her mother's place with the father. But such theorizing ignores the plain fact that children often play at being horses or engines, and that when they play at being other people, it is often not a member of the family. For example, Y at 2:8 would sometimes play at being an imaginary Mrs Jones with her baby doll. Most unusual characters may be 'played at', if they have been seen by the child. Thus Sully's boy, at $3\frac{1}{2}$ years, was immensely interested in watching the coal being brought in one morning. He played at being a coal-heaver all day, refusing to respond to any other name, and that night he prayed to be made 'a good coal-heaver' [99].

I think parents may safely ignore the suggestion that there is anything highly significant or abnormal if a little child plays at being Daddy (or Mummy), though it may be interesting and illuminating to us as parents to note what kind of person the child thinks we are. I recall watching a group of little children playing at school in a public recreation ground. The shouting and scoldings and general bad temper shown by the little girl who was the teacher cast an unfavourable light on the goings-on in her class. We shall see directly that there is evidence that the type of behaviour adopted by children playing with a family of dolls may reveal something of their own home environment.

Imaginary companions. Closely allied to the imaginary play just described is the invention by the child of an imaginary playmate. Usually this is another child, who may continue to be brought into imaginary play over a long period, at least six to twelve months. This is far from rare or peculiar. From statistical records it looks as though an only child is more apt to invent such companions than are those with brothers and sisters near their own age. Out of 210 cases studied in the Yale Guidance Nursery 41 children had imaginary companions, 30 being humans and 11 animals. The peak age for these phenomena was 3:0 to 4:0 in this group, but over half of the children were under 5.

Nearly half were only children. On the other hand, some who were very sociable and had good friends had nevertheless invented these companions. I agree with the author of this report that the creation of an imaginary companion seems to depend much more on the type of imagination of the child than on his being lonely or dissatisfied. For example, our little girl Y, who had ample companionship and was a very happy, sociable infant, had an imaginary companion, and indeed her imagination was so active that she was constantly inventing fantastic situations. Thus, shortly after being told (at 2:4) some stories about a lion, she told her sister that she had met a lion in the park and it had kissed her and went with her to see the ducks. At about 2:9 to 3:0 Y at times played at being someone else, adopting another name and insisting for a time on our calling her by that name. In the Yale inquiry the imaginary human companions were most often (sixteen cases) merely general playmates, but in six cases they were allowed to do things the child was not allowed to do; in three cases they were very weak and were either bossed about or cared for by the child; thus they gave an opportunity of expressing impulses maturing at the time in a way we shall exemplify in a later paragraph.

The authors of the Yale Report consider that there might be a good number of the other children who had imaginary companions, but whom they had not discovered; and some children over 5 or 6 may be reluctant to reveal such imaginings, but they have been reported by adults as going on beyond the age of 5. An extensive inquiry as to such memories of imaginary companions was made at Columbia University among 700 high-school and college students. Of these, 31 per cent of the women and 23 per cent of the men clearly remembered having had an imaginary playmate. Among the women this was relatively more frequent among only children, but not so with the men, and imaginary playmates were not infrequent even in families of three or more children. 'Being lonesome' was given as the occasion of the first appearance in only about 20 per cent of the cases; being scolded or unjustly treated or 'not being able to get on with real friends' accounted for 9 per cent of the cases among the women and 19 per cent of the men. The peak age for these appearances among girls was 5 to 8 years; among boys more about 7 to 9 years. In one-third of the cases the occasion for the disappearance of the imaginary companion was forming friendships with other children; but clearly this was not always so.

Further evidence as to the importance of the type of mind in the creation of an imaginary companion is supplied by some results gained by Lewis M. Terman in his important research on specially gifted children [100]. These children were all much above average intelligence, and among 554 of them (ages 6 to 13) it was found that 85 per cent of the girls and 51 per cent of the boys had had imaginary play-mates, including fairies and animals, or had assumed roles of characters in books. The figures for actual imaginary personal companions seem to be about 72 per cent for the girls and 37 per cent for the boys – decidedly bigger proportions than those in the Columbia University Report. Incidentally I may mention that my secretary tells me that she, an only child, and her best friend (not an only child) together invented imaginary companions, both human and animal, to join them in their games, and in addition they themselves assumed roles of characters read about.

This phenomenon of the imaginary companion has been interpreted by some psycho-analysts and others as an indication of abnormal day-dreaming. No doubt it appears in some of the genuinely maladjusted or neurotic children, especially as a means of satisfying cravings frustrated by reality. But the evidence is clear that in itself, while by no means universal (partly perhaps because so few children are so imaginative as to indulge in it with pleasure), it is not in the undesirable sense abnormal. Indeed, one might regard it merely as a small step beyond the imaginary play with dolls who are companions, though the doll companions are almost invariably regarded as younger and more helpless than the child herself.

On the other hand, the imaginary companion does lend itself to wish-fulfilment in day-dreaming, and it is not surprising to find records of seriously maladjusted children who have indulged freely in such imaginings.

Other play in later infancy. The tendency to play especially at newly matured capacities continues of course through childhood, and in an active-minded child it reveals itself even in intellectual processes. Thus the boy B, when he first grasped the meaning of 'two', repeated the words continually for days when the opportunity arose. Thus on a walk he would point and say with evident delight, 'Two boy', 'two gee-gee', 'two puff-puff', and so on.

Various psychologists have commented on the delight in drawing with a crayon when sufficient skill has developed to draw something even moderately recognizable. The activity may be concentrated on for days at a time. Equally familiar is the tendency to pull things to pieces, sometimes to see what is inside, sometimes apparently to enjoy the manipulation required, and sometimes perhaps to enjoy a feeling of power in smashing something, often seen when a child carefully makes a sand castle and then jumps on it, and wildly scatters the sand. Such play may be closely allied to a new type of play which appears about 2:0–3:0 namely, the delight in experiencing a novel emotion or maturing impulse. Thus several of my children would love me to 'play at lions'. Roaring like a lion (somewhat), I would chase the child up the stairs until when I nearly caught him he would scream in real earnest, tears rolling down his cheeks. Then at once I desisted, only to be begged a few moments later to play lions again! I can only suppose that the impulse to experience a novel emotion was greater as a motive force than the unpleasantness at the extreme moment. Another psychologist noted that her little girl of

2:6 greatly enjoyed a game which consisted entirely of her Nannie saying 'No' and the girl shouting 'Yes', a dozen or more times. My psychologist son reports precisely the same of his little girl at 2:5. Several of our own children devised similar games of playing at assertiveness and contradiction, e.g. when the mother asked, 'Does B love Mummy?' B would say 'No' emphatically. Then he would suggest, 'Daddy' and his mother would ask, 'Does B love Daddy?' and he would exclaim 'No', and so on.

Notes by other psychologists report children apparently playing at being naughty in some defiant way, yet with much merriment; of course, we are all familiar with the fact that little children, especially boys, will play at fighting, with no more real wish to hurt than is shown by a young dog engaged in a romping fight with a canine friend or with his master, yet showing bared teeth and uttering fierce growls. One of my students told me she could clearly remember at the age of about 3:0 being deliberately naughty for a day or so and enduring the punishments for the sheer joy of the fight, and repeating the process at intervals of a few weeks.

So far in this section I have given examples from the records of psychologists on their own children, possibly a selected type intellectually, though one can see no reason why they should be peculiar as regards assertiveness or fears, even if they are usually above average intelligence. But reports on large groups of infants of this age confirm these individual reports. Thus Gesell records, as a characteristic of the average child of 2:6, that he demands to do things *by himself*, even though he may not be able to do them properly. K. Bridges noted among her children of this age a 'love of the sense of new-found power' leading to the refusal of adult assistance. Various more recent reports confirm these findings.

At the same time, however, there is going on a maturing of social impulses, and by 3:0 children in nursery schools or kindergartens show an increased interest in playing with other children, and by 4:0 there is usually a preference for playing in a small group.

By 5 years the customary playing in groups, and the increased skill and interest in dealing with various kinds of toys, bring complications which carry us beyond the study of play as a basic impulse, but which we shall meet again in our general study of social development in childhood.

Some reports and interpretations of play. As one special concern of this book is to study normality in childhood and to examine suggestions as to underlying influences, we must refer briefly to some experimental studies of children's play at this period. A considerable number of reports have been made as to the play of children from 3 to 5 years with dolls and dolls' houses. Some experimenters have sought to show that the children tend to represent conflicts occurring in their home life. Others have pointed out that the fantasies of the children often produce events which could not possibly represent real events in the home life. Some who have interpreted actions as giving release to repressed impulses have failed to allow for the natural tendency of little children to practise all kinds of activities with materials and to revel in exaggeration and fun. One psychiatrist was so convinced of the fact that the play of a little boy with a 'family' of dolls would prove representative of the situation in the boy's home, which the boy would have an urge to express, that he naïvely records how he kept bringing the boy back to the dolls when the boy wanted to play with engines instead!

As a sample of the play of unselected children of ages 5, 6, and 7, I will give the results gained by one of my former research students, Miss E. Hall [49]. She studied the play, with plasticine and clay, of 200 children in their schools, two in towns and one in the country. The fact which emerged most clearly through the inclusion of town and country children was the decided influence of the environment; e.g. children living near a canal made horses, barges, and bridges. Recent topical events showed their special influence, e.g. logs for bonfire night, pancakes for Shrove Tuesday, presents at Christmas. And the child's special interests appeared, e.g. football was represented. The new prominence of aeroplanes at the time (1937–8) resulted in aeroplanes topping the list of objects made – 61 times. After that came cakes, sweets, etc. (45 times), animals (41 times), and people, including soldiers, only 37 times. The author concluded that of only six children was the play so divorced from reality as to be termed fantasy – apart from such dramatic play as 'Indians' and shooting by the boys.

Now in such an experiment the nature of the play, though to some extent limited by the material provided, is not determined by the material. Where the object has been to study especially the child's relationship with his family, this has been effected by providing a family of dolls and perhaps a doll's house.

Dramatic play with dolls. Much of such research on the play of problem children in clinics has been of little value for lack of a comparison with a control group of normal children. It is too often assumed that the child in his play is expressing what the observer knows he tends to show at home. Some samples, however, of the better type of research do provide evidence that home conditions can affect the type of play. I shall describe one inquiry as to the effect of father separation on the aggression showed by children in playing with dolls [90]. This dealt with twenty-two boys of each of the ages of 3, 4, and 5 and twenty girls of the same ages. Within each age and sex group half of the children were from homes from which the father was absent – usually in one of the armed forces (U.S.A.).

It was found that less aggressiveness was shown in the play of the boys whose fathers were away than by those whose fathers were at home. The authors consider as a possible explanation that the father-separated boys missed what the authors called the 'sex-typing' of their fathers; in other words, they missed the example of the more aggressive male to imitate. The authors, however, favour the view that the father's presence operated as a frustration and so issued in aggression in play. This may be; I am prepared to admit that repressions in real life may be expressed in play, but it seems possible that the greater aggressive play of the children whose fathers were at home can be explained largely as the mere imitation of recent experiences at home, in which the father himself acts more aggressively as a disciplinarian towards the boy. The fact that no appreciable difference appeared in the aggressive play of the girls whose fathers were at home constitutes a difficulty for either view. It might be understandable if the fathers were gentler in handling the girls, and the girls' frustration due largely to their mothers' discipline. On the other hand, it might be interpreted as due to the girls merely imitating the one aggressive towards them – the mother.

A similar inquiry was made at Columbia University [5] among twenty older children (ages 6 to 10) whose fathers had been away from home in the Forces for from one to three years. These children were all 'normally adjusted' children and there was a control group of children of similar ages and intelligence whose fathers were at home. In each group half the children were girls. Again they had a doll's house and doll's family to play with. The main finding was that 'Father-separated children produce an idealistic fantasy picture of the father, who has a good time with his family and who is enjoyed by them. He gives and receives much affection and has little marital discord. This fantasy-father shows very little hostility and does not exert his authority. The children of the control group, however, living as they do in daily contact with their fathers, elaborate significantly more upon the punitive function of the father and his contribution to intra-family hostility.'

In this research reports were also obtained through home interviews and through teachers' reports as to how the father was spoken of by the mother to the children –

whether he was represented as a model to be imitated, the kind provider of good things, or a loafer, devoted to the family, or escaped to the army, aggressive or gentle, and so on. Typical of some mothers was the warning they gave to the children, 'Don't you be like your father'. This rather bold and intimate inquiry only provided four children whose fathers were undoubtedly very badly spoken of by their mothers and four whose fathers were certainly only highly praised. But so far as the results went, the former group showed very much greater aggressive action by the fathers in the doll play. Had the numbers been larger the results might have furnished some further evidence of the assertion confidently made by one psychologist that the children's attitude to the father is almost entirely determined by the mother's own attitude to him.

That extreme caution must be observed in interpreting the play of children is emphasized by the findings of a more recent and extensive research by A. F. Korner [69]. The children were between the ages of 4:0 and 6:0 in a kindergarten. There were only twenty of them (described as 'presumably normal'), but the technique of the research was good. The observation on the play (with dolls, clay, and paint) were compared with information gained by careful questioning of the parents and with independent ratings by their teachers. Very little relation was found between hostility represented in play and that reported at home or in the school. Some children, indeed, showed strong hostility in play and very little in real-life situations, and *vice versa*. Those who received severe corporal punishment at home were reported as 'strongly hostile' in behaviour. The author seems to regard this as an imitation by the children of their parents' behaviour. It does not seem to have occurred to her that the children who were strongly hostile in behaviour were for that reason more likely to receive corporal punishment.

Finally I must refer to an inquiry by one of Burt's research students on the play of a group of twenty (normal) boys, ages mostly 10 to 11, in a mixed junior school. Observations were made as to aggressiveness, unselfishness, and twenty other traits seen during play with sand tray and dolls. When these estimates as to aggressiveness and the other traits shown in play were compared with estimates of aggressiveness made by the head teachers and class teachers, an average correlation of 0·42 was found. This means a definite but slight resemblance between the two estimates. (See p. 230 for explanation of 'correlation'.) On the basis of observations of the boys' play at a tea party and games, the average correlation fell to 0·27.

Summing up all the evidence we have given we may say that, while interpretations of play must be made with great caution, nevertheless, allowing for differences of personal judgements in interpreting signs of aggression, etc., even children supposedly normal may at times reveal something of their temperament in free play; such a revelation is, however, more likely to be found in seriously maladjusted children. Especially may some persistent forms of play give useful clues, and in any case the use of play-therapy in clinics may at least be the most valuable method of establishing good relations between the children and the clinic psychologist, which I believe is probably the most important factor at the clinic in influencing the behaviour of the 'problem child'.

Play in later childhood. The basic impulse to play which we detected in the first two or three years arose from the delight in exercising newly matured capacities. Naturally as the child grows older all the simpler skills will be mastered. Mere running will cease to interest him, but he may like to race another child, for then there is the added element of competition. For this the impulse to surpass others must have matured. There is indeed a stage in early infancy varying with the child, when it is very difficult to organize a really competitive race, unless there is a visible prize to be seized. In middle childhood, however, we find many competitive games, and even in some of the simpler of these some degree of novelty is ensured through seasonal changes, e.g. there seems to be a 'close season' for marbles and hopscotch. In other games there is included the thrill of an emotion not often experienced in the ordinary daily life, as in the dangerous game of 'last across the road'.

The ordinary games of childhood are so familiar that we need not discuss them here, but one special topic has been so excellently investigated and yielded such interesting results that it deserves notice.

The play of gifted children. There is a valuable report on this by Terman in the book already referred to [100]. There were 643 highly gifted children, nearly all with an intelligence quotient of 140 or over. (See our p. 236 for an explanation of this term). The great majority of the children were between the ages of 6 and 13. Preference ratings were assigned to ninety plays, games, and other forms of amusement. The forms of play include a wide variety from cycling, skating, and football to chess and puzzles. The gifted children show appreciably greater interest than the control group of average ability, in activities that require thinking and that are mildly social and quiet. They show slightly less preference than do the control group for competitive games.

The *masculinity* of the games was determined by the extent to which a game was liked more by boys than by girls. The mean masculinity ratings of the gifted boys were slightly higher than those of control boys at all ages except 13. The means of the gifted girls did not differ consistently from those of control girls. So there seems to be no truth in the idea that clever boys are more effeminate than the average, at least in play. In general, gifted children tended to prefer activities which, among control children, show increasing rather than decreasing popularity with the increase of age from 8 to 14.

A *sociability rating* was also derived for each child, based on the proportion of preferences which fell to social and competitive games. This was somewhat lower for gifted than for control children. The gifted showed much less sex preference than did control children in the choice of play-mates and the girls showed far less sex preference than did the boys. A somewhat larger proportion of gifted than of control children were said to be regarded by other children as 'queer' or 'different'.

CHAPTER 4

Self-assertion, Anger, and Aggression

In tracing the development of play in the first few years we saw that there comes a time when the child takes a special delight in doing things for himself, and later a pride in beating another child in competition. The well-known game of 'I'm the king of the castle' is an early example of the tendency. It is impossible to determine the precise point at which there is a consciousness of the self and an enjoyment in the feeling of superiority in winning. The emotional reactions of the baby seem at first to be very general, as indeed are most of the bodily reactions. Differentiation into specific emotions and specific impulses and movements appears only gradually. In reference to emotions, as distinct from actions, we are in a special difficulty. Until the child is able to describe its own feelings we must adopt a purely 'behaviourist' attitude. We can only describe the child's reactions to various situations. We can note easily that it cries when it falls, but cannot say whether it feels pain or fear or both. Even some behaviourists who have belittled or ignored the study of consciousness by the psychologist have had to reflect on their own experience in certain situations and to infer that the infant feels *fear* when it screams at a sudden and loud noise because such a noise also startles the psychologist himself.

All we can say with confidence is that gradually the expressions of feelings (cries, stampings, trembling, wide-open eyes) become more and more differentiated, and if stampings and shouts occur when the child's actions are strongly restrained and frustrated we guess that he feels anger, because that is what we adults tend to feel when frustrated.

In the first year or two at least it behoves the adult to be very cautious in interpreting the precise significance of an infant's expressions of feelings. Indeed, what may appear an expression of feeling may not be genuinely such at all. As we have seen in the chapter on play, the child may enjoy activities for their own sake, including at times such as may be easily misinterpreted as expressions of genuine feeling. But the crudest misinterpreting of infantile behaviour I have come across does not need even a reference to the play impulse to refute it. I refer to the interpretation of the baby's biting of the mother's breast or hands as a sign of aggressiveness and ambivalence (love and hate) towards the mother, and to the statement that there is a marked increase in destructive impulses at the teething period. Such fancies make one wonder if the psychologists have ever handled a baby in the teething period and found how it loves to have a hard rubber ring or cool spoon to bite, apparently to ease the discomfort in the gums.

The beginnings of self-assertion. Some element of self-assertion may have been present in the examples of teasing by the child which were common in the second year. It may also have been present when the frustration of even simple wishes led to anger. Sometimes before 2:0 the boys A and B showed what certainly looked like anger when they were prevented from doing just what they wanted at the moment – screaming, kicking, and hitting out at us. B even struck his mother several times as early as 1:4 when taken out of his bath, which he loved.

Anger, however, may apparently occur without actual pugnacity. Thus I noted that B at 1:8½ 'shows temper by throwing himself on the ground and waving his arms to and fro.' At 1:10 B wanted his engine and, when not given it at once, he fell into a temper and hit his own hand in his excitement – a curious example of blind aggressive excitement, not directed against another person. Yet, as I mentioned in Chapter 2 (p. 29), this boy later developed admirable self-control. Once again such tempers cannot be taken as signs of coming abnormality.

Another curious note was made on Y at 2:0¾. Her mother took something from her, and she screamed and stamped her feet, then just afterwards she slapped a paper on her mother's chair two or three times. It looked as though the aggressive impulse to smack must out (as with B when he hit himself), though it is not directed against the person causing the trouble. It reminds me of the behaviour of a little puppy of 4 months which I saw a few days ago. I was teasing him, and, though he sat on his haunches some feet away, he made lunging movements at me with his clumsy paws.

Numerous records of temper tantrums in the second and third years, with or without the hitting of others, could be quoted from other observers. I have given most of my own examples of self-assertion and aggression in earlier books, but I must report two notes on the girl X as they illustrate especially the possibility of self-assertion in infancy without any untoward signs of anger or of pugnacity. This indeed was characteristic of the girl X, and to a large extent of her sister Y, as contrasted with the pugnacity of the boys A and B. True, as already reported, Y once boasted that she 'did bleed' the maid with a knife, but Y was rarely angry and then usually without any hitting of others. Especially typical of X was the following note at 3:6. 'X is very self-willed just now. Longs to assert herself. Dances and stamps with rage if her will is crossed. One day I locked her in my dressing-room till she should stop. She was silent a moment, so I unlocked the door and said she could come out. She would not, however, but held the door and said she "did not want to come out" – a final resort to save self-respect when resistance was futile.'

Precisely the same kind of cold pride was shown by B at about 3:6 and Y at about 4:8. B would pretend he did not want to do something which he had been forbidden to do. I took the trouble to inquire of my university students about the appearance of such self-assertion in infancy. In one class of about eighty university graduates, three-quarters of them had seen similar behaviour in their own little brothers and sisters or in the infants of friends. In two other classes, numbering 200 in all, nearly all the women and the majority of the men said they could actually remember adopting such attitudes themselves.

So far we have chiefly discussed assertiveness in antagonism to others, but we must emphasize that it can appear quite independently of this and with no alliance with anger. The clearest evidence of it is when the child can use the term (my)self. Thus a note on Y at 2:4 runs: 'Just now there is a great development of determination to do things "myself" – e.g. dress herself. Wanted to go a walk in park "myself"! Shortly after this Y would constantly boast that she had done things herself. Even at 2:0 Y, when doing something with a piece of wire, called out to her mother, "See *me*".' Indeed, such boasting and occasional self-display seemed to be the form in which self-assertiveness revealed itself in Y rather than in assertiveness against another.

The observations on groups of little children by several investigators show that aggressiveness is more frequent in boys than in girls; already the little ladies are beginning instead to use the art of self-display as a means of satisfying the desire for self-importance, though display of prowess and boasting is certainly found also in boys of about 3 and over.

Assertiveness, competition, and individual differences. At the ages of 2 or 3, although self-assertion already shows itself in the child's effort to do what it wants and to do things itself without help, it does not yet show itself in trying to beat others in some form of competition. Even in an experiment in which a large group of children from 2 to 7 were encouraged to compete with one another in seeing who could build the biggest house or tower, it was found that at the younger ages (2 to 4) the children paid little or no attention to what the others did. Something needed for competition had not yet matured. Towards 4 years, however, there was a great increase in grabbing bricks from others, and so on. Even among the older children there were some who, while interested in building well, showed none of the competitive spirit; they were not concerned in beating others. This is only one of many reports which bring out the great range of individual differences among children as regards assertiveness and aggression.

Even before the age of 1 year marked individual differences have been found between babies when faced with another baby of the same age and only one toy between them. Some will vigorously grab the toy, some refrain from competing for it; some will fiercely resist the taking of the toy from them, some will meekly yield it.

In view of the many reports of marked individual differences in the earliest months of life, the most reasonable hypothesis seems to be that such differences are at least partly due to individual differences in some innate temperamental traits or tendencies. As regards babies and infants assembled in groups for experimental purposes, it is of course always open to the psychologist to suggest that there have been differences in the training even in the first few months. Personally I have noted such enormous individual differences in respect to these and other temperamental tendencies in my own children which I could not possibly explain by differences in training, and similar differences between the little children in families of my friends, that, in view also of the evidence of reports on larger groups of children, I have no doubt about the existence of large individual innate differences in such temperamental traits and tendencies.

Striking differences have also been found in the frequency of anger outbursts in children of the ages of 1 : 6 up to

6 or 7. In Professor F. Goodenough's well-known inquiry [46], the reports were made by intelligent parents
on behaviour in the homes, so here it is highly probable
that differences in the treatment of the children had considerable influences at least on the older children. There
were no doubt some differences as to standards in estimating
outbursts of anger. Even so, it is worth noting that among
the small group of eight children of ages 1:6 to 1:8 one
boy only averaged one outburst in about two and a half
days, while another averaged about three and a half outbursts per day. Of the fifteen children between 2 and 3
years of age one boy averaged only one outburst in about
five days, another over three in one day!

The strong behaviourist movement in psychology of forty
or more years ago tended to minimize the influence of inborn differences and to explain temperament and character
as a huge system of 'conditioning' through experience. Yet
we find such psychologists constantly requiring some
original impulses and emotions on which to begin to build
up their 'conditionings'. For other psychologists to explain
any differences in such original impulses or emotions as
due to physiological differences (e.g. in the endocrine
glands) does not get rid of the fact of corresponding psychological differences.

In more recent years the reports of anthropologists have
been quoted in support of the view that personality is
determined entirely by training and the influence of tribal
culture and customs. I have dealt with this kind of evidence
elsewhere [101], but I may give one example here. One
anthropologist reporting on the children of a very unaggressive tribe stated that a teacher, when she told a class
of children to solve an arithmetical problem and the first
one who had finished to let her know, found that the
children who had finished early were waiting for someone
else to report that he had finished first. This, it was inferred,
proved the influence of the non-competitive culture of the
tribe. But the least assertive of my three boys asserted at one

time that he would hate to be first in class; one of our girls expressed a very similar attitude. Another very clever boy whom I came across admitted to me that he was deliberately doing badly in school examinations so as not to be top, which he had been the previous term. Our British home and school atmospheres are not noted for absence of competition, but innate individual traits may be too strong for them, as anthropologists have to admit they can be even among primitive peoples, where tradition and custom can be even more rigid than our own.

In concluding this section I may refer to investigators who have shown that, while home environment certainly has a marked influence on aggressiveness in the young child, nevertheless boys from the same homes tend to be more aggressive than girls. Their conclusion that this is largely an innate difference seems the most reasonable; and further, within the same sex and similar homes, the individual temperamental characteristics of each child are big factors in deciding the degree of his aggressiveness.

The rebellious period. The records of nearly all the psychologists who have published detailed reports on the mental growth of their own children contain evidence of a marked development of rebellious assertiveness somewhere between the ages of 2 and 4 or 5. Typical of them is a report by that pioneer of child study, James Sully, who refers to 'the sudden emergence of self-will' in his boy of 2 :1. 'He began now to show himself a veritable rebel against parental authority.' At 2 : 2 he would sometimes strike his father or mother and 'follow up the sacrilege with a profane laugh'! In the extensive inquiry among parents which we outlined in Chapter 2, about one-quarter of the parents complained of *excessive* temper tantrums between 2 and 5. As I remarked about that report, the parents were probably allowing for a certain amount of rebellion as normal, and we must note that, in Prof. Goodenough's inquiry already referred to, reports by parents showed that all the twenty-nine children between the ages of 2:0 and 5:0 showed some outbursts in the hours during which they were observed.

All these reports about rebellion against parental authority during this period (*a*) by psychologists on their own children, and (*b*) by parents co-operating with psychologists, are of special value because in the records of the behaviour of little children in groups the frequency of aggression is complicated by the increase in general sociability after the ages of 2 or 3. It has been found that there is a slight tendency for those infants who show most aggressive actions to reveal also more friendly approaches than the average. Their very sociability brings them more contacts, and so more likelihood of situations which arouse controversy. Apart from the effects of this partial cause, however, it seems that aggressiveness is a definite characteristic of this period.

As to relations with other children, we saw in Chapter 2 that Gesell describes the typical 2-year-old as showing much 'snatch and grab' in play with 'frequent kicking and pulling of hair', while the 4-year-old is 'usually quarrelsome with much boasting', and 'frequently resists mother's authority'. We may emphasize also that K. Bridges found that one main characteristic of the nursery school children of 2:6 to 3:0 whom she observed was resistance to adult influence and not merely aggression towards other children.

There seems general agreement that aggressive actions are more frequent among boys, at least so far as physical interference is concerned. In one inquiry 'calling another child names' appeared far more, frequently among the girls than among the boys!

I may conclude this section by reference to another inquiry in which it was suggested that some rebellious behaviour during these ages – about 2:0 to 5:0 –is actually a good sign. Follow-up studies were made on a group of 100 children who showed marked refractoriness between 2 and 5 years, and on a control group of 100 who showed no such period of rebellion in those early years. It was found that, of the young rebels, some eight years later 84 per cent were developing satisfactorily in adolescence, with sufficient firmness of character, and what is popularly called 'strength of will'. Of the other group – the non-rebels – only 26 per cent were developing satisfactorily, the majority being described as 'weak-willed' [54].

It should be noted that this inquiry refers to Austrian children, and the reports as to personality at the later ages were made on the basis of consultations with the parents. Clearly therefore much will depend on the standard adopted in estimating the character or the supposed 'strength of will'. In any case the numbers given show a fair proportion (one in four) of the non-resistant children of 3 or 4 as turning out 'strong-willed'. Whether we might not also prefer some of those markedly submissive ones is another question. It is possible that some of those who seem defective in securing their own way or advantage in life may gain something which is in the end more worthwhile. The author of this report, however, maintains that the children who pass through no 'refractory' period are usually too apt later to depend upon adults for forming plans for them and keeping them sticking to those plans. It is very desirable that further researches should be made on this point, in other countries, and with more precise technique.

Adler and the goal of dominating others. A chapter on the place of self-assertion in the development of the child would be incomplete without some reference to the work of Alfred Adler, who declared that the chief purpose in life for the child is to dominate those about him, though, as we shall see later, Adler points out that the child may do this not merely by asserting himself in the way in which he sees adults do, but by making an appeal through his weakness [1].

First a word or two about Adler himself. He was not, as

is often thought, an actual student or colleague of Freud, though he was a member of Freud's discussion circle in Vienna and claimed that Freud's views needed serious study. When, however, Freud demanded that his discussion circle should accept unconditionally his sexual theory, Adler resigned, together with some others. This report is stated by Adler's biographer to have been given her by Adler himself [84]. Adler, indeed, so far from making sex fundamental in the study of neuroses, claimed that often the disturbances in the sexual life were really due to a fundamentally wrong general attitude to life.

As Adler emphasized so much the influence on the child's development of his awareness of weakness, and particularly the tendency to compensate for specific weaknesses, especially organic, a word or two about Adler's own childhood is of interest. He suffered from rickets when he went to school, and this was, of course, a hindrance in games; and he kept very much to himself at school because he thought himself ugly. Such early experiences no doubt helped to intensify his sympathy with, and understanding of, the handicapped child, and may partly explain the excessive prominence in his doctrines of the influence of a feeling of inferiority and of the urge to compensate and even overcompensate for any specific weakness.

Adler did not attempt any very systematic and consistent doctrine of human nature. His teaching, as a whole, tended to emphasize the importance of environmental influences, that of the family being supreme. Yet here and there he reveals his acceptance of supremely important inborn tendencies. Thus, for him, the urge to dominate can only be balanced and checked by what he calls the child's 'social feeling', which he describes as 'inborn' and varying in strength in different individuals [1]. Of course, he goes on to expound the need to encourage and guide this social feeling; but that he was right in asserting the existence of some innate element in social feelings will, I hope, be clear from our next chapter.

Adler's whole position seems also to require an innate element of assertiveness as a starting-point for the will to dominate. He is, I think, right in his general estimate of the very little child in, say, the second and third years, as feeling his own inadequacy and his dependence on his parents. He is right, too, in thinking that the treatment for the child should be a happy medium, avoiding extreme indulgence on the one hand and on the other extreme severity or excessive restraint of the child's natural impulses.

Assertiveness and the inferiority complex. Where, I think, Adler's doctrine is inadequate is in his underestimating the great range of individual differences in the strength of the 'will to dominate', or assertiveness. These differences lead, I think, to very different reactions in different children, not only to the child's general feeling of dependence or inadequacy, but to any awareness of specific weaknesses compared with other children, say, of lack of physical prowess, of skill in games, of good looks (at least as regards girls), of intelligence and ability to keep up with others in school work, and so on. A child aware of any such weakness, or in other words having a conscious feeling of inferiority, if he has also a comparatively weak impulse of self-assertion, may meekly accept his position and remain submissive to the superiority of others and possibly their domination. He may, in fact, be a very lovable child, and may indeed eventually gain more devoted friends than his more dominating brother or friends, but that is by the way and not essential to our present argument.

On the other hand, the child endowed with a very strong tendency to assert himself, may find any specific weakness in himself or inferiority to others intolerable to contemplate. He may, as Adler contends, seek to compensate for such a weakness, or even over-compensate, as did the 'strong man' Sandow, who as a child was a weakling, but later claimed to be the strongest man in the world. If poor in school work the child may try to compensate by excelling in sports.

Now he may indulge in such compensation quite deliberately, fully conscious of where his weakness lies; in which case there is no repression – no influence of a buried complex. He suffers from a feeling of inferiority, but not an inferiority *complex* in the sense in which that term is generally used now, the sense in which Freud used it. Adler, however, uses the term as covering a conscious awareness of inferiority – an inferiority feeling.

As we saw in Chapter 1, we may find a complex due to 'dissociation' of the original cause without repression to the extent of complete forgetting; and such are probably the more frequent type of inferiority complexes which lead to excessive unjustified boasting, and perhaps bullying, by young children. It is only such extremely foolish and irrational behaviour then that we should label 'abnormal' in the sense of neurotic or maladjusted. The conscious feeling of inferiority is very common; one inquiry I made among about 300 university graduates showed that the great majority had had a persistent feeling of inferiority in intelligence and in social capacities.

The moral significance of aggression. It is not the business of the psychologist as such to judge what is morally desirable or otherwise in human conduct; but in our consideration of the limits of 'normality' and the beginnings of abnormality in the undesirable sense, we have had to assume at least some generally accepted moral or social standards. The topic of aggression is clearly one in which we cannot help referring to such standards. It makes a great difference to our judgement of aggression according to whether it is directed against the weak and helpless or against the strong and tyrannical; and it is possible that in a boy of, say, 8:0 or 10:0 (*a*) teasing or hitting *younger* boys may be a sign of the future bully or tyrant, and in some cases of the germ of an inferiority complex in the proper sense; while (*b*) occasional fighting of those of his own age may be of no special significance, whereas (*c*) the attacking of *older* bullies, like

> Some village Hampden, that, with dauntless breast,
> The little tyrant of his fields withstood –

may be actually the sign of later courage of a nobler type.

The example above gives us a reminder of the fact that one cannot finally consider one trait like aggressiveness alone. It is convenient to study it and other traits and tendencies first separately and to estimate their strength or the characteristic behaviour at different stages. But we shall see in the next chapter how, for example, a strong assertive impulse may be checked when, in the same individual, sympathy and the protective impulse are strong.

CHAPTER 5

Sympathy and the Impulse to Help

THE original meaning of sympathy is 'suffering with'. In everyday use the word 'sympathetic' when applied to a person generally implies also that he is disposed to help someone in need or trouble. For psychological purposes we need something more precise than these usages, especially in studying the early years of childhood. In the first place, there seems to be a type of mental reaction which consists of 'rejoicing with' and not merely 'suffering with'. Both kinds of feelings and emotions can be roused in some people when they see them expressed by others, especially by those they care about; they share their joys as well as their sorrows. These constitute the good friends *par excellence*.

This merely rousing in a person of a feeling or emotion which he sees (or hears) being expressed by another, needs a special term, and I know none better than William McDougall's – 'the sympathetic induction of emotion' – though he changed it in later writings to 'passive sympathy'.

As an example of this I may mention a common experience of my own in watching television. I knew little or nothing of ice-hockey when I first watched it, or even now. I turned it on once or twice to make sure of getting the next item on the programme, but keeping the sound down to nil. It interested me very little; but when I turned up the sound and heard the excited commentator's voice rising to a shout and then dropping to an intense whisper I gradually found my own excitement rising to a climax. I have noted the same when only listening to the radio, and so must many, or the B.B.C. would not attach so much importance to first-rate commentators.

Many examples could also be given of the effect of a companion at a theatre or concert who is also being thrilled or bored by what appeals strongly to us. Merely to know this is to be affected; in the one case pleasure is intensified, in the other it is deadened. These are true examples of sympathetic induction of feeling, but not of 'sympathy' as the word is ordinarily understood.

The second reason why we need a special term other than plain 'sympathy' is because we want to avoid the suggestion that an impulse to help is necessarily associated with sympathetic feeling. Clearly if a feeling of joy is experienced because my friend is happy, there may be no need to do anything about it, and some people seem to feel at least momentary distress at seeing or hearing of others in trouble, but yet do nothing about it. Sometimes indeed the sympathetic distress felt is so great that it even produces a revulsion and may unfit the sympathizer for helping. Thus one woman graduate student wrote as follows: 'I am very sensitive to sympathetic pain and there has always been a struggle between sympathy and tender emotion in the case of illness or accident. When I was small I was quite useless, for I used always to run away and hide. When I was 11 our dog was run over and, though I cared for him very much and wanted to help him, I could not bear to see him suffer and I ran away and crept through a gate.' Two other women students reported that their inability to help the mental state of mentally defective children made the children 'physically repugnant' to them.

Responsive laughter. The most obvious primitive form of mere sympathetic response is laughter induced by seeing or hearing another laugh: together with a feeling of at least light hilarity. A number of psychologists have noted, as I did, that laughter merely in response to laughter, may occur at as early an age as 2 or 3 months. Among my own children there were considerable individual differences, one boy only smiling in response to laughter at 0:4, whereas B and Y showed responsive laughter at 0:2. In several of the children this tendency was so strong that when the baby was actually crying, our laughing at him would cause him to burst out laughing. This was noted at 0:3 and 0:4. Still at 0:8 I noted of B: 'Does not cry when laughed at; he was crying bitterly himself because something was taken away from him, and when we laughed at him, he laughed too.' G. V. N. Dearborn's little girl, who clearly was a merry child, would also break into laughter in the midst of crying, at 0:6 [33].

Responsive laughter does not carry us far in social development, simply because of its dissociation from any impulse to help or any germ of co-operation; though it is true that if you can get someone to laugh with you, you are sometimes preparing the ground for further advances. Much more important, of course, is sympathy with distress, to which we now turn.

Sympathy with distress. Possibly an early sign of this is sympathetic crying – the crying of a baby when it hears or sees another cry. This, however, may often only be the crying at a loud or unexpected noise, which even the most rigid Behaviourists have admitted may be an innate response. When, however, a little child has frequently heard a baby or another infant cry, the loud or surprising noise explanation becomes inadequate. Indeed, a child may cry at the sight of weeping when there is no noise, as Baldwin reported of his child at 0:5. Furthermore, I have noted sometimes a delayed sympathetic crying – only after several cries of the other baby.

Crying in response to crying, however, again does not carry us far. But there are numerous reports of crying at merely seeing or hearing the story of distress in others. Thus Dearborn's child of 1:4 invariably cried when told about Little Tommy Green putting pussy in the well.

It is recorded of Robert Southey, the poet, that about the age of 2:0 he wept at the fate of '*Children sliding on the Ice*' and at the death of 'Billy Pringles's Pig', and was so distressed that he begged his mother not to go on with the tale.

My boy B at 3:11 was heard crying in his bed one very stormy night. When I went up and asked what was the matter, he said he was thinking of the poor sailors at sea. Incidentally this provides one example of the possibility of sympathy with trouble of a kind the child himself had certainly not experienced. When B was 4:11 I described a soldier wounded in the knee so that his knee was a pulp. B shuddered and almost cried and said, 'Oh! That gives me a pain in my knee.' B's acute sympathy is notable because he himself was extremely tough; he bore bruises through falls with indifference. At a later age, when, on a wet afternoon, the children had arranged a 'fair' with sideshows, B established himself in a tent as 'the leather-skinned man', and the other children for 1*d* were allowed to scrape him on the bare thigh with a nutmeg grater!

Stern reports of his girl, H, at 2:5: 'When an aunt sat down on a rocking-seat and rocked up and down the child called out in fear, "Leave off, leave off!"' [97]. Again, at 3:6½: 'We happened to mention when talking one day that many poor children had no shoes or stockings. Then said H, "Oh, then their feet will be cold; (adding joyfully) then we must buy the children shoes and stockings and gloves too," and she added several other things we were to buy.'

The records from several psychologists on their own children reveal that this sympathy with distress may appear to a very different degree in different children brought up on similar lines in the same family. In any case, it is extremely difficult to see how actual distress can be roused in a child at the sight of another's distress merely by training. To say that he feels it because the mother shows signs of it does not explain it away; that very 'feeling' with the mother implies the sympathetic induction of feeling. Furthermore, there are many records of sympathy shown to animals and pictures of persons for which reactions there were no adult examples – as noted by that pioneer of child study, W. Preyer. When human figures were cut out of paper to amuse his little boy of 2:3 'He would often weep if a paper figure was in danger, through hasty cutting, of losing an arm or a foot'.

So far as there is mere sympathetic feeling with distress without action, again we are not carried far towards social development. It does seem that sympathetic feeling can appear without the impulse to help, but clearly it is often the precursor of active help, even if not the essential stimulant. It is, I think, undoubtedly an important element in those early social responses to others which form the total quantum of social feeling, as Adler labelled it, and which he rightly regarded as so important a counterweight and balance to the urge to dominate.

The impulse to help or protect. From the age of about 2:0 there were frequent occasions when our children did something about the distress of another child or parent, sometimes kissing and consoling. Such comforting was shown by the Kelloggs' little boy at 1:4 even towards the little chimpanzee with whom he was brought up. If the chimpanzee was put on a chair and made to stay there as a punishment the boy would run to the chair, stretch his arms up and embrace her [68].

At 2:6 one of our boys was heard crying in the nursery. It was found that he had been thinking of a poor little boy who had no toys, of whom the nurse had told him. Later he insisted on giving me four of his toys for the boy.

Active sympathetic helping and protection is also shown by infants to animals. Stern gives a report of a boy of 2:8 who carefully carried a crippled butterfly, lying on the ground, to a tree-stump saying, 'Come, poor man, so the hares may not eat you'. A little girl of 4:0 in a nursery school was seen by my daughter tenderly covering up a worm which had been uncovered in the school garden.

In some children the impulse to help appears even when there is no question of distress. Thus I noted of B at 2:7: 'Very thoughtful nowadays, e.g. when I came in this morning he said, "Daddy want slippers" and ran to get them.' Y at 3:11 looked after a little boy guest in a motherly way, putting his shoes on for him, and so on. The common interest in 'helping mother' shown by children of these ages involves special affection, which will be discussed later.

Let us turn now to some attempts to determine the frequency of signs of sympathetic feeling and sympathetic action and see if we can conclude whether it is abnormal, in the sense of extremely unusual, for them to be quite absent at the early ages. Before doing so, however, let me say that the impulse to protect and help has been regarded by some leading psychologists (including W. McDougall) as the very essence of the maternal 'instinct', if for the moment we may use that term. Even so, it would not be surprising if it should appear in early infancy. For there are many ways in which nature seems to begin the maturing and the exercise of functions long before they are of serious biological importance. We saw that in our chapter on Play. On the other hand, even if the impulse to help and protect is primarily the germ of maternal (or better, parental) concern for offspring, it may obviously play an important function in the relations with the herd or community.

The frequency of sympathetic responses in infancy. Here we get little help from Gesell, in his study of the first 5 years, apart from the general statement that 4-year-olds in general will share their toys with others and the 5-year-olds are 'protective' towards younger playmates and siblings (i.e. brothers or sisters); and that they like to help about the

house. Even the reports on the 6-year-olds are much fuller
of the child's own individual doings and demands on others
than of any responses to the distress or needs of others. No
doubt the conditions of the observation and playrooms, and
perhaps the kind of homes from which Gesell's children
came, did not provide many occasions for sympathetic
responses.

Dr K. Bridges, in her observations on nursery-school
children over a period of three years, gives a number of
examples of sympathetic responses and states that 'it is
quite common for a 3-year-old to try to comfort another
child in distress, or to give actual assistance'. But she provides no precise figures, though she emphasizes the fact that
in this respect there are great individual differences. Most
of the many large inquiries into young children's personality and behaviour have been inspired by the wish to
discover causes of misbehaviour and the traits of the problem child, so sympathy and friendly helping have tended
to be ignored.

The most important research for our present purposes is
the one by L. B. Murphy [82], though even here the numbers are not great enough for confident generalization. The
report is rich, however, in evidence as to wide individual
differences. The survey covers five groups of children
between the ages of 2 and 7, with intensive observation for
432 hours from two nursery school-groups, W and H, over
a period of 94 and 117 days respectively. Group W included
twenty children of ages 3:1 to 3:11 and Group H nineteen
children of ages 2 : 4 to 4 : 6. We may note that Mrs Murphy
also made observations on two of her own children in the
home and she makes the following comment, which is, I
think, very significant as coming from one who had done
so much thorough research among schoolchildren. 'Studies of
social behaviour would gain enormously if extended observations could be made in home situations, and if the inter-
play of social responses between children, parents, visitors,
and helpers could be recorded there.' That is true partly

because the nursery school at once introduces complications owing to the variety of the children and the presence of teachers; even shyness may inhibit an impulse to help, and fear of a relatively strange child may check the tendency to sympathize with him. Another reason is that often it is only the parent (with a psychological training too) who is likely to understand the nature of the responses of a child of only 2 or 3.

Mrs Murphy's 'Social Behaviour Scale' was an admirable one for the purpose. It was marked on a five-point scale, the extremes being (1) meaning 'Never' and (5) 'Almost always', 'a characteristic response'. The items referred to definite actions, not vague qualities, for example:

Takes away another child's toy
Defends right of smaller child
Pushes away child making friendly advances
Offers spontaneously to share materials
Responds to another child's distress by staring with no signs of distress
Offers to share toy brought to school
Attempts to comfort another child with pats, embraces and the like
Tells child 'I like you' or equivalent
Gets toy to give to another child (not just to exchange it for one he wants)
Cries when hears the crying of another child not in sight
Laughs when hears another child laugh

Two general facts must be mentioned in reference to the type of child in the nursery schools specially studied:

1. Their parents were mostly connected with the university, as teachers or students, or with some profession, and in the home discipline by corporal punishment seemed largely taboo.

2. All the children were above average intelligence so far as could be judged by one intelligence test at these early ages.

One main conclusion was that there was a striking

advance in sympathetic and helpful responses among 3-year-olds as compared with 2-year-olds.

Examples of sympathetic behaviour. I quote now a few samples of the sympathetic actions observed. The first set are from group W, all aged 3:0 to 3:11.

1. Daniel approached the bus. Peter pushed him away and pulled his hair. Daniel squealed. Wallis (3:7), watching, shuddered and tensed as Peter pulled Daniel's hair.

2. Mary fell and cried. Douglas and Evan were near; they looked, and went off. Winifred (3:2) approached, looked, then put her arms around Mary and kissed her.

3. Daniel approached the group. Nancy pushed him. Evan hit him. Daniel knocked Evan down. Evan cried. Alice looked anxiously at Evan and patted his face.

4. Kirk walked around crying, 'Me have no Mommie', Agatha (3:8) followed him, looking very concerned, and put her arm around him. Agatha asked, 'What's the matter, Kirk?' in a solicitous tone. Agatha turned to the observer and said, 'That little boy has no Mommie' in a worried tone, looking serious.

The next set are from Group H, ages 2:4 to 4:6.

5. Gwen and Saul were playing together on the jumping board. Gwen ran up the incline and was bumped by another child. Saul (4:3) approached: 'Did he hit you on the head?' 'I'll rub it for you, Gwen'. Saul felt Gwen's head and rubbed it (the way the teachers in this group often rubbed a bump).

6. Reinhardt and Heidi were playing with the big ball. Reinhardt threw it. Heidi stooped down to catch it and got accidentally hit. Heidi ran to Miss S: 'Reinhardt hit me', she cried. Julius (4:1) ran to the teacher and asked, 'Why is Heidi crying?' Julius patted her six or seven times and kissed her. Patrick (4:2) came over, patted her and looked at her. Julius hit her hard: 'Why don't you stop crying?' Julius to Miss W: 'Why doesn't she stop crying?' Julius left.

Heidi continued to cry. Patrick rode up again, reached out to her arm (comforting). Seth (4:3) came over: 'Hello, Heidi', watched her, but did nothing.

In a day-nursery (all children aged 3), the following happened:

There was a new boy, Albert, at the nursery school. When his mother left, he sobbed for ten minutes. Three children said nothing to Albert at that time. They merely went near him and stared at him. Later, when Albert was playing on the floor with blocks, and sobbing quietly, Christopher went to him, put his hand on his head and patted him. Then Christopher found some coloured blocks and took three of them to Albert, saying: 'You can play with these'.

Group W of twenty children gave, in the 188 hours observed, 318 sympathetic responses against 195 unsympathetic.

Group H, of nineteen children, in 234 hours, gave 395 sympathetic responses against only sixty unsympathetic.

These results show the great preponderance of sympathetic over unsympathetic responses. They are a useful counterblast to the reports of so many investigators, who are concerned with problem behaviour in children referred to clinics, and who even in their reports on any control group (of children not referred to a clinic) may present such a poor picture of them, because the personality items referred to relate almost exclusively to unpleasant traits, and give so little space, if any, to sympathy and kindliness.

For our present purposes, however, the totals and means of groups are not sufficient because of the enormous individual differences to which we now turn.

Individual differences. Mrs Murphy shows that the score of sympathetic responses for Group H was 25 per cent more than that for Group W. This she attributes partly to the facts that (1) H had wider play space, and (2) H group was divided roughly into two age groups. Thus one group of eleven children (ages 4:0 to 4:6) in H were older than the oldest in W (ages 3:1 to 3:11), while all the rest of H (except one) were younger (2:4 to 2:11) than the youngest in W.

To my mind this last fact seems the most important; the weakness and need of the very young would appeal more to the elder children. As Mrs Murphy herself remarks: 'In Group H there were only five girls and two of these had almost the role of "pets" in the group. One of them, Joyce, who was also one of the youngest children in the group, was lowest on "responses given" and next to highest on "responses received".'

The table giving the scores of each child of the sympathetic responses given, shows very great individual differences. I give a small selection of the extremes, together with the record of the sympathetic responses received by the same child.

Child	Sympathetic Responses given	Unsympathetic Responses given	Sympathetic Responses reced	Unsympathetic Responses reced
Group W				
Theodore (3:8)	1	0	7	1
Elda (3:7)	2	0	8	3
Agatha (3:8)	46	22	26	7
Douglas (3:10)	70	6	11	2
Group H				
Gregory (2:11)	0	0	15	1
Jesse (2:11)	5	0	16	0
Alex (4:2)	5	1	3	0
Davis (2:7)	1	0	45	1
Heidi (3:11)	10	1	56	14
Heinrich (4:0)	47	5	9	2
Janet (4:6)	38	4	27	6
Julius (4:1)	56	20	17	1
Seth (4:3)	27	0	18	4

Here we see all types – the little pets, Gregory and Jesse, just receivers; the sympathizer, who is never otherwise, Seth; the vigorous active Julius, who scores high in both sympathetic and unsympathetic responses. Mrs Murphy makes the following interesting contrast between Julius and Alex: 'Julius, a child of great social responsiveness, gives many sympathetic responses, while Alex, with little social contact, gives very few. Alex is an imaginative, bright boy who remains aloof from the group, absorbed in his own dreams except on occasions when he can co-ordinate the activity of other children with his elaborate dramatic patterns. Julius's scores for conflicts were quite as conspicuous as his outstanding score for sympathetic responses to distress situations; but his sympathy by no means consisted chiefly of defence or sympathetic uses of aggressive techniques. It was Julius who offered a toy to a new child, and who leaned over a hurt child, inquiring warmly what was the matter. His sympathy included warmth and a resourcefulness that were beyond that of the other children in the study.'

Others besides Mrs Murphy have noted that there is a slight tendency for the more generally active and sociable child, by achieving more social contacts than most in a given period, to show more aggressive actions, as well as more sympathetic ones.

A further interesting finding was that boys proved to be as sympathetic as the girls, though here again the smallness of the numbers must be borne in mind.

Summing up as to the frequency of sympathetic responses noted by Mrs Murphy, we may recall first her own summary that such 3-year-olds generally, though not universally, made sympathetic responses to certain kinds of distress. On inspecting her detailed tables, we find that out of thirty-nine children there were only eight who gave less than three sympathetic reactions and of these five were under 3 years of age. Among the thirty-two children of 3 or over all gave some sympathetic response; but one only gave one and two only gave two each.

Very marked individual differences in sympathetic response are recorded in another report, which dealt with the relationship between young sisters [76]. Twenty pairs of sisters were observed, the older sisters varying from 3:5 to 6:9, the younger from 1:4 to 4:11. One markedly indifferent older sister made only one sympathetic response in thirteen instances of her little sister's distress; the younger made one sympathetic response in the two instances of her elder sister's distress. At the other extreme another older sister showed eleven separate sympathetic responses on the three occasions of her sister's distress. It was observed that this girl was so sympathetic that she was affected by hearing about the distress of children unknown to her.

So far from the sympathetic responses being mere imitations of the mother's behaviour, in many families the older sister would comfort and try to entertain the little sister when the latter had just been punished by the mother.

The effects of experience and training. While the process of sympathetic induction of feeling seems to be essentially an innate element, experience widens its range as the child comes to understand the signs of distress, and later even to infer distress in another from the latter's circumstances even when he gives no signs of distress.

Again, while there seems to be a fundamental and innate impulse to help and protect, this is, of course, soon complicated and modified by experience. The very satisfaction of the impulse when the helper sees the pleasure of the helped one (conveyed back to him also to some extent by sympathetic induction) tends to encourage such impulses in the future.

Where the impulse is very weak experience may show the child in turn that at least it pays to be co-operative, and the actual helping of others may be carried out partly as an imitation of others, or through the suggestion of those admired and loved, as we shall see in the next chapter. We see the first of these types in the man who gives generously to charitable funds for the sake of the public prestige that it brings him, but without the inner urge to relieve the distress. We also meet the youth whose capacity for sympathetic feeling and impulse to help or protect are extremely weak, in some types of bullies and young toughs, and among some of the young delinquents brought before the courts. Deficiency in the helping or protective impulse and in sympathy, combined with excessive innate assertiveness, seem to be the true innate bases of what some people have miscalled lack of 'inborn moral sense'.

CHAPTER 6

Basic Affection, and Early Attitudes to Parents

In studying early child development it is well, I think, to use the term 'affection' rather than 'love', retaining the latter for the very complex sentiment which develops later. Even affection is hard to define, though we know it when we feel it; but at least one sign of affection for another is delight in that other's presence, and other signs particularly useful in studying infancy are certain spontaneous expressions which we shall describe.

First, as we are specially concerned to find out whether there is any innate tendency towards affection without experience, let us leave on one side for a time records as to the response of babies towards their mothers, for it might reasonably be argued that such affection is due merely to having received food and comfort from them. The manner in which babies of 1 to 2 years show their affection for their mothers is, however, a useful clue as to their attitude to other babies, dolls, and animal pets. As everyone knows, the little infant loves to get close to his beloved mother, snuggles up to her, strokes and hugs her, and such behaviour may be shown also to other babies, to dolls and animal pets, from whom the infant has never benefited. That such love of physical contact with the mother, though sensuous, is not sexual I hope to show in a later chapter.

Affection shown by babies to other babies. There is ample evidence that babies of a year or less behave in the following way towards other babies, from whom they have received no benefits. I quote first the record of a very acute observer, Professor G. V. N. Dearborn [33]: 'For the first time in her life L today (age 0:10½) had hold of a little girl about her own age, and it was surprising to see how delightedly she hugged her and how emphatic were the signs of instinctive "natural" affection for even an entirely strange little girl.' Again, at 1:0 L was 'distinctly jealous when another baby sat in her nurse's lap a moment. A few moments later, however, she offered him all her toys and voluntarily ran through all her little accomplishments (dancing, throwing kisses, etc.) for his entertainment, besides hugging him violently on every occasion presenting.'

Note that the feeling and impulse were strong enough to overcome jealousy, though jealousy was not surprising in the circumstances. Again, at 1:0½ L offered Johnnie all her favourite toys; at 1:8 she became very fond of a little baby boy when away on a visit and when she returned home would kiss his photograph. At 1:11 'L's instinctive interest in and even love for young infants is now very strong – she pays no attention to a playmate of 2¼ years, but is interested solely almost in the latter's sister of 6 months'.

Some of my own records suggest something that looked very like the dawning of at least a mild liking even earlier than the reports on L. Thus B at 0:5 had rarely if ever met a baby of his own age. Yet he and another baby of 0:6½ 'showed great delight in each other and stretched out their hands to one another when sitting with feet not quite touching'. Such behaviour, however, might be interpreted as merely a form of keen interest. The reports gathered by Miss M. Shirley [94] include a number as to apparent affection for other babies, nearly always about the ages of 0:8 to 0:10. As to two twins it was reported, F at 0:8 'crazy about his sister W is the only way to describe it. He tries to attract her attention and laughs and coos with her'.

Early affection may be disinterested. At a somewhat later age we get more remarkable evidence of affection shown towards baby brothers or sisters where we might expect jealousy to dominate. Thus of one of our boys I noted: 'By 2 : 6 the elder boy's sentiment for the baby of 0 : 5 is considerable. He likes to stroke and kiss him; is very gentle with him; puts his arms round him and often patting him said, "Billie (his own pet name) like Baby".' At 2 : 7. 'Is much more demonstrative to baby than to us; often wants to kiss him and puts his arms round him. This is done practically never to us except when one of us pretends to cry, and of course at regular times, like going to bed.' At 3 : 5. 'Very fond of baby; affection seems instinctive. He often has to give up to baby and sees us petting him; and he himself of course gets no advantage from baby. Yet he makes a great fuss of him and began to cry in the train when he could not see baby and we pretended he had gone away.'

Such affection cannot, of course, be explained by any association of advantages gained as might affection for the mother, and often the mode in which affection is expressed, e.g. crying when the baby has gone out of sight or thrusting toys upon it, cannot have been mere mechanical imitation of what the infant has seen the parents do. In passing I may remark that those who, in minimizing the importance of innate tendencies, have sought to explain nearly all infantile social behaviour as due to imitation and suggestion, seem to need as a foundation an enormously strong and general innate tendency to imitate, but this they seem to slur over. That imitation and suggestibility are of great importance in social development we certainly do not question – as will be seen in a later chapter; but their influence is apt to be slight when a natural spontaneous impulse is not also present.

If further examples of early affection are needed, we may refer to the extraordinary fondness mere infants of under 2 usually show for dolls and animals. This is so well known as hardly to need exemplifying, but I quote a description by my psychologist son on his daughter, J. at 0 : 11. 'Great excitement at sight of aunt's dog (her first close contact with dog or any animal); shrieks of delight, whole body held rigid, fists clenched and unclenched with excitement. Tried to grab dog and pat him vigorously. Movements of hands very vigorous and she had to be restrained lest dog became angry and bit her.' 'From 0:11 to 1:6, always great excitement and pleasure at sight of dogs and cats. Always tried to pursue and fondle them. From 1:6 to 1:9, still great pleasure at sight of dogs and cats, but is now able to handle them with more restraint. At this age, great fondness for neighbour's cat; spends much time watching and stroking it and cries bitterly if removed from its presence, sometimes falling to ground in fury. She often goes out of house to look for this cat and if she cannot see it seems to find comfort in saying "'ussy bobos" (Pussy in bed).' 'From 1:3 onwards: great interest in and affection towards babies and young children. Often runs after them and tries to cuddle them; this applies to complete strangers as well as to local infants. One of the first words she said was "baby".'

The frequency of disinterested affection. Unfortunately we have inadequate evidence to say whether such disinterested affection as we have been discussing is revealed by all or nearly all infants. K. Bridges, who observed about fifty nursery-school children over a period of three years, gives no precise figures. She writes that 2-year-old children usually show more affection for adults than for other children, but that 'three- and four-year-old children show mutual affection, and apparently take even more pleasure in hugging and kissing than in being hugged and kissed. Some older children take special delight in looking after the little ones, carrying them about, sitting beside them, or holding their hands. This parental affection begins to develop about the third or fourth year, while filial affection develops before the pre-school period. There is no evidence of sex preference in the affections of pre-school children. Little boys are as much attracted to each other as they are to little girls; and similarly the girls show as much affection for one another as they do for the boys.'

D

The babies studied by M. Shirley were all under 2, and she relied partly on the reports of parents as to personality, though the babies were also seen in their homes by the psychologist every week during the first year and every fortnight during the second year. An examination of the records of the individual children shows definite evidence of affection in ten out of the twenty infants, doubtful in six cases, and no evidence in four, and we must bear in mind that K. Bridges reported expressions of affection for other infants as rare before the second year.

Age of maturing of disinterested affection. Some slight evidence that the period of 1:6 to 2:0 is a critical one for the appearance of signs of affection, or at least of friendliness towards other strange infants, is afforded also by another research on nearly 100 infants, ages 0:6 to 2:1. Here the conditions were such as to stimulate rivalry, as the babies were put in playpens in pairs, with a variety of partners at different times, and only one toy provided between them – a bell or ball and a drum. Hence there was plenty of selfish or aggressive behaviour – 'negative' social behaviour, as it is often labelled. Nevertheless, smiling and babbling at the partner, touching him, caressing him and co-operation (unfortunately grouped with mere looking at him) were as frequent as 'negative social reactions' in the twenty-one infants in the age groups 1:2 to 1:6 and appreciably greater in the group of twenty-four from 1:7 to 2:1. (In defence of the researchers' including 'looking at the partner' as a positive social behaviour, it may at least be said that it implied not grabbing for the toy and indeed showing more interest in the partner than in the play material.) Unfortunately in this report all the results are in averages and percentages and there is no statement to show whether any child showed *no* signs of affection. The omission of such evidence of individual differences is the more surprising in that the numbers are in any case too small for generalization about any differences between the age groups. Still, so far as it goes, this research supports the view that the period round about 1:6 to 2:0 is an important transitional one for friendly, including affectionate, behaviour towards infants of the same age.

As we saw, Dr Bridges' report on the frequency of affection is not backed by precise figures, and we are unable to generalize about the usualness of this trait of affection at 2 or 3 years or say whether entire absence of the signs under circumstances when some children at least show them (e.g. in the presence of an infant of the same age or less) must be taken as ominous.

We have some further evidence as to affection between sisters in the report already referred to in our chapter on sympathy [76]. The signs of affection recorded were patting, hugging, kissing, and some verbal expressions of affection. In the five periods of observation of three-quarters of an hour each, eighteen out of the twenty older sisters (3:5 to 6:9) showed some affectionate approaches to her younger sister. The range in scores was as great as 0 to 17. Of the twenty younger sisters (1:4 to 4:11) eleven showed affectionate approaches, with a range of 0 to 8.

Of course, we must bear in mind that these five periods of observation might not be truly representative of the children they dealt with.

One further thing, however, we can add. Tender affection, combined with sympathetic help, may be shown in most unpropitious homes by children who are also at other times very obstreperous. I quote one report by my daughter on two children in a nursery school in a very poor neighbourhood. 'K, age 4:0, of low intelligence (mother for a time in mental home). I had observed him for over four months. He was very rough, a member of a small gang of older boys (4:0 to 5:0), noisy and pugnacious. Today I saw a completely new side of his character. His little brother, F, aged 2:0 came to school. F cried and howled continuously. K sat with his arms round him and tried to comfort him, e.g. pointed out his cousin, saying, "Look,

Harry's here" and offered his own milk (which he generally loves). All morning K devoted himself to his little brother; when F started crying again, K sat by him with his arms round him and began to cry himself and finally said, "I am going to take him home, he wants his mum". Then at dinner he seemed proud of his little brother, telling the others his name. Later K still sat with his arms round F, in spite of the temptation to play with the much-loved special "wet-weather toys" which were put out for use just then.'

'Jane, aged 3:0. Very big for her age. Often inclined to be pugnacious – suddenly hits, pinches, or even bites other children and then laughs; jeers noisily at others, e.g. "Silly old Doreen"; yet never seems very angry. Sometimes rushes up to me and hugs me and says, "Miss, I like you". When little Fanny (aged 2) joined older children in a running-round game and was in danger of being knocked over, Jane stopped her own running and took F's hand, saying "Come on, Fanny", though she thus stopped herself joining effectively in the game.'

Kissing as a learned sign of affection. I have not mentioned kissing among the natural signs of early disinterested affection, because I believe that kissing in the very early years is usually a learned process, and may at times be used quite mechanically by the child and not as a sign of affection; it may indeed sometimes be found rather boring by the child. Most mothers indulge in kissing their babies from the earliest months and soon try to get the baby to kiss them back, and so by imitation, or by request when that is understood, the baby obliges. Undoubtedly a baby, even during the early suckling period, will turn its lips to the cheek of its mother (or of father or other person in whose arms it feels at home) and will often try to suck. But kissing in the conventional sense seems in early childhood to be a learned action and apparently needs to be learned if it is to occur in the second or third year. At what stage it would be indulged in, if the child were never kissed and never saw others kissing, it is impossible to say. We can only speculate that it would be likely to appear after puberty when the characteristic excitement appears with it, in its association with sexual attraction.

My own observations agree with those of Preyer [86], who reported of his boy, at 1:1, 'The child has absolutely no idea of what a kiss signifies, for he always turns his head away when he is kissed, no matter by whom.' The baby learned to 'give a kiss' when told by 1:3, but only at 1:11 did Preyer think the boy realized that a kiss was a mark of favour. Here are some of my own notes.

Y, 1:0. Kissing does not seem to be an expression of feeling; it seems rather to be done as a game. Sometimes she will offer all members of the family kisses in turn repeatedly.

X, 1:0. Offers kisses when she hears anyone else kissing or when being taken out of a room; has done this for two or three weeks.

The boy B, though very sociable and responsive to suggestions, seemed often bored with kissing about the age of 1:0. Just afterwards I noted the following at 1:2½. B's kisses are now a sign of either (1) gratitude or happiness, often offered when very pleased, or (2) saying good-bye. He will kiss when leaving M or me if he is willing to leave, *but not if he wants to stay*. Today he seemed to offer a kiss to M as a hint that she was to go when Mrs D took him. 1:3. Climbed on top of his tub and then, when facing away from me, made kissing noises several times. He seems to do this when pleased.

1:5½. When he kissed his mother (by request) he insisted on giving me one, and *vice versa*. Today after kissing me, he went off towards lawn and then turned back, went into the house, found his mother and kissed her. This looks very like the following of a routine procedure.

B, 1:5½. After kissing his mother and me he took hold of my chin and pulled my face near his mother's, apparently for me to kiss her. On my doing so he released me, kissed his mother and me again, and then again dragged me to his mother, and so several times.

At least by the end of the second year, our children clearly realized that kissing was a sign of affection. As already exemplified above, it may accompany the words 'I like you'; yet even now the child's throwing his arms round his mother's neck was probably a more unlearned expression. Concurrently (as other psychologists have noted in their own children) with this growing use of the kiss as a sign of affection there was also an increasing practice (from early in the second year) first of accepting kisses on bruised fingers, etc., to make them better, and later a child might kiss his own injuries.

Affection towards parents. As stated at the beginning of this chapter, I deferred any reference to the attitude of babies towards the mother because she does so much for the baby that many pleasant experiences come to be associated with her, and we were searching for evidence of disinterested affection. Long before the time of maturation of such disinterested affection (which we have seen seems to be about 1:0 or 0:9), such associations with the mother have been taking place, indeed from the first weeks. In the more popular modern term, the baby is being 'conditioned'. This term adds nothing of value as a description of the process, but has a nice aroma of scientific experiment about it because of its origin in connexion with Pavlov's famous experiments on reflexes in dogs.

Let us recall then the familiar facts that the mother satisfies the child's craving not only for food, but for other elementary things, such as warmth, bodily support, and very soon for mere company. The tremendous power of such experiences in building up a strong bond between infant and mother is unquestionable; and I need hardly give evidence of affection in infants towards mothers.

On the other hand, the child's affection is not dependent merely on the satisfaction of its hunger or thirst, or on some sensuous or even sexual satisfaction through suckling at the breast. For at least some time during the second year a strong

bond may also be set up with the father. This may be shown
by a look or cries of delight and smiles, by inviting the father
to share sweets, and so on. In my own case the greater
opportunities of companionship and play with the children
after the age of about 1½ or 2 led to signs of increased affection, in spite of the fact that I was usually called in to act as
the disciplinarian for any naughtiness. B's first explicit
declaration of affection for his father came indeed only one
day later than that for his mother. Thus I noted:

B, 2:6. Suddenly put his arms round M and said, 'B
like Mummy', and kissed her spontaneously. (He has heard
the word 'like' before in reference to things to eat.) The next
day he came to me in the garden, put his arm round my
neck and said, 'B like Daddy'. Again I noted at 2:9: A
very little playing with him affects his feeling towards one.
After I had been playing with him today he came up to
me and said, 'I love you very much'.

About the ages of 3 or 4 our three boys became even
better friends with their father. On the other hand, the fact
that affection may reveal itself in babies from whom all
expression of affection has been deliberately withheld by
adults is indicated, by what seems a rather cruel experiment,
on twins (girls) reared in an experimenter's house from the
age of 1 month [34A].

The twins were fed and cared for entirely by the experimenter and his wife. They were kept in individual 'coops',
with an opaque screen between them. The experimenters
did not smile at them or play with them or talk to them.
Only when a baby cried did they enter the room and deal
with what seemed the cause of the crying. This treatment
was continued until the babies were about 6½ months old.
Careful notes were taken as to the appearance of many
activities, including social behaviour, and the dates of first
appearances were compared with those of about forty
infants of whom biographical records were available. In
nearly all points, except motor activities and talking, the
twins exhibited the usual items of behaviour as early as the

majority of the other babies. Thus both the twins showed 'smiling at a person' and laughter at about the average age—the former at about 2 months. The investigator's general conclusion was: 'Fondling is not necessary for the development of interest in, and every sign of affection for, the adult'.

The supposed Oedipus complex. Some readers of this book may be rather hazy about Oedipus; indeed, I have known some people who talk freely about the Oedipus complex to be ill-informed about the origin of the term. Oedipus was the son of a mythical King of Thebes; the latter had been informed by the oracle that he would be killed by his son. So he ordered his wife, Jocasta, to destroy her child at birth. She, however, merely told a servant to expose her child on the mountains. He was rescued and brought up by another queen and later met his father (without knowing who it was) and killed him in a quarrel. Later he met Jocasta, without his (or her) knowing she was his mother, and married her. When he discovered the facts he blinded himself, went to the place where it was foretold he must die, and was swallowed by the opening earth.

Freud's use of the term Oedipus complex covers much more than the experiences of Oedipus himself; for Freud's use is based on the dogma that boys are sexually attracted to the mother during infancy and are already antagonistic to the father then.

It should be stated here that Freud based his doctrine of the Oedipus complex partly on the results of analysis of adult neurotics. Later he concluded that some of what he had thought actual memories of his patients were fantasies, and, though he still thought these were important, he came to the view that the complex does not affect, in adulthood, normal people. But he retained his view as to the behaviour and experiences of infants in their relations to mothers and fathers, and some of his followers have gone even beyond their leader.

Freud's enunciation of the doctrine of the Oedipus complex is essentially bound up with his view that sex development is already emerging during the first years of life, and that in particular after the second year the boy is attracted towards the mother and the girl towards the father. A discussion of this is incomplete without an examination of the evidence as to early sex development which we shall undertake in the next chapter. This, however, is an appropriate place to consider Freud's statement about the usual attitude towards parents in these first years. He declared emphatically that the direct observation of children up to about 6 years shows the following: 'It is easy to see that the little man wants his mother all to himself, finds his father in the way, becomes restive when the latter takes upon himself to caress her, and shows his satisfaction when the father goes away or is absent. He often expresses his feelings directly in words and promises his mother to marry her; this may not seem much in comparison with the deeds of Oedipus, but it is enough in fact; the kernel of each is the same' [39].

That this attraction is not due to the mother's doing so much for him is shown, so Freud argued, by the fact that she does as much for her little girl and yet that does not produce the same effect. Indeed, he asserts, the little girl turns more and more to the father, thus: 'The loving devotion to the father, the need to do away with the superfluous mother and to take her place, the early display of coquetry and the arts of later womanhood, make up a particularly charming picture in a little girl, and may cause us to forget its seriousness and the grave consequences which may later result from this situation.'

Now Freud does not say this happens merely in abnormal children who were later to become neurotics. No, it is to be regarded as the normal process. Let us see what evidence 'direct observation of children' does provide. Freud seemed to be content with a general impression plus a very few individual case studies. First we may recall that the psychologists Stern, C. S. Myers, W. McDougall, each with three, four, or five children, on whom they made many precise observations were all opposed to Freud's idea of an Oedipus complex. My own observations on five children led me to the same conclusion. However, this gives us only seventeen children in four families. So I planned an inquiry about the children of sixteen friends of mine, all professional psychologists except three who were university teachers in other subjects. Between them they had thirty-nine children – twenty-four boys and fifteen girls. I also included reports on our own five children. The parents were asked to report on the attitude of each child to each of the parents at the ages of 1 to 6 or 7 or over, and to do so in close consultation with their wives. They were also asked as to signs of jealousy and curiosity about sex. They were assured that in any publication of results their reports would be kept anonymous. The full details of this research are given elsewhere [102]. Here I will briefly summarize the main findings.

The first question was which parent, if any, was dominant in the affection of the child. The parents were asked to put '?' if they were doubtful and 'equal' was, of course, also an alternative. Further questions referred to apparent reasons for changes at different ages, which parent undertook the more severe discipline at different ages, any signs of special sex interests, jealousy – of parent or other child – and so on.

Taking first only those children reported on up to at least 5 years of age, I got the following results:

Boys Year	1	2	3	4	5
Preference for mother	14	13	10	9	9
Liked equally, or doubtful	4	4	6	6	6
Preference for father	0	1	2	3	3
Total	18	18	18	18	18

Here we see at the ages of 3, 4, and 5 actually a small *decrease* in the number of boys who preferred the mother, and a small increase in the number preferring the father or liking him as much as the mother. Small as these numbers are, if we compare the scores for ages 1 and 2 against 4 and 5, this trend in favour of the father is statistically most unlikely to be due to chance; whereas if Freud's views were right there should be decided changes in the opposite direction.

Girls Year	1	2	3	4	5
Preference for mother	10	10	8	8	7
Liked equally, or doubtful	2	1	2	2	3
Preference for father	0	1	2	2	2
Total	12	12	12	12	12

Here also we find some decline in the number of mothers preferred, but it is actually somewhat less marked than it was among the boys.

We can approach the results in a different way by contrasting fathers' and mothers' scores with boys and girls. Taking the children of ages 2 to 6, we find: *Fathers* become more instead of less popular with *boys* during ages 3, 4, 5, and 6 as compared with 2 : 0.

The father's score with boys at
    2 years is 11 per cent of possible score.
    3 years is 20 per cent of possible score.
    4 years is 28 per cent of possible score.
    5 years is 28 per cent of possible score.
    6 years is 23 per cent of possible score.

Fathers' scores with girls are remarkably like those with boys:

Father's score with girls at
    2 years is 10 per cent of possible score.
    3 years is 28 per cent of possible score.
    4 years is 26 per cent of possible score.
    5 years is 25 per cent of possible score.
    6 years is 15 per cent of possible score.

Mother's score with boys at

    2 years is 77 per cent of possible score.

    3 years is 61 per cent of possible score.

    4 years is 57 per cent of possible score.

    5 years is 57 per cent of possible score.

    6 years is 68 per cent of possible score.

Mother's score with girls at

    2 years is 87 per cent of possible score.

    3 years is 66 per cent of possible score.

    4 years is 66 per cent of possible score.

    5 years is 66 per cent of possible score.

    6 years is 78 per cent of possible score.

The reasons given by the parents for any changes in children's preferences supported strongly the views I expressed in reference to our own children – e.g. the father taking more interest in the child, or one parent beginning to take over more of the disciplining, and so on. In particular, there was a strong relation between preferences and easier discipline.

The parents had been asked to state which was the more strict disciplinarian to each child at each age, and during the period 2:0 to 7:0 the more severe parent only scored thirty-three preferences against fifty-five for the less severe, and the severe parent would have scored far fewer but for the fact that in twenty-two cases the girls persisted in preferring the mother in spite of her being the more severe.

There were not many reports of jealousy, and they were nearly all about jealousy of another child, not of the father or mother. There was one record of a boy, aged 7:0, who was thought to be jealous when his father and mother were showing affection to one another, but there were several examples of a girl's being jealous when her mother displayed affection to anyone else – father, brother, or sister. The only marked jealousy of this type was shown by our own girl Y. Thus: 'Y, 3:5½. Saw me kissing M (her mother) fondly. Said, "Dear Mummy" and came running up to kiss her. This was rather typical of her behaviour on such occasions. No jealousy of M yet. Y, 3:11. M kissed Y's brother and Y immediately asked M to kiss her. Then her brother wanted another kiss and Y flew into a rage and begged M not to kiss him. Y even struck him and said he was "naughty". Y, 4:0. Y's brother kissed M at table. Y got off her chair next to M and fondled her too.'

I may add here briefly the results gained in another very careful investigation as to children's preferences for the father or mother [95].

Fifty boys and fifty girls at each of the ages 5 to 9 were interviewed. Taken together about 22 per cent of the boys preferred the father and about 28 per cent of the girls. There were clear indications that preferences were affected by the frequency with which a parent 'spanked' the child. The preference of the youngest groups of boys and girls were also affected by the frequency with which the parents played with them.

CHAPTER 7

The Development of Sex and Sex Interests in Childhood

FOUR or five different types of evidence have been brought forward in favour of the view that sex-feelings and the behaviour prompted by them appear already in the first few years of life. We will begin by considering what is perhaps the weakest type of evidence of all.

Curiosity about sex. It has been argued, especially by psycho-analytic writers, that the little child's curiosity about sex affairs, e.g. as to how babies come or as to the differences between a boy's body and a girl's, when this is first noted, is a sign of actual sex-development beginning in the child. It seems hardly possible that such a view can be held by any parent who has brought up even one child of average live-liness of mind. The questions 'Why?' and 'How?' come in torrents about all sorts of things, especially about the ages of 3:0 and 4:0. Such questions are put about the most trivial things; how much more must they be expected about such a thrilling event as the arrival of a little brother or sister. As to the child's body, that has been a central point of interest from the early months, and what more natural than intense curiosity when he finds his sister is different from himself?

If the parents try to repress such curiosity, to reprove the child and say he must not ask about such things, then of course curiosity will be further reinforced, and the idea grows up that there is something specially secret or even

naughty about these matters, and it is not then surprising if
there is something like an appearance of guilt or shame in
the child, which at once the psycho-analysts seize on as
highly significant. I once roused great curiosity in our four
children by an experiment in which I placed an (empty)
box on a high shelf, and said that no child must touch it.
The youngest went on asking what was in it for three weeks!

My questionnaire on the attitude of infants to parents,
described in the last chapter, included three questions referring specially to sex. Since I have given full details
elsewhere [102] I will only say here that the answers as to
curiosity decidedly support the view I have put forward
above, with one little girl of 3½ as a doubtful exception –
and that on the basis of a report by a parent who was a very
strong supporter of Freud's views. In particular three pairs
of parents who had accustomed the children from the first
months to seeing their parents in the nude in the bathroom,
as well as older sisters and brothers, reported a marked lack
of interest in sex differences.

Considerable attention was attracted in this country by
reports from the Malting House school at Cambridge,
formerly run by the late Dr Susan Isaacs. Some thirty
little boys and girls, ages mostly about 2 : 6 to 8 : 0, mingled
there, and as there was a remarkably free discipline, it is
not surprising that there was considerable curiosity about
sex organs. As Dr Isaacs herself wrote: 'They began to
wake up to the fact that over a large area of their desires
and impulses the customary checks and penalties were
removed. They found not only that they were free to run
about, and to occupy themselves in any way they liked,
either with real material or fantasy, but also that at the
first hint of quarrelsomeness they were not forcibly separated
or scolded or spanked' [59].

In particular one would expect a specially keen curiosity
especially in boys (or girls) of 4 or 5 or over, who had no
sister (or brother) at home and had never seen a naked
member of the opposite sex. Considering the fact that

Dr Isaacs's observations lasted over a period of three and a quarter years, the records of curiosity about sex differences, or as to excretory processes, are by no means surprising. Incidentally they include reports of the curiosity of *girls* about Mrs Isaacs herself. That one of the boys, however (aged 4), did seem to have some quite exceptional and persistent curiosity and impulses which looked very suspicious, we shall see in the later section on masturbation. On the other hand we shall also see the marked tendency of Dr Isaacs, as a convinced Freudian, to read sex-interpretations into some commonplace everyday activities of little children.

Some further evidence as to sex curiosity is provided in an excellent record of observations on two groups of nursery-school children in the U.S.A. [35]: Group I contained eleven boys and eleven girls, between the ages of 2:3 and 3:6; Group II consisted of eight boys and eight girls between 3:6 and 5:2. They were observed during the dressing periods for twenty-one days. These children showed very little curiosity when seeing one another naked, or about going to the toilet. The behaviour of most of the children in Group I during elimination was 'as matter of fact as when brushing the hair'. As to the older group, 'The most noticeable behaviour of the children of Group II when undressed in the presence of other children or adults, was an absence of any sense of impropriety.'

Only seventeen observations were made in Group II which indicated an interest in their own bodies or those of other children. Here is a sample: 'Mildred stood beside the toilet while Ted was urinating. "What is that?" she asked. "That is my penis." "Girls do not have a penis," she remarked, looking up to the teacher for confirmation of her statement. "That's right, Mildred," replied the teacher. "Only boys and men are made that way." "And my Daddy, too," the child added. The tone of the conversation was exactly the same as if it concerned hats or spectacles.'

It is noteworthy that one little girl showed great curiosity about her navel. These examples are typical of the children's attitudes as described in this report. Certainly there is no hint of any penis envy in the girls, or fear of castration in the boys, as asserted by the Freudians. The general trend of this careful report strongly supports the view that there is little curiosity about sex differences in children at these ages, when they are accustomed to seeing one another naked, and few signs of special sex interests or sensations. Here again, however, there were one or two children who appeared exceptional, to whom I shall refer again in the later section on manipulation of the genitals.

The 'castration complex'. Closely allied with the question of anxiety about sex is the 'supposed 'castration complex'. Some psycho-analysts confidently assert that the little boy, when he discovers that his sister has no penis, is terrified lest his own should be cut off; and that the little girl, when she finds out the difference between herself and a boy, is filled with envy. This is how Freud puts it; the little boy, he says 'is horrified at the possibilities it reveals to him; the influence of previous threats occasioned by too great a pre-occupation with his own little member now begins to be felt. He comes under the dominion of the castration complex, which will play such a large part in the formation of his character if he remains healthy, and of his neurosis if he falls ill, and of his resistances if he comes under analytic treatment. Of little girls we know that they feel themselves heavily handicapped by the absence of a large visible penis and envy the boy's possession of it; from this source primarily springs the wish to be a man which is resumed again later in the neurosis' [39].

In a later article on 'Female Sexuality' [40] Freud adds that the little girl regards her mother as responsible for her deprivation of the penis, and so arises the girl's strongest motive for turning away from her mother; and that she even 'clings obstinately to the expectation of acquiring a similar organ sometime'. But evidence for such things is sadly lacking, except for the extremely unreliable reports of patients.

Of course, if parents do threaten a boy that they will cut off his penis if he plays with it, we can understand such fears. But Dr Isaacs, who states that *many* children are so threatened, only gives as evidence the report of one patient who said he was so threatened by his father, when he was 14. An eminent psychiatrist, Dr R. G. Gordon, with undoubtedly far more experience with adult patients, has stated that evidence of a fear of castration was entirely absent in his own experience [48].

As I have stressed several times in this book, evidence about the behaviour of children and its interpretation are often difficult to assess because of the danger of subjective influences and prejudices. So it is relevant here to give a sample bearing on this question of a castration complex of Dr Isaacs's tendency to interpret children's behaviour as symbolical. She quotes the report by the mother of a boy of 2 : 7, as follows [59]: 'At bath-time he got his duck out of the stool and put it in the bath near the plug-hole, saying, "Duck want wee. Duck wee in hole. Duck have penis." I asked him which was the duck's penis and he pointed to a place on its underside and said, "Penis dere", but there was nothing like a penis there.' Dr Isaacs interprets this as 'Denial of castration' anxiety! Another note on the same boy is no more convincing: 'Said to his mother, holding his own nose – "Got nuvver penis". His mother asked, "Where?" He said, still holding his nose, "Dere – penis dere."' This is interpreted by Dr Isaacs as 'Reassurance against castration anxiety'!

I may conclude this section by stating that Miss Dillon, in all her very detailed and careful report mentioned above on thirty-eight children under very stimulating conditions, gives no hint of any jealousy by the girls as to the boys' genitals, or of any fear of castration among the boys, though, as we shall see, she gives intimate details as to manipulation.

Erections and anticipatory development. Another fact often brought up as evidence of sex development in infancy is that erections of the penis appear in some boys even in the first year. One psychologist who made careful observations of a large number of infants in a maternity ward noted four erections just after birth and one at four days. There is other evidence to show that such erections may occur in at least a proportion of infants, though spontaneous erections seem to disappear after the first few years. (It is notable that the Freudians hold there is a 'latency period' in sex development in infancy, usually from about 5 to 10 years of age, when repression of earlier impulses and memories is supposed to take place.) Naturally the evidence of spontaneous erections becomes harder to gather as the infant grows older, and the complication that some manipulation of the penis may begin at least towards the end of the first year makes it uncertain whether an erection observed is entirely spontaneous.

It is, however, quite unjustifiable to assume that the sensations in the child due to an erection are at all comparable to those of an adult or adolescent. It is indeed possible for erections in oldish men to occur without any sex impulse or specially pleasant sensations. I would suggest that these infantile erections are another example of what I called 'anticipatory phenomena' in a study I made of reflexes in infancy, some forty years ago. I quote from the article in which I reported my observations [106]. 'As early as D.2 (i.e. the second day) I noted, as to one of my boys, B, "When held, and feet just allowed to touch floor, performs quite regular walking movements: progressive, forward movements, not mere pressure against floor, or lifting up and down".' D.9. 'Walking reflex still present, as decided as before.' The movement is something distinctly more than the response pressure of the foot when pressed by the hand. There was a movement upwards and forwards of the foot, which was then rather heavily stamped down.

The tendency seemed so unusual that I checked the

observation on another boy, and on D.11 noted 'Walking reflex very evident, much more so than on second or third day when his nurse tried it; in fact, it did not then show perceptibly.'

The same phenomena were noted in the girl X and the boy A, but in them it had disappeared before the age of 3 weeks. With B it continued up to 6 weeks or more. The various psychologists who studied the development of their own children seem to have missed this phenomenon in the first 2 months. But some years later two observers reported finding such a 'stepping reflex' in the majority of the 125 infants tested before the end of the 'neo-natal period' [25].

In observations on my own children I also noted another evanescent reflex – the jerking up of the arms when startled, which occurred in the earliest weeks but which was much less marked later on, though something like it appears at times in some adults. Physiologists have indeed reported that crude reflexes may occur even in the foetus in the womb, and reappear later after birth in a more co-ordinated form.

These various examples of what I have called anticipatory developments may seem hard to explain, as they may serve little or no purpose for the moment (apart perhaps from the arm-raising in alarm). We might perhaps regard them as relics of earlier stages of evolution, for we know that the foetus passes through stages in which it resembles more primitive forms of animals; or we may regard them as puzzling examples of the way in which Nature proceeds in maturing and developing the mechanisms of the living organisms. She has to begin with preliminary preparations long before any mechanism can function efficiently. It seems to me that erections in the first year or two may well be of the nature of anticipatory mechanism developments not genuinely sexual, and that they cease after a few years without any such repression as is suggested by the Freudians.

Manipulation of the genitals. Here, again, we are up against differences both in observations and in interpretations. In the first place we must recall that the mere baby is intensely interested in all parts of his body. He will play with his toes and his hair, and the baby boy at least inevitably comes across the sex organs and plays with them. It may be that even as early as the second year these parts may be more sensitive than other parts of the body, but it is quite unjustifiable to assume that this is so on the mere grounds that the genitals are played with. For one thing fidgeting with the trousers or knickers near the genitals may be due to tightness of the garment; and it is as justifiable to assume that the fidgeting is to gain greater comfort as that the tightness has stimulated the genitals and the fidgeting is always done to increase the stimulus, though that may be true in some cases.

The term 'masturbation' has usually been used for all playing with the genitals. With some others I prefer to use the term 'manipulation' except where it is continued to the point of orgasm, as it often is in adolescence. But even so, differences of interpretation as to what is manipulation for the sake of pleasurable sensation and what mere playing comparable to playing with the ears or toes, is no doubt partly responsible for very different results reported by different observers. Thus Dr Charlotte Bühler, discussing a wide range of findings in Germany, concluded that evidence of masturbation in infancy was rare, one survey of 1,000 children in a Berlin clinic showing only fifty-three cases of masturbation, the highest percentage being for boys during the age period of 7, 8, and 9 years. In an American nursery school, however, among about 280 boys and nearly 300 girls between the ages of 2:0 and 5:0 34 per cent of the boys and 21 per cent of the girls were observed to 'masturbate', but there was no description as to what exactly constituted masturbation.

My own questionnaire to parents, already referred to above, asked for signs of 'sex interest or feeling'. Among forty-two infants none was reported as having masturbated to the extent of causing any unusual facial expression, except for two boys in the same family; one boy played with his genitals about the age of 2 : 0, while having teething trouble, and the habit ceased about 2 : 3. With the other boy it recurred even at 7 : 0 when he was excited and it seemed to be a 'nervous mannerism'. Full details of the results of my questionnaire on sex interests are given elsewhere [102], but as this problem of masturbation is so disturbing to some parents and teachers, and the differences as to interpretation and frequency reported are so substantial, I think it well to give in detail the figures from some other careful inquiries.

Turning to the admirably precise report of M. R. Dillon, already referred to, we find that in her younger group of twenty-two children (ages 2 : 3 to 3 : 6) in twenty-one periods of observation there were fourteen instances of 'play with the genitals in some form' by seven children (one boy contributing four of them) and four of these cases seemed to be mere curiosity. In four instances, however, 'the behaviour, although of an absent-minded character, was prolonged. In these cases, the children were exceedingly unstable and the tic-like manipulation of the genitals accompanied crying, refusals to comply, interference with the activities of other children, and failure to persist in the task of dressing.'

In the older group of sixteen children there were twenty cases of play with the genitals in some form, one boy being responsible for eleven of these, five of them prolonged. In general Miss Dillon concluded that such playing seemed 'to be related to a state of emotional instability. The activity usually was not accompanied by a conscious sensory response apparently, but was a mechanical, motor reaction which served, perhaps, as a release of tension. Masturbation was much more frequent among the boys than the girls.' Also 'In no case was there an attempt to conceal the play nor was there any indication of a sense of guilt or shame.'

Now let us turn to an inquiry on much larger numbers,

namely, 244 children selected haphazardly from the same number of families, but superior in education to the average family [77]. Half the children were in a 'Guidance' group. The children were studied from the age of 1 : 9 with follow-up observations and reports from parents, visiting nurses and teachers up to the age of 5 : 0 or over. The rest of the children were a control group, with much less precise observation, and I give only figures from the 122 children in the Guidance group.

In this inquiry very precise definitions were given to the parents and visitors, as to the various types of behaviour to be noted. As to masturbation the classifications were as follows, according to degree and frequency.

1. At least three or four times a week or more, vigorously stimulates genitalia by manual stimulation with or without orgasm, depending upon physiological maturity; or involving orgasmic equivalent (excitement followed by relaxation); rubbing against furniture, floor, causing friction with clothes. Includes severe cases where child publicly and compulsively masturbates. (Only direct stimulation of genitalia classified under this heading; e.g. rocking, where there does not appear to be actual friction occurring, is not so listed.)

2. Vigorous stimulation once or twice a week or mild habitual touching more frequently (tic-liking pulling at genitalia many times a day).

3. Absence of overt behaviour but considerable tension about it; or infrequent episodes (one or two times in six months).

4. Occasional or perfunctory touching of genitalia (when child needs to go to toilet, during bath, or in response to physical irritation or too tight clothes) with absence of tension about it.

5. Absence of overt behaviour and no apparent tension.

Only items coming under (1), (2), and (3) were listed as 'problem behaviour'. Unfortunately Miss MacFarlane does not give separate figures for (1), (2), and (3), but the totals for the Guidance Group were as follows:

Ages	1:9	2:0	2:6	3:0	3:6	4:0	4:6	5:0
Percentage incidence of masturbation	4·2	4·3	7·9	6·0	6·6	3·4	2·1	3·4

At all age levels the boys showed a slightly higher incidence than did the girls.

Miss Macfarlane comments. 'These figures are so much lower than psycho-analytic literature suggests that to many their accuracy will be under suspicion. We wish to point out that the education of our parents relative to the frequency of such behaviour, and the desensitization of our parents relative to sex behaviour and conflicts, has resulted in their having a much more relaxed and objective attitude than most groups of parents. We have only one or two suggestions to offer. First, the more frank and open attitudes of the parents may have reduced tension which frequently may express itself in masturbation. Second, better habits of hygiene may have appreciably reduced masturbation due to external irritation. We can hardly believe that openness and an easier attitude on the part of parents led to greater secretiveness on the part of the child; and yet these figures are sizeably smaller than the author obtained with a similar age-group of dispensary patients.'

I have kept till the end of this section any reference to masturbation in the observations of Dr Susan Isaacs in the Cambridge school. It is very notable that, in spite of her predilection for finding sex phenomena, she writes that only one instance of masturbation was recorded in the three years, and that for 'quite a short period'. It seems that she (rightly, I think) ignored examples of momentary touching, for she writes in the Introduction to her book as follows: 'If one could win parents generally to realize that occasional or mild masturbation, for example, or other open expression of sexuality, is a common happening belonging to a normal phase of development, and one best dealt with indirectly, then the real danger of too harsh treatment might be avoided. But, on the other hand, if one could get it widely understood that where masturbation is continuous or persistent, the child is in urgent need of skilled therapeutic help, *not* whippings or leg splints, then a great deal of serious mental disturbance in later life might be happily forestalled.'

To sum up all the evidence as to manipulation mentioned above is not easy in view of the differences as to estimates of what is and is not genuine manipulation. On the whole I think the evidence strongly suggests that, with the great majority of infants of about 2 to 5 or 6, manipulation is very trivial, so trivial indeed that it is only momentary and easily inhibited by very ordinary distractions.

On the other hand one boy in Miss Dillon's older group did behave in a very extreme way. He was, she reported, 'exceedingly unstable during the entire period. He interfered with others, dawdled, and, when not occupied, manipulated his penis.' One leading authority on the sex life of childhood [81], while taking the sceptical view as to Freudian evidence on sex in infancy which I have advocated here, does give at least three examples from his own experience with patients of marked sex precocity. One girl of 6:0 seemed to get a definite orgasm through masturbation; one boy of 5:0 masturbated with penis erect and frequently tried to stimulate his little sister by playing with her genitals. One of his men patients reported that he masturbated often after the age of 9, with seminal emissions as early as 10:0.

The wide range of individual differences which we have repeatedly stressed in this book is known to be true in reference to sex development. Menstruation may begin in girls in extreme cases as early as 3:0 or as late as 20:0. Sex maturing in boys is harder to determine precisely, but there is little doubt that the range is very great. We may expect, then, in large groups of children one or two at least who are highly precocious in sex, and incidentally they may try to initiate other children. But the fact that a few are sexually abnormal in both the statistical sense and the sense of betraying highly undesirable behaviour, is not to be taken as evidence that in the great majority of children the experience of genuinely sexual sensations begins before puberty. In the chapter on adolescence we shall refer to sex interests and masturbation again.

CHAPTER 8

Innate and Acquired Fears

IN contrast to the topic of sex, we have many reports from hundreds of children themselves as to what fears they suffer from; but naturally these reports can be relied on only when they come from children past the stage of infancy, and by that time various influences may have been at work producing or at least accentuating specific fears; for example, a painful fall when climbing, the bite of a dog, or the more subtle influence of suggestion.

The value of fear. In much of the literature about children's fears the background assumption seems to be that all fear is deplorable and even 'abnormal' in the sense of something which we should seek to eradicate. In fact, however, fear and the associated impulse to escape danger, by flight or concealment or (especially in infancy) by cries for help, is one of nature's greatest safeguards against injury or death. Indeed, though it is unusual, we find some children in whom a stronger element of certain kinds of fear would be a good thing. Certainly in at least two of my own children there were times when I wished they were more fearful and so more cautious. Lest it might be thought that I tried to 'molly-coddle' them may I say that we allowed them, even at the age of 3 or 4, to climb trees in the garden. The eldest boy (about 10 or 11) then devised a game of climbing up a fir tree with horizontal projecting branches, crouching down with his arms protecting his head and then letting himself bump from branch to branch down to the bottom, and some of the younger ones imitated him. Only when I discovered this, and that they were then planning to climb the tree and descend roped to one another, as in mountain climbing, was the veto applied.

Anyone who has seen children playing 'last across' in front of fast-moving traffic, knows that a little more fear might be a good thing in some children. Burt, in his study of juvenile delinquency [21], still unequalled for its combination of strict critical examination of extensive evidence together with a great human interest in, and understanding of, individuals, writes as follows: 'Many delinquents suffer not from too much, but from too little fear. They are reckless, headstrong, and venturesome. In some this unflinching fearlessness, the utter absence of all prudence and precaution, may be the direct result of an inherited shortcoming; for, if the excess of an instinct may be inborn, so equally may the lack of it.' Though Burt goes on to say that such lack of fear is just as often due to lack of understanding, he is right, I believe, in holding that it is sometimes due to an abnormally small element of inborn tendency to fears.

As the main purpose of this book is to study the 'normal' in children together with the occurrence of extremes in certain tendencies, this passing reference to the possibility of a lack of fearfulness is not out of place, though we shall see that most children suffer from many fears which are unnecessary and due largely to environmental influences.

To get at the original and innate factors in the causation of fear we must study its very first manifestations, though, of course, any fear, even suddenly caused, say, as late as the age of 7, by the bite of a dog, implies a pre-existent tendency to feel the emotion of fear in the presence of, or at the idea of, danger of pain or injury. No amount of learning or 'conditioning' can produce the actual ingredients of an emotion.

From the point of view of motivation in everyday life, to establish the existence of certain innate tendencies to fear is not as important as, say, in reference to assertiveness or active sympathy. Nevertheless, it is of interest in that it might explain great individual differences between children having the same upbringing and with the same suggestive influences.

The first innate fears. As we saw in discussing anger, it is impossible for us to say with certainty when the specific emotion of anger, or fear, first occurs. But a careful observer who spends much time with the same baby daily over a period of months can finally learn to discriminate between the cry of hunger, which is pacified by feeding, and the cry of pain, relieved only when, say, the baby belches or a projecting pin is found in his garments. The cries which arise when the baby is frustrated in some way and which we therefore tend to assume are expressing anger, are not at first easy to distinguish from the cries at, say, a sudden loud noise; but there soon appear trembling and wide-open eyes, characteristic of the adult when feeling intense fear.

The psychologist who was probably the most sceptical about there being many innate tendencies to fear, and who argued that any fears of animals or of the dark were acquired, was J. B. Watson, one of the chief early exponents of behaviourism. Yet even he admitted that there is an innate tendency for the baby to experience fear, or rather, as he would say, to 'show the fear response' (*a*) when it hears a sudden loud noise, (*b*) when the support of its body fails and it begins to fall, (*c*) on experiencing pain, and (*d*) probably at some sudden movements made by others when it is falling asleep [112].

As no psychologist, to the best of my knowledge, has disputed that an infant tends to show signs of fear, or alarm, or at least 'nervous shock' under such circumstances, I need not give here any of the ample evidence I gathered of such reactions in the first months of life. I will only add three things clearly observable in my own five children:

1. There were marked individual differences between the children in the tendency to show such fears, and other types later.

2. The fear response tends to cease when a particular noise is frequently repeated.

3. Fear responses to a sudden loud noise were less likely when the baby was comfortable in my arms, or in those of the mother, though they might occur then, even during feeding. Thus, when B, at the age of $0:3\frac{1}{2}$, was being suckled, a band outside started playing. He stopped sucking, went on a moment (he was getting sleepy), then his mouth squared and he yelled, lip trembling, and he had to be comforted. Put down in the cot (band still playing), he squared his lip again, but the windows were closed at once, and he did not cry again.

Nevertheless, it is generally true that the total situation is an important factor in deciding whether a specific stimulus will produce a fear response.

Fear of pain. The view that all fears, other than the two or three innate ones which even J. B. Watson admitted, are due to painful or very unpleasant experiences, and, in short, are really conditioned reflexes, is not supported in the case of my own children by observations on their reactions to pain. Pain produced surprisingly little fear, provided it was roused in circumstances under the child's own control. Thus, B at 1 : 8 'fell down half a flight of stairs on his back; kept his head from bumping till the bottom. Screamed loud for about half a minute. I took him from the maid's arms, but he at once wanted to be put down and started climbing stairs again! No fear here.' Also C at 1 : 3 'climbed on a chair; it fell over, C banged on the floor and screamed. Within two minutes C climbed again; a worse fall and more screams. In two or three minutes C climbed up again!'

Others of the children showed similar fearlessness as to pain, at least pain in an expected form and a familiar situation. This was especially true of B, who was particularly fearless in later boyhood when in the sea, in the first experience of horse-riding, and in climbing dangerous cliffs.

Fear of the very strange and uncanny. Before we discuss the fears most commonly reported as occurring in infancy, e.g. of animals and the dark, let us consider one type of fear which it is extremely difficult to explain as the outcome of experience. I give first a few examples.

A, at 1 : 9, showed great fear of a velvet rabbit which was among his Christmas presents. He screamed and ran away from it; yet I am confident that he had never had any unpleasant experience with a rabbit or anything resembling it. At 1 : 2, X showed great fear of a Teddy bear *when it was moved toward her;* she turned away, trembling in every limb; but when it was still she would pick it up and kiss it. Two German psychologists report that 'a hare mask caused a child of 1 : 0 to wince and strike out, one of 1,: 5 to scream, and one of 1 : 9 to cry, but to laugh at the mask when it was taken off by the experimenter.'

Of the boy B I noted at 0:11 : 'Yesterday he had a new toy given him, an elephant. He seemed frightened of its trunk; he touched it once or twice, drawing back his hand quickly.'

The late Professor William McDougall reporting, I imagine, on one of his own children, wrote [75]: 'A courageous child of 5 years, sitting alone in a sunlit room, suddenly screams in terror, and, on her father hastening to her, can only explain that she saw something move. The discovery of a mouse in the corner of the room at once explains and banishes her fear, for she is on friendly terms with mice. The mouse must have darted across the peripheral part of her field of vision, and this unexpected and unfamiliar appearance of movement sufficed to excite the instinct.'

As to my own daughter Y at 1 : 5, I noted: 'M (mother) in room. I crawled towards her (Y) on hands and feet, monkey wise, with head down. She retreated to end of room, looking frightened and cried out, "Mamma," in an alarmed tone, half a whimper. Even when I looked up and smiled there was still an expression of distress, and wagging of hands at me afterwards. Then she ran to M and, when seated on her knee, Y showed no such signs when I approached right up to her.'

At 1 : 7½ 'Y showed great dislike of a doll, the top of whose head, with the hair attached, opens backwards. She cried, moved away, and wriggled her body repeatedly. When the head closed and said "Baby", Y said, "Baby" and took the doll in her arms, but again horror was suggested when I opened the head. Yet she can scarcely have any idea of the injury caused by opening a head.'

Stern [97] gives the following reports: 'H (2 : 7) started back in fear from her toy drawer with the words "Got a fright". What was the reason? A couple of doll's eyes joined by a wire that had dropped out of a broken doll! I took the eyes out of the drawer, examined them closely with the child looking on, and even spoke to them to calm H's fear. But she would not hold them, and knocked them out of my hand on to the floor.' 'G (1 : 10) was given a little metal dog that ran about gaily when wound up. The boy set up a terrible cry and ran away from the animal; on the other hand, when it was still he liked to pick it up. A mechanical top that played a hymn-tune excited and terrified him much more. He could not think how to escape from the dread object, and even in my arms cried bitterly.'

H (3 : 3). 'Her parents for fun were making an elephant by covering themselves with a big rug and moving one arm from side to side like a trunk. Although the child had been told beforehand that they would make an elephant, at the sight of it she burst into frightened tears, so that we showed ourselves at once. H got somewhat calmer as we explained our make-up to her, but later on asked several times: "*But not make another elephant, No!*" As we knew she had never shown any fear of a real elephant, it was therefore its mysterious character and that alone which frightened her.'

In all these examples there is a certain element of strangeness; and it is possible to see some usefulness in an inborn tendency in infants of very primitive ages to scream for help when faced with something extremely novel. In a wide inquiry among parents as to fears shown by 153 children (ages from 0 : 3 to 8 : 0) it was found that half the children in each age group (*a*) under 1 year, (*b*) between 1 : 0 and 2 : 0, and (*c*) between 2 : 0 and 3 : 0, had shown some fear of strange objects or persons (including masks) or strange situations, and even one-third of the children between 3 : 0 and 4 : 0 [64]. To some extent a tendency to fear the entirely novel may explain the fear of the sea to which we now turn.

Fear of the sea. It seems to me that the element of great strangeness is probably the important factor in producing fear of the sea. I was with four of our children when they first caught sight of the sea. There had certainly been no suggestion that would make them fear it; on the contrary, it was something spoken of as a coming pleasure. Here are some of the notes I made. The first is of the usually fearless B at 2 : 2. 'Showed some slight fear when taken for first time to edge of the sea. At least he said "No, no" when I urged him to go into (or even nearer than 2 feet to) a quite shallow, calm, narrow passage between rocks.' 2 : 6 'Would not go even to the edge of the sea with M, who was paddling.' The boy A at 1 : 4 'Showed fear when held in my arms near sea; would not put his feet in it at all. Screamed when his feet were put in. No forcing, of course, was attempted.'

X (who later showed herself remarkably courageous), when she first saw the sea, at 2 : 5, 'was very frightened at first. Would not even paddle for several days; but by end of a week she loved it though she would not lie on her back even in very shallow water.'

Preyer noted of his child at 1 : 8 [86]: 'My child showed every sign of fear when his nurse carried him on her arm close by the sea. He began to whimper, and I saw that he clung tighter with both hands, even during a calm and

E   129

at ebb-tide, when there was but a slight dashing of the waves.'

On the other hand Sully writes of several infants who showed no such fear; but two of the three were only 1 : 1 and may not have been sufficiently mature. We will consider in the next paragraph this essential factor of maturation in fear. First, however, I will report that four at least of our children soon lost their first fear of the sea, by gradual familiarization; B and X in particular eventually became too venturesome. It seems clear, however, that some children take a very long time to lose their fear of the sea. In such cases indeed early pressure to go into the sea, or constant suggestion by parents to be careful, or unfortunate accidents such as slipping into a hole in the sands and falling into deep water, may establish a fear which is never overcome.

Maturation and the fear of animals. In some observations on my own children I had what seemed to be clear evidence of the importance of maturation in connexion with the fear of animals, and fear of the dark, as we shall see later. But the clearest evidence for the effects of more maturation are given by an experiment by Gesell in which infants of different ages were confined in a small pen. At 0 : 2½ there was little or no response to the seclusion; at 0 : 5 some signs of slight disturbance; at 0 : 7 such vigorous crying as suggested fear. As to fear of animals let us first consider the remarkably fearless B. A note at 0 : 6 says 'No fear of Tweed, the big sheepdog' (at the farm where we were staying for a holiday). 'Intensely interested in the dog's moving tail. Grabbed it later.' This was typical of B's attitude to animals until the age of nearly 1½ years, except for a half cry at the sight of a cow, and he might have previously heard a cow low. Then at 1 : 8 I noted 'Our neighbour's dog tripped on string of B's horse and yelped. B cried and showed fear of dog on its re-approach. The first apparent fear of a dog, I fancy.' At 1 : 8½ 'He cried a little (apparently afraid) at a bull-terrier, though the latter did not bark. But he was frightened by the roughness (playful) of a dog some days ago.'

There were other notes of fears of a dog just later, and though there may have been yelping or rough play, I want to emphasize that B was thoroughly familiar with the barking and romping of dogs, and even if knocked over we knew how indifferent he was to that.

The attitude to animals of B – and of the other children – strongly suggests a lurking innate tendency, not maturing in the earliest months, but soon afterwards ready to be called forth by a very slight stimulus. I will not repeat the various similar observations on my other children, as I have given them in detail elsewhere [102], but here is a note by William James on two of his own children. To one boy he gave a live frog, the first time at about the age of 0 : 7, the second time at 1 : 6: 'The first time he seized it promptly, and holding it, in spite of its struggling, at last got its head into his mouth. He then let it crawl up his breast, and get upon his face, without showing alarm. But the second time, although he had seen no frog and heard no story about a frog between whiles, it was almost impossible to induce him to touch it' [61].

As to his little girl he writes: 'One of my children from her birth upwards saw daily the pet pug-dog of the house, and never betrayed the slightest fear until she was (if I recollect rightly) about eight months old. Then the instinct suddenly seemed to develop, and with such intensity that familiarity had no mitigating effect. She screamed whenever the dog entered the room, and for many months remained afraid to touch him. It is needless to say that no change in the pug's unfailing friendly conduct had anything to do with this change of feeling in the child.'

Experiments have been made with harmless snakes showing that children under 2 : 0 showed no fear of them, while at 3 : 0 and 4 : 0 they were hesitant. It was, however, possible that children of 3 : 0 might have heard that snakes might bite them, though here again we must bear in mind the difficulty of suggesting danger to many children unless there is some inner tendency to respond readily to the suggestion.

In illustration of the ineffectiveness of suggestion when *contrary* to an innate tendency to fear (or perhaps disgust) I quote notes by a former research student of mine, made on his own child, E. W.: '$1:3\frac{1}{2}$ whimpered and came running to her mother when she accidentally touched a worm while playing outside. $1:4\frac{1}{2}$ tried to accustom her to worms by showing them to her and saying "Nice worm". She repeated – "Worm", but whimpered and apparently alternated between fear and curiosity – sometimes put her hand out to touch the worm but always withdrew it before actually doing so. On several occasions during this week she has found a worm while playing and came whimpering to M saying "Worm, worm!" and not satisfied until her mother came and threw it away.' '$1:6$. Some time ago showed disinclination to stroke a cat, and recently, when she was quite on friendly terms with cats, was frightened at two kittens about a week old – would not touch them and shrank away, clinging to M. This furnishes an example of fear of *strange* animals – she had never seen a tiny kitten before.'

Experiments with fear. Lack of attention to this factor of maturation vitiates most of the inferences in J. B. Watson's famous experiments in which he produced the fear of a white rat in a child of $0:11$ by striking a steel bar, making a loud noise, when the infant touched the rat, of which he had shown no fear before. As I have given a thorough examination of Watson's experiments elsewhere [102] I will not repeat it here; but I may record an experiment in which I quite failed to set up in Y at $0:11\frac{1}{2}$ any fear of a pair of opera-glasses by blowing a loud whistle when she touched them. Nor did she even start when the whistle was blown but just looked round to see where the noise came from – and so several times. Then, instead of the opera glasses she was shown a woolly caterpillar on her brother's hand. She had seen one before but had never touched it or been plagued with one or had fear or disgust of one suggested to her, to the best of my knowledge. Her brother had only just discovered his caterpillar and assured me that he had not attempted to tease Y with it. (I had complete confidence in his truthfulness; and even if Y had been teased, such teasing implies a pre-existent dislike. And even if, to go further, fear of the caterpillar had been suggested to Y, this would not affect the most interesting result of the test, as will be seen.) She repeatedly turned away with a shrug of the shoulders or slight shudder, 'waggling' her hand from the wrist at it (as she did sometimes when annoyed), but without touching it. When she turned again to look at the caterpillar, I loudly blew the wooden whistle. At once Y gave a loud scream and turned away from the caterpillar. This was repeated four times with precisely the same effect.

Note that the whistle which previously the same day had caused not even a slight start, now in conjunction with the caterpillar caused a loud shriek. It might seem at first indeed almost Watson's experiment with a reversed association or 'conditioning', to use the modern term; the nervousness about the caterpillar produces genuine fright at the sound of the whistle. In fact it is the conjunction of the two causes which results in the fear.

Some years later similar experiments to mine were done in the U.S.A. with fifteen healthy infants between 0:8 and 1:4, using not animals but inanimate objects in conjunction with a loud electric bell, and were found to produce no fear 'conditioning' even after six days of experiments.

Fear of the dark. None of our five children evinced any fear of the dark during the first year. They were accustomed to be left to go to sleep at night without any light. Six of my former students reported the same of their children. The exceptionally fearless B never showed unmistakable fear of the dark, but once at 4:11 after he was in bed, he cried because the blind was up and said he did not like the 'light mixed with darkness'. Y, at 3:1 showed a similar fear of what she called 'the dark light' on the first night of the change from 'summertime', though she had never before shown any fear at being left alone in bed in the dark. One of my former students also reported that her child showed distress at 1:5 when, in a lighted room, she saw the darkness outside.

There are a large number of reports by other psychologists to the effect that no fear of the dark was shown by their infants during the first year, and it seems quite clear that it is only long after the child has become accustomed to darkness that the fear first arises. Whether when it comes it is due to maturation of some innate tendency (as seems likely in some examples) or always due to suggestion, it is impossible to say, though here again the ease with which fear of the dark can be suggested makes it more comprehensible if there is some tendency just maturing which is quickly responsive to the suggestion. To that argument we may add that suggestion *against* fear of the dark and encouragement to face it, is often so difficult. Thus as to Y at 2:1 'M went down the greenhouse steps into a dark cellar saying "Come into the cellar." Y was unwilling, saying, "No, no." As she came away she said "Dark, kikky" (nasty).'

A word must be said about '*seeing things*' *in the dark*. In Chapter 2 I have already mentioned that the girl X about the age of 5:0 suffered from vivid and unpleasant imagery in the dark. She said she saw 'horrid things – cabbages all round the room and a girl going out of the window'. For some weeks she would come downstairs crying. Her descriptions of the images were so vivid that it seemed clear they were of the type labelled 'eidetic' imagery, the type not very rare in childhood, even in broad daylight. The image is 'placed' as it were on a seen background – the wall or ceiling – and resembles a genuine hallucination. We tried putting her elder brother to sleep in her room and though night visions continued for a time, they were now only 'nice things'. Now this girl X was the one who was so exceedingly brave in the sea and with horses, at the age of about 3 and onwards.

Our boy A also experienced vivid night imagery about the age of 5 and so did the boy C at 7:7. But the latter said that if they were horrid things he stared at them and made them turn into nice things. Once the images remained even when I went to the boy's bedroom and he could not understand why I could not see them. Some other psychologists have reported similar unpleasant night imagery in their children about the same age. For example, Stern reports of his daughter, Hilde, at 4:9 that she said she saw 'Such ugly children and women keep coming, so black, and then they go away from one another again; so ugly! And when I shut my eyes, I still see them'.

It seems clear that such night imagery *need* not be a premonition of future neuroses, though Dr Susan Isaacs includes it among her examples of 'Neurotic difficulties in children'.

Group studies of fears in infancy and middle childhood. We may now turn to some findings of researches on large groups of children, including inquiries among older children who can be asked to report on their fears. One of the earliest of these was made by Burt on 250 children in Liverpool [23]. I give the table summarizing the result.

Children's Fears

	Age 5–7 years		Age 8–10 years	
	Boys Per cent	Girls Per cent	Boys Per cent	Girls. Per cent
Animals	39	50	82	61
Persons	26	20	9	26
Inanimate objects	22	8	9	5

As some of the children may have reported more than one fear we cannot be sure as to how many reported *no* fear, and, if any, perhaps even they had fears they did not wish to confess. But it is clear that the great majority of the children of ages 8–10 had some fears and almost certainly at least half of those between the ages of 5 and 7. Certainly the proportions are enough for us to say that fears in children of these ages cannot be regarded as abnormal in the statistical sense, or as 'neurotic'

Some of the details are of interest. The large percentage of boys who at 8:0 or 9:0 are afraid of animals is explained partly by the fact that they include animals they *might* meet rather than do meet; thus lions are mentioned by 44 per cent of the boys, while 26 per cent of the girls mention cows. 'Persons' include robbers and drunken men.

In the U.S.A. the extensive inquiry, already referred to [64], among parents in which they were asked to report fears occurring in their 153 children (all ages up to 8:0) during a period of three weeks, revealed the following further interesting facts, some of which have a close bearing on the reports on individual children given earlier in this chapter.

(i) None of the eight children under 1:0 showed any fear of the dark; but of those between 1:0 and 2:0, 8 per cent did, and 11 per cent of those between 2:0 and 3:0.

(ii) More than half the sixty-eight children of ages 1:0 to 3:0 showed some fear of a strange object, person, or 'situation'.

(iii) About 60 per cent of those between the ages of 1:0 and 3:0 showed fear of 'noises', 'noise plus motion', or 'events associated with noise'.

The normality of some fears at the ages of 1:0 and 2:0 is again exemplified by (ii) and (iii).

Unfortunately there are no figures showing whether any children showed no fear at all in the three weeks, but of each age group at least half revealed at least one of the types of fears, and as the different types of fears observed numbered twenty-three there is little doubt that the great majority revealed several types.

The group of children between 4:0 and 6:0 numbered

only twenty-four. Of these half revealed, in the three weeks, some fear of one or more of the following: dreams, ridicule, death, robbers, the dark, being alone, and imaginary creatures. Nine of the children showed fear of some animal, seven of bodily harm; and there were some entries against nearly all the other items. So again, so far as these small numbers go, we cannot say that having some fears is rare in children, but rather that it is the normal thing. As to the point at which it becomes a serious abnormality, everything depends on the degree and persistence of the fears. That they can be seriously disturbing to some parents is shown by some figures given by Dr Susan Isaacs [58]. At one time she dealt with inquiries from parents addressed to a popular weekly. Out of 402 cases on which advice was asked, fifty-nine were those of 'Fears, night terrors and anxiety', very nearly as many as difficulties in reference to the children's attitude to parental authority (sixty-nine).

It has been shown by one of Burt's research students (Miss H. F. Campbell) that there was a general factor in estimates of different fears among 350 schoolchildren, i.e. fears are not merely individual items acquired by some specific experience. Children tend to some extent to be fearful on the whole or brave on the whole, though there are a few marked examples of those with only one or two highly specific fears, as we saw was the case with X whose only fears, almost, after 4:0 or 5:0 were night visions. Miss Campbell also found that some children were mainly afraid of physical dangers, whereas others were more afraid of personal or social situations.

If the general tendency to fear is especially high, we may get the child who is popularly called a very 'nervous' child. Such is likely to be highly suggestible to warning of danger and resistive to suggestions that the objects he fears are really harmless. The combination of the temperamentally fearful child with a mother herself constantly afraid for the child, is clearly the condition most likely to produce the abnormally fearful child.

I do not wish to underestimate the effect of suggestion as a cause of fears. But as we shall see in a later chapter, suggestion works much more easily when it is working with a natural tendency rather than against one, and the difference of fears of children within the same family is easier to explain if there are some innate differences in the children. A good example is the following [64]: 'Extreme contrasts in the tendency to be fearful may occur among siblings. An instance of this character appeared in the reports of the fears of a girl aged 9 years and a boy aged 7 years. The older child was extremely fearful on her own account and was also apprehensive about the safety of her younger brother and other members of the family. She would fear to enter a dark room, refuse to go downstairs alone even during the daytime, show apprehension in crossing a bridge, and in scores of specific situations manifest a similar tendency to be afraid. Her younger brother was quite immune to fear in numerous situations which alarmed his sister.'

Now here the younger child would be exposed to the suggestion of fear expressed by the older; yet he remained impervious. Apparently he was exceptionally lacking in innate fear tendencies while his sister was very prone to them, partly, as the authors say, owing to her physical condition; she seemed to be 'somewhat lacking in vitality'.

Such children may be difficult to distinguish from those suffering from what is more precisely labelled 'general anxiety', which may again be a product of a constitutional proclivity combined with unfortunate experiences, for example, deprivation of the mother's love or separation from the mother at some critical early period. To examine these extreme cases, however, would take us beyond the scope of a book on the normal child, so we will return to some more findings about unselected children.

Nearly 400 children in the U.S.A. between the ages of 5 and 12 were asked to describe their own fears [66]. The types of fears most frequently mentioned in the whole group were: (1) ghosts and other supernatural agents, witches, corpses, etc., mentioned by 19 per cent of the children (the inquiry was made some twenty-three years ago); (2) being alone in a dark place, or being lost (14 per cent); (3) animals (13 per cent); (4) bodily injury, illness, accident, pains (nearly 13 per cent). It may be noted that the first three closely resemble the main types in which I have suggested an innate element – fear of the very strange and uncanny, fear of the dark, and fear of animals.

School and home worries. Yet another inquiry made was among over 1,100 American children of about the ages 11:0 and 12:0 [65]. The children were asked what they worried about. A list of possible 'worries' was given them and they were asked to indicate whether they worried about each particular thing 'often', 'sometimes', or 'never'. Twelve items were related to school; twelve others, some of which are clearly of the nature of fears, were non-school items. Combining the 'often' and 'sometimes' scores the highest score was for 'being scolded by father or mother' – about 78 per cent of the boys and about 75 per cent of the girls. The earlier types of fears which we have especially discussed above still remain – 'being alone in the dark' being marked by about 43 per cent of the boys and 43 per cent of the girls; 'being bitten by a dog' was mentioned by about 32 per cent of the boys and about 37 per cent of the girls; 'ghosts and spooks' were feared by 21 per cent of the boys and 18 per cent of the girls. Of special interest to us are some marked individual differences. Thus about 9 per cent of the boys and 11 per cent of the girls say they were *often* worried about being alone in the dark, while 56 per cent of the boys and 56 per cent of the girls said that *never* worried them. 'Dying or being killed' worried about 10 per cent of the boys 'often', about 67 per cent 'never'. The figures for girls were also about 10 per cent 'often' and 71 per cent 'never'.

As to school worries the most frequent was 'having a poor report card' – about 68 per cent of the boys and about 73 per cent of the girls.

On the average among boys, worries connected with school were nearly half as many again as home worries; among girls it was about the same. Of course, one cannot generalize on the basis of this investigation: in other countries, with different schools, or homes, results might be very different.

The establishment in the child's mind of some specific fear may result sometimes in a remarkably permanent fear. It may remain only a mild feeling, such as a slight nervousness in the dark even if one knows there is no danger; it may be a mild horror approximating to disgust rather than fear, as in my own strong revulsion from earwigs which I imagine was established by the suggestion, which I know I believed in boyhood, that they might crawl into one's ear and get into the brain.

CHAPTER 9

Motivation and Environmental Influences

Learning and conditioning. In our earlier chapters we have discussed several tendencies in which there seems to be some innate element, e.g. the play impulse and the urge to practise new capacities, assertiveness, sympathetic feeling, active sympathy (helping and protecting), affection, and some fear tendencies; and we have seen examples of the ways in which these tendencies can issue in actions, at first with little or no modification due to training or experience. From the earliest, or almost earliest stages, however, environmental influences can begin to modify these tendencies, encouraging or deflecting or checking. One of the most obvious ways is the checking of an action or impulse by consequent pain; though, as we saw in the case of the infant who repeatedly tried to climb stairs in spite of painful falls, an impulse, if it is strong enough, may persist in spite of frequent checkings and penalties. The other obvious influence is seen when an impulse and action leads to satisfaction, which tends to encourage its repetition. These influences are, of course, familiar in connexion with rewards and punishments.

When an action, say an infant's hitting another on first entering a nursery school, results in the former being hit back (which may surprise an infant who has never before played with children of his own age) the next time the impulse is felt it may be checked by the recall of the previous experience of being hit back. This is often expressed by saying that the child (or the impulse) is '*conditioned*' – a term which has become far too loosely used. Its original use was in the phrase 'conditioned (or conditional) reflex' and referred to the widening of the original stimulus of a reflex, e.g. Pavlov's dogs whose saliva began to flow eventually merely when a bell was rung, after a learning period in which the bell was rung when meat was given to the dogs. It might just as accurately have been called an associated reflex; and so in many of the wider uses of the term 'conditioned', the term 'associated' could be substituted; but psychologists familiar only with the old, rigid form of associationism (exploded by James Ward, G. F. Stout, and others half a century ago [98]) revolted against any use of the term 'association' and insisted on appearing right up to date.

The checking, encouraging, or modifying of original impulses and actions is, of course, constantly taking place during childhood, and the nature of such influences may profoundly affect the issues. Original fears can have |the range and variety of stimuli which produce them widened through associations; aggression can be checked by penalties, and so on; but the ease with which, and the extent to which, an impulse is likely to be modified by a given experience depends also on the inherent strength of that innate impulse in the child himself; not all infants of $1\frac{1}{2}$ years, having climbed the stairs only to bump to the bottom and yell with pain or fright, would just afterwards proceed to climb again. We shall refer to this question of the importance of the innate factors later in this chapter. It is not entirely unconnected with the growth of intelligence and the power to form ideas and to look ahead; but the little child's actions are affected by the immediate consequences, and not until later can he be influenced by the thought of remoter consequences.

The limitations of environmental influences. Having stressed the fact that innate tendencies can be modified at an early age by environmental influences, we must stress equally the fact that environment is not by any means the sole determinant of the development of conduct and character. Common observation has noted the 'black sheep' in families brought up under the same influences as their brothers and sisters of irreproachable repute. Most of the brothers and sisters of young delinquents are not themselves delinquent; and though a substantial proportion of 'problem children' referred to clinics come from broken homes, the majority of children from broken homes do not themselves become problem children.

Sometimes, indeed, there emerges in the most unpromising home environment a character of a type one would never expect in such a setting. I give one example in some detail. It refers to a home in which there were two boys who had been committed to a Remand Home for repeated thefts. These boys and their home were studied by an investigator over a period of six months; he was also a teacher of the girl Madge referred to later [27]. In this record I have changed the names of the children. The father of the family was a man of low mentality with a poor sense of social awareness. He was a bricklayer's labourer and had held his job by hard work and by his popularity among his workmates who treated him as a halfwit. His feeblemindedness was an object of derision in the immediate neighbourhood. The investigator found him to be inoffensive, ineffectual, and completely dominated by his excitable nagging wife.

Madge had two brothers older than herself (the delinquents) and there were also younger children. As to the eldest brother, he seems to have been the worse delinquent; the younger, Tom, displayed many of the features which normally characterize a boy who is a victim of parental neglect. He was dirty and untidy in his habits, ill-mannered, and lacking in discipline. He fought for his food like a wild animal, and he was generally irresponsible in his conduct.

Out of school Madge now assumed an outstanding social dominance over her parents and siblings during all the interviews which the investigator conducted with the family as a group. Her two older brothers whose individual physical strength surpassed that of Madge often threatened to attack her, but she was always able to repel them with her expressions of disdain. When the mother took some outside work, Madge assumed responsibility for the material, intellectual, and moral welfare of her brothers. The home was extremely filthy, untidy, and its furniture was of poor quality, but Madge was intensely proud of it. She reduced the truancies of her two elder brothers to a bare minimum, and she exercised a forceful interest in their school and leisure activities.

During the six months which were involved in the investigation of this case, there was a noticeable growth of the social and moral dependence of both the parents and the siblings upon Madge herself. She controlled the social life of the siblings and supervised their attendance at the day school and even the Sunday school.

How are we to explain such a remarkable emergence as that of Madge in such a home? The most probable explanation seems to be that there were some inborn qualities in Madge which were not in her elder brothers or her parents. Great intelligence was apparently one, but hardly enough to explain everything. Incidentally it is worth noting that the paternal grandparents were regarded as mental defectives and very feckless people. The maternal grandparents, on the other hand, were honest, hardworking people who acquired some social standing. Madge seems to have inherited more from the latter than did her brothers, and less from the former.

A book of this type is not the place for a thorough examination of the difficult problem of the relative importance of inherited or innate tendencies as compared with environmental influences in the development of the child. Yet I hate dogmatism without evidence in psychology, and there is already more than enough of it. I shall therefore try to present very briefly viewpoints which at least would have the support of a goodly company of leading psychologists, including some who have tended to stress rather the influence of environment.

Prejudice against the idea of innate individual differences. First, however, I wish to warn the reader of a tendency evident in several quarters to allow emotion or even prejudice to sway the judgement on this problem. Some worthy people who are intensely devoted to the service of neglected children, not unnaturally want to think that the aberrations of young delinquents and the aggressiveness or selfishness or other abnormalities in temperament of many younger children, are always due solely to broken homes, bad discipline, or other environmental influences. They are glad to think this, because much can often be done about such influences.

If, however, trouble has arisen even partly because of some extremely strong (or weak) innate impulse in the child, then in the long run we shall be more able to discover the best kind of influences to apply in such cases, if we can detect these disabilities and face the unpleasant facts rather than shut our eyes to the truth.

Prejudice on this question of innate individual differences is also shown by some who seem to get their minds entangled by misinterpretations of the phrase 'All men are equal'. Let us admit at once the great truth here expressed, primarily in reference to political equality; some would like to add 'in the sight of God'; others may prefer to put it that all men have the right to equal consideration or to equal opportunities; and so on. But it is then so easy to slip into the assumption that, if so, all are born with equal mental capacities and equal temperamental tendencies. Whereas, as I once heard a witty statesman put it, the ideal is rather that all children should have an equal opportunity to display their inequalities.

The fact of great inborn differences in mental abilities will be more fully expounded in our later chapter on 'General Intelligence', but I may anticipate at least with one point, namely that strong prejudice is shown by some against intelligence tests and the findings through them of differences in mental abilities. Such critics urge that the superior average performance of children from homes of higher social or economic rank is due to superior environmental influences. They ignore the plain fact (some of the critics do not even seem to know it) that a large number of children from the poorest and worst types of homes do far better in intelligence tests than do many children from the homes of higher social or economic or cultural levels; and even in half a dozen children of the same family the range of intelligence may be enormous.

Prejudice against the view that innate factors can be important in the development of character and conduct is shown in a rather subtle way by some psychological writers. I have noted it in books, in theses presented for the degrees of Ph.D. or M.A. which I have examined, and in papers offered to a psychological journal which I edit. The writer begins by asking: 'Can heredity or innate tendencies explain our findings?' (e.g. as to problem children from broken homes). He then shows that it cannot be proved for certain that innate factors are the cause, because it is conceivable that this or that environmental factor may have had such and such an influence in the first months or years. He thereupon concludes that the results under consideration were *certainly* due to environmental causes. He does not apply the same stringency of proof to the environmental factor, whereas, if quite impartial, he should have been equally prepared to argue as follows, starting with the environmental influences: 'We cannot prove for certain that our findings are due to environmental factors because it is just conceivable that innate hereditary factors were at least of substantial influence, i.e. the children of broken homes may have become problem children largely because they inherited from one or other parent some temperamental weakness which was itself the cause of the home being broken – as indeed one eminent American investigator maintained was usual. Absolute proof on either side of this controversy seems out of the question. We have to be content with probability, but at least we should approach the question if possible without prejudice, and begin by admitting that both environmental and inborn factors may be operative.

Some illustrations of innate differences. May I say here that my own position is not extreme; I find myself on the whole in close agreement with Dr Arnold Gesell, who has done more research on the earliest months and years of life than any psychologist living or dead; and shortly I shall show that so representative an authority on child psychology as Professor A. T. Jersild, and such a severe critic of the view that innate tendencies are supreme as G. W. Allport, seem to concede all the points which appear to me essential in reference to our present problem.

First, however, I would like to emphasize the point that the clearest evidence on inborn differences in temperamental tendencies comes from the study of children within the same family. The remarkable differences in temperament shown by some (unlike) twins are notable, for one thing, as Gesell himself has pointed out.

As regards differences in intelligence in the same family I know of no more striking example than one given by Gesell [44]. He repeatedly tested six brothers and sisters in the same family between the ages of about 1 : 0 and 15 : 0. Three of these children scored repeatedly on Gesell's development scale, and other tests, average scores or very little below. The three others were persistently at the level of low-grade mental defectives. Yet, says Gesell, there was no history of illness or injury to account for the mental deficiency. Dr Gesell reports that when a child had been tested the mother would ask anxiously, 'Does he take after me or after the father?'

In view of the overwhelming evidence in favour of inborn differences in intelligence, it is difficult to resist the view that inborn difference can occur in temperamental tendencies also. We do know that nature allows indeed enormous physical differences in babies; so great that sometimes life itself is endangered in the earliest days. Some of these physical differences are connected with glandular defects. Possibly temperamental differences may some day be shown to be due to glandular or other chemical differences, i.e. the physical make-up of the child; for the moment we can leave that on one side. We do know, however, that babies in perfect health can in the first few weeks and with the same physical care and friendly hospital treatment, show great differences in liveliness and cheerfulness; e.g. when laughter begins, some laugh a great deal, some hardly ever.

To a psychologist who is the father of a large family, including children of very different temperaments or personalities, those differences may be fairly convincing that environmental influences are at least not omnipotent. When the youngest of our five children was approaching adolescence I filled in for each child parts of a report form on temperamental traits which I had published some time before. One question was concerned with the most outstanding of the following traits in the child: 'Co-operative, friendly, popular, aggressive, dominating, taking the lead, submissive, timorous, indifferent, sympathetic, protective, excitable, placid, cheerful, morose, obedient, conscientious, impulsive.'

Taking this list I marked for each child the five most characteristic qualities. A list was also marked independently by a woman psychologist who had known all the children intimately since the earliest years, sometimes having taken charge of our home when we were away. Her markings coincided almost exactly with mine.

The differences between the children were extremely great; e.g. four qualities were marked in one child's list and not in any others; another child had three qualities to himself; no one quality was marked for all the children, and the only quality marked for four children was 'cheerfulness'. When each of the eighteen qualities was assessed for each of the children on a five-point scale (A B C D E), the individual differences were even more remarkable. [Full details of the reports are given in No. 102 of the bibliography.]

I can only add that, try as I could, I was quite unable to attribute these differences to any differences in our training of the children or any other environmental or physical cause; e.g. the one who did not include cheerfulness in his five main traits, had had much better health in early childhood than one whose list did include cheerfulness.

Some questions of innate differences on which there is substantial agreement. Here let me first quote some views of a great American psychologist who has taken a leading part in stressing the effects of environmental influences and experience in the building up of personality. In G. W. Allport's book on Personality [3], a book which brings forward some new arguments and ideas on motivation, readers are so apt to miss or forget the force of Allport's admissions which yield certain points to the other side. Here are some remarkable concessions in Allport's book: 'The three principal raw materials of personality, physique, the endowment of intelligence, and temperament, are genetically determined through structural inheritance, and are only slightly altered by conditions existing subsequent to birth'. . . . 'Sometimes they accelerate the moulding influence of the environment; sometimes they place limitations upon it; but always their force is felt.'

Temperament is defined by Allport as follows: 'The characteristic phenomena of an individual's emotional nature, including his *susceptibility to emotional stimulation*, his *customary strength and speed of response*, the quality of his prevailing mood, and all peculiarities of fluctuation and intensity in mood; these phenomena being regarded as dependent upon constitutional make-up, and therefore *largely hereditary in origin.*'

Note especially the words I have italicized. Again

Allport writes: 'Within a family where very similar environmental influences exist for each member, the differences between siblings are probably due, paradoxical as it may seem, chiefly to heredity.' 'Shyness in one person, for example, may be due to hereditary influences that *no amount of contrary pressure from the environment has been able to offset*.' 'No infant is socialized though some temperaments seem from the beginning to respond to the socializing influences of the environment more readily than others.' '*Hereditary endowment in terms of temperament contributes to this stabilizing of the course of development.* . . . Nature sets limits beyond which the variation in individual development may not extend.'

Elsewhere Allport also admits there is an aversion to a feeling of inferiority, which he says invokes a painful tension; and so provides a basis of a 'drive'. But this surely implies a pre-existing impulse to be the equal or superior of others, and so seems equivalent to what we have discussed in Chapter 4 under the title of the impulse of self-assertion.

The trend of opinion on motivation. With no room in an introductory book like this for a full examination of evidence about innate impulses and tendencies, it will perhaps be best if I give a brief account of the broad trends and changes of thought, during the present century, as to inborn tendencies. The nineteenth-century psychologists had chiefly dealt with the intellectual, sensory, or general cognitive aspects of the mind, though in this country Spencer and Bain were marked exceptions. Then William James and William McDougall brought forward the view that instincts in man are dominant motive forces, and some followers exaggerated their views and ignored the emphasis that McDougall himself put upon the modification by experience of innate propensities, as he called them later. Then came the revolt and the development of Behaviourism and its view that almost everything in man was learned through experience and 'conditioning'.

Now we are seeing a reaction again. As to these last extremes may I quote the view of one of America's leading psychologists, H. S. Langfeld, Professor of Psychology in Princeton University. In his address to the International Congress at Edinburgh (1948) he said that 'There has been a great change among American psychologists as regards the attitude to McDougall's views on instincts. Now the trend is to recognize more decidedly the great influence of innate tendencies, and of individual differences in these, rather than to regard environmental influences as supreme.'

Just after I wrote the above paragraph there reached me the new edition (1955) of the *Manual of Child Psychology* which has already established itself as an authoritative book of reference on the subject. In the article there by Professor A. T. Jersild, whom I have already referred to as one of the most eminent child psychologists in the U.S.A., I find the following: 'Writers in recent years have stressed the need for a broad conception of human motivation. Many of the "propensities" which McDougall (1926) listed before Behaviourism was in full cry have stolen back into the literature, although under new names.'

These frank statements will be welcomed by those of us in England (outstanding among whom has been Sir Cyril Burt) who have persisted, in the last quarter of a century, in resisting the attempts to explain human conduct almost entirely by 'conditioning' or some other environmental influences, and have maintained that most if not all of the 'innate propensities' listed by William McDougall are of profound importance as bases for conduct. Some of us have, indeed, long been urging that psychologists who have used especially the terms 'drive' or 'urge' often imply at times some underlying innate factor.

Some indeed have frankly stated this, for example Jersild himself. In the third edition of his standard work on child psychology [62] published in 1947 he recounts a group of 'drives' or 'needs' which, if I understand him, he thinks have an innate basis, though greatly modifiable by experience.

Among these he includes even curiosity, the impulse to explore the environment, as well as the seeking to 'have a status with his age group' which would appear to involve the impulse of self-assertion as I have represented it in an earlier chapter. In Jersild's article in the *Manual of Child Psychology* he mentions also, with approval, the 'parental drive', with a probable beginning in childhood – comparable with what we have called the 'protective or helping impulse', which comes to its most intense form usually in mothers. A reference is also made with approval to a writer in 1948 who maintained that there is even a drive to use the intellect. It is not easy to avoid a smile at reading this new pronouncement if one recalls that as long ago as 1914 Graham Wallas contended that thinking was as genuine an innate tendency as the instincts in McDougall's list [111].

Generally recognized innate tendencies. If now I try to draw up a list of innate tendencies as to which there is substantial agreement it seems that they would include most of the list of unlearned 'motives' or 'drives' given by that very representative American psychologist, R. S. Woodworth, also recognized as one of their leading authorities. He includes in his list [114] the following, and he emphasizes that individuals differ widely in the strength of any 'drive': A general activity drive, exemplified in the play of children; an exploring drive; sex activity; mother love with elementary desires to succour and protect, which do not need to be learned; the impulse to escape from danger and to feel fear in its presence; fighting and its accompanying emotion of anger; the 'mastery motive' – overcoming resistance, in the exposition of which Woodworth comes very close to the one I have given as to the first year or two of life in Chapter 4. Woodworth even adds an innate drive towards self-submission as McDougall did. I have not thought it essential to discuss that separately in this book, though elsewhere I have examined its importance as an element in hero-worship and the following of a leader.

The tendency I discussed under the heading 'passive sympathy' would not in any case come under the heading 'drive', for it does not, as we saw, contain in itself the impulse to act, though usually it is closely associated with it.

Individual differences in innate tendencies. One of my purposes in stressing the innate factors in most of the drives or urges described in modern textbooks, is to emphasize the fact that it is not necessarily 'abnormal' if one child is very different from another in response to the same treatment. As we shall see, the innate elements in general intelligence vary enormously with a gradual increase in the frequency of cases from extremely low to average and then a gradual decrease to extremely high innate ability.

A similar wide scatter seems to occur in the more special abilities and indeed in all the human characteristics which we can measure. There seems on general grounds no reason for expecting that the case will be any different in reference to the innate elements in drives, or innate tendencies as we have called them. Even in animals the primary instincts vary in their strength; some hens make much better mothers than do others; some dogs in puppyhood show more aggressiveness than do others, even of the same breed, and still more than those of some other breeds.

General emotionality and the intensity of drives. So far in this book we have usually been studying individual tendencies and emotions separately – the impulse of self-assertion, sympathetic feeling and action, fears, and so on. Presently we shall refer to the problem of co-ordination and unification into a well-integrated character or personality.

Everyday observations of children and the many records of inquiries we have studied all indicate that a little child may show a high degree of aggressiveness but a low degree of fear or sympathetic feeling or active sympathy. On the other hand everyday observation also suggests that some children (and adults) are very emotional in general, or very placid in general. Now this might be explained theoretically by assuming that, in the haphazard distribution of innate tendencies of all degrees of strength or weakness, a very few children will be born with the germs of all in a strong degree, and a very few will inherit all in a weak degree, though in most there will be differing degrees of strength in the various tendencies. Statistical evidence has, however, been provided by Burt to the effect that there is a common factor in estimates of the strength of all innate tendencies and emotions, and the most reasonable explanation of this is his own theory that there is some general element of emotionality, and that this is largely innate [14, 20]. If this general element is present in a marked degree, the child tends to be very emotional and impulsive in general: if it is weak, he tends to be placid and inhibited. In addition to this general element, however, each innate tendency and the corresponding emotion (if there is one), has its own strength or weakness, so that a child, who on the whole is not very emotional, may, because of a very strong tendency to fear, appear to be very timid and nervous. Strong emotionality may be to a great extent controlled and guided by good intelligence and sound training, and then may often be of great value in the person's social life. But closely allied with this high general emotionality is emotional instability and lack of 'dependability' [107], and possibly the tendency to develop a neurosis, for the hereditary determination of which by the way there is evidence, among other types, from the study of twins [37].

The unification of individual impulses in the whole personality. In adults we look for a co-ordination of tendencies, with a general control of momentary individual impulses in accordance with thoughts of future consequences and with some dominating aims and ideals. Even adults, however, often fall short of this, and a man suddenly overwhelmed by a spasm of anger or of sex-impulse may act in a way which the next day his calmer, more unified, total self bitterly regrets.

In the child there is still less co-ordination of tendencies. We may see rapid fluctuations between rebellious conduct and obedient submission. Teasing and even minor ill-treatment of another child may be followed in a short time by friendly help. For the co-ordination of independent tendencies and the building-up of a properly integrated personality and character, the growth of relatively stable and permanent sentiments and attitudes and the development of general ideals of behaviour are necessary; and these are most likely to be acquired through the suggestive influence first of parents, and later of admired friends, teachers, and others who have dominant prestige in the mind of the child and who win his affection. These processes we shall discuss in the next chapter, which I hope will help us to see more clearly the element of truth underlying that popular, vague and indeed inaccurate phrase about the child '*identifying himself*' with his mother (or father, etc.).

CHAPTER 10

Imitation and Suggestibility

The main environmental influences. The main environmental factors in the building of a stable and integrated character are as follows: the early modification of innate tendencies by experience and training, especially in the home; the building up of desirable habits (though mere 'habits' are apt to be highly specific and limited in their scope); the application of, and reaction to such discipline as is applied to the individual child; and the response to the suggestion of ideals of conduct, made by parents, teachers, and others. Now this little book only seeks to be descriptive and explanatory. The theory of the development of the integrated self is extremely complex, and practical questions of training and discipline constitute further problems. For neither of these have we room here, and in any case I have tried to deal fully with both elsewhere and must not repeat myself [101, 103].

There are, however, two fundamental processes which should be considered briefly – imitation and suggestion, or suggestibility. They are not 'drives' of the type which we have been considering, nor can we assume without examination that they are always effective in varying circumstances or that individual differences do not occur. Those psychologists who write as though the child's conduct and personality were almost entirely determined by environmental influences, often seem to assume that nearly everything is picked up through imitation of parents and others, or as the effect of suggestion by elders or contemporaries. Yet imitation and suggestion are rarely considered independently by such writers, nor are their mode of functioning and their limitations expounded. Thus in the very comprehensive *Manual of Child Psychology* (edited by L. Carmichael, 2nd edn.) the author of the important section on Character Development states that the gang influences the individual through imitation and suggestion. Yet the term 'suggestion' does not occur even once in the *Manual*'s enormous index – numbering about 7,000 items (including names), and there is only one reference to imitation, outside the section on language. One of the articles, however, makes much of what another author had called 'behavioural contagion' – the spread of one child's mode of behaviour to others of the group – as though this were a new discovery.

The role of imitation. Let us consider imitation first. On this again we find great fluctuations in opinions in the last century. Time was when the popular and admirable motto 'example is better than precept' often carried with it the implication that example would inevitably be followed. Some psychologists indeed regarded imitation of a rather mechanical type as the most important process by which a child learned social behaviour. This over-emphasis led to the expression of a scepticism as to whether there was any general tendency to imitate, except, of course, when, say, a child saw that someone's way of doing some particular thing (which he himself also wanted to do) would be a good way to try: whether it be the opening of a bottle of lemonade or glancing a fast ball to leg. No one has doubted this very obvious type of deliberate imitation.

The divergence of views has been partly due to different interpretations put upon the term 'imitation'. This is one of the difficulties the psychologist is constantly meeting. Shall he continue to use the everyday terminology for mental processes – instinct, imagination, imitation, memory, and so on? If so he runs the risk of being misunderstood by the general public, and of not being precise enough for his psychological colleagues. The alternative is for him to devise new and more precise technical terms, and then he is criticized by the general public for indulging in 'jargon'. My own custom is to start with the popular term, then to show if it is not adequate, and to add qualifying terms as we shall do now, speaking (*a*) of reflective or purposive imitation and (*b*) of non-deliberate imitation. Furthermore, we shall confine the term to the imitation of actions. Some writers have used the term in a very wide sense, including the imitation of feelings and of ideas or ways of thinking. As to feelings we already have our specific term 'sympathetic induction of feeling, or emotion', or more briefly 'passive sympathy'. As to the imitation of the ideas of others, that is better brought under the heading of suggestion and suggestibility.

The conscious, deliberate imitation by a boy of some greatly admired hero, or a girl's imitation of the hair style of a film star are familiar enough: that type of imitation has such a close resemblance to certain phenomena of suggestion that we will deal with it later. Here we will take the earliest forms of imitation and see how they develop.

Early examples of primary imitation. The very earliest imitations are cooings in response to cooings. Experimental tests suggest that this may occur in the second month; there is first, of course, the spontaneous impulse to coo and babble and the example simply serves to set it off. There is not precise imitation of specific sounds, but some sound-making by the baby in response to sound-making by the parent, which later changes to more definite attempts to imitate specific sounds.

Imitation of hand-waving, familiar to most mothers as 'waving ta-ta', began in my own children about the age of 0:9; but the most striking examples of imitation were of my smoking a pipe, by children about the age of 1 year. The child would gaze as though fascinated at my puffing out the smoke, and then finally he would throw back his head slightly, as I did, and make a puffing sound. All the five infants imitated this smoking.

Y, who was very prone to imitate, began to imitate our reading aloud at 1:3. She would put her face to a book and make soft mutterings. So B at 1:8. 'Imitated reading this evening. Sat on floor with book on floor and put his face close to it, moving his head across it as if reading.'

To my amazement I found that Y at 1:1 had been led to imitate the nurse in winking one eye! Repeated testing proved this beyond doubt. Such imitations of smoking and reading cannot be reconciled with the view that primary imitations are confined to actions prompted by specific instincts: nor can they (or, I hope, the winking at this early age) be regarded as purposive or 'involving insight'.

On Y at 1:1 I began an extensive series of tests of imitation, spread over two weeks. It comprised thirty-seven items, and included such things as tearing a newspaper, putting a basket over my head, and putting two hands above my head. About halfway through the series I asked the older children to suggest things they thought Y would *not* imitate. In thirty-one cases there was clear imitation, and in several of the other cases there was good reason for no imitation. Thus 'shaking the head' had come to imply a refusal, and hand waving meant 'good-bye'. (Details are given in [102].

Most of these tests were repeated on Y between the ages of 2:0 and 2:3 and again nearly all the actions were imitated; in a number of cases imitation did not follow when I or one of the other children performed the action, but only when the greatly beloved mother did it. Thus when I stretched my arms up, Y looked and said 'Mummy do it'. Her mother now stretched her arms up, and immediately Y imitated her.

A psychological colleague of mine kindly applied thirty-four of my tests to his boy of 2:0 and twenty-five actions were imitated, most of the rest already 'meaning' something to the boy.

These two infants – and two of my others – may, of course, have been exceptionally prone to imitate; but examples of similar imitation at this period are given by Stern, Piaget, and several of the other psychologists who have made observations on their own children. Furthermore, Gesell found that over 65 per cent of the infants he tested at 1:0 imitated scribbling with a pencil, and the same percentage at 1:6 imitated building up three bricks.

The marked superiority of the mother in eliciting imitations, however, quite convinced me of the importance of the imitatee; and the ignoring of this affects the findings of some experimenters who say they have failed to get much imitation by children of 1:0 to 1:5 in the laboratory. Thorndike, for example, stated that nine times out of ten an infant does not imitate a simple action. In my experiments and those of my colleagues it was almost precisely nine times out of ten that the child *did* imitate the action.

The scope of primary imitation. By 2 years and even earlier, reflective imitation for the sake of specific purposes begins; and the primary imitation remains only in reference to external influences which are not deliberately and purposefully attended to and yet in a way may be subconsciously noticed, as, for example, the local accent in speech and the manners of those around.

In this way both good habits may be picked up and also bad, as for example, the habit of sniffing, or some quaint mannerisms of a teacher. I obtained anonymous reports from two classes of university graduates as to examples of involuntary, primary imitation which they could remember they had indulged in since early childhood. The totals were 58 out of 81 women, and 23 out of 75 men. Burt reports that: 'A school in Vienna had to be shut for some weeks owing to an epidemic of hiccups which affected more than half the pupils; another at Budapest was closed owing to a wave of hysterical coughing which prevented all work in the classrooms; at Wildbad 26 out of 74 pupils were suddenly affected with what appeared to be St Vitus's dance' [20]. It is possible that primary imitation is an important factor in many of the cases of nail-biting we reported in Chapter 2.

If, as seems certain, there is an innate element in the tendency to imitation of this non-reflective type, then we may expect some individual differences. I certainly noticed marked differences in my own group of five children, as Stern did in his; and M. Shirley gives examples of individual differences in her group. When primary, non-deliberate imitation appears in adults, great individual differences still appear. Thus when I attended holiday courses in France with other teachers, I noticed towards the end of the course that I tended to shrug my shoulders and gesticulate with my hands somewhat in the fashion of the French people, but most of the others did not. Similarly, after a family holiday for a few weeks in Wales, on return home I would find myself speaking unawares with something of a Welsh sing-song intonation, and so did one of our girls, but not the rest of the family. Another form of unconcious imitation I have noted in snapshot photos I have taken at college sports, in which spectators have been revealed as imitating the movements of students jumping.

Summing up, we may say that, while primary, non-deliberate imitation of actions is one medium for young children in the acquisition of language and of customary manners, its scope is limited to very specific forms of behaviour. Of greater importance is the adoption of ideas and ideals through suggestion, to which we now turn.

Suggestion and suggestibility. Readers will be familiar with the extraordinary power of suggestion under hypnosis. A patient can be told that he will feel no pain when pricked with a needle and he will feel none, even if a needle is stuck right through the skin. Hypnosis is outside the scope of this book, but I want to call attention to the fact, often overlooked, that the process of putting the patient to sleep by quietly repeating to him 'You are going to sleep', over and over again, is one of conscious waking suggestion and in itself evidence of its efficacy.

If the patient is to be hypnotized it is necessary that he should yield himself to the influence of the hypnotizer and have some confidence in him. This gives us a clue to the process of suggestion in waking life. The prestige of the suggester is important. People are more ready to accept the ideas of one by whom they are strongly impressed or whom they greatly admire. Sometimes this may have a partly rational basis; obviously if we think highly of someone's knowledge of a subject it is reasonable to bow to his opinion. But the suggestibility often goes beyond this, and indeed, we are likely to be suggestible to one we greatly love, even if we do not think very highly of their knowledge.

Careful everyday observation should be enough to convince the experienced reader of these facts, but there is also experimental evidence that the acceptance or rejection by large groups of persons of the soundness of some general social or political principle can be changed (though they may be unaware of the change) when at a later date the same principle is presented to them with the added information that it was stated by a prominent person whom they greatly liked (or disliked).

Suggestibility in infancy. It is readily understandable that little children are especially suggestible. The greater knowledge, experience, and power of adults gives them prestige, and warm affection for a parent adds to that. With our own children, by the age of 2:0 and onwards, I had repeated evidence that slight pains could be banished by our 'kissing them better' – as several other psychologists have reported. With B the procedure of kissing apparently acquired efficacy in itself. B would kiss his own fingers better, and at 4:9, if the part hurt was not within reach of kissing, he kissed his hand and touched the hurt part with the hand!

Suggestion also at times changed the children's attitude

to a food at first disliked; but much easier than that was to elicit fear or disgust by suggestion, because here I was working in accordance with an innate impulse, only awaiting a mild suggestion to be set off.

When Y was 2:7 I noted: 'In suggestion the power of the specially loved mother which was shown in Y in imitations of actions, was again shown in some tests on Y. I gave her at 2:7 Binet's test with pairs of faces – one pretty and one ugly. Y discriminated between these correctly and would not reverse her judgement at my suggestion or that of her older brother; but she did (rather reluctantly) respond to her mother's suggestions, though they were contrary to her own first judgement.'

Prestige and suggestibility. That the prestige of a special visitor to a school may be very effective for some children was shown by the following experiments [4]. Professor Aveling tested sixty-five children (aged 12 or 13) individually. Sitting opposite the child he held out his own hand, and told the child to hold out his, but to keep his eyes fixed on his (the psychologist's) hand. The psychologist told the child he would feel a tingling in his hand and then, 'Now! You will find that tingling and stiffening increase, so that your hand becomes *quite* stiff; so that you can't bend your fingers at all or close your hand. Do you feel it? It's getting much stiffer now – quite stiff and rigid. Now you *can't* move your fingers. You can't *close* your hand. You can't close it at all. Try!'

There were different degrees of success with different children. Some could not close the hand, but could move the fingers slightly – remarkably like the response of some partially hypnotized patients. About 33 per cent of the children could not close their hands in spite of apparent effort, about 16 per cent could with apparent effort. With about 50 per cent the suggestion failed to work, but even so the experiment was a substantial success. It might be suggested that some of the children were 'pulling the psychologist's leg'; but children are just as prone to enjoy proving someone wrong. One might not, however, attach much importance to these results with children were there not ample evidence of the effects on adults of suggestion as to body movement and even as to sensations.

Aveling performed another experiment with thirty-eight children, suggesting to each child that his hands would lift up from the table with Aveling's own resting on it, but without the child willing it. This was successful in 40 per cent of the cases and failed in 60 per cent. Several other tests were applied in which the prestige of the psychologist was not involved: a comparison of results suggests that in the 'prestige' experiments the children tended to divide into two groups, (*a*) very suggestible, and (*b*) contra-suggestible.

Influence of suggestion on conduct. In this book we are more concerned with the influence of suggestion on ideas and on ideals of conduct than on such things as are dealt with in the above sections. I have described them in order to bring out the surprising effect that suggestion can have under certain conditions. The conditions there were an impressive personality (as I know Professor Aveling to have been) and no strong motive in the children against yielding to his influence. One possibility, however, was that the impulse of self-assertion might be roused in some and so a resistance created, and in fact we find that with about half the children the suggestion failed.

Suppose we concur, then, in the view that assertiveness is the enemy of suggestion, even if we do not also posit an innate tendency of self-submission to the recognized superior, which is very weak in many children, but strong in some, and an important factor in determining the success of a suggestion. We have, however, to bear in mind that in matters of everyday conduct strong individual motives to act in this or that way are often present, and the attempted suggestions of parent or teacher may be in opposition to these. This is where the general attitude of the children to the suggester is so important: the greater the child's affection or admiration for the suggester, the more likely is the suggestion to work. If, however, there is neither much admiration nor affection, or if there is apparent to the child a lack of sincerity and conviction or authority in the suggester, then no amount of reiteration of what the children should do or think will in itself have much effect. Indeed it is likely to arouse antipathy and a strong inclination to do the opposite to what is suggested, and so satisfy the impulse of self-assertion. This motive force then would be added to the attraction of the alternative line of conduct to which the child was originally inclined.

The situations in which suggestion is attempted with children are no doubt usually dominated by two factors: (*a*) the child's own impulses and desires, and (*b*) the influence of the suggester, through prestige or affection. Yet, in addition to these, there is the question of innate individual differences in the children. If, as seems to me probable, those psychologists are right who posit an innate tendency of self-submissiveness, which conflicts with assertiveness in the presence of obvious superiors, then this submissive impulse may be strong enough in some children to encourage the yielding to suggestion. In others it may be very weak and assertiveness very strong, and so suggestibility is lessened. All this may be true even if there are other elements or mechanisms connected with this process of suggestion, e.g. unconscious factors and inhibitions.

Contra-suggestibility. At least the importance of assertiveness as a factor in limiting suggestibility seems clear. Even psychologists who do not recognize suggestibility as dependent partly on a specific innate quality, seem to require this to explain contra-suggestibility. For example let us consider the view of that eminent American psychologist, G. W. Allport. I said above that most contemporary American child psychologists failed to examine the nature and importance of imitation and suggestion. Professor Allport, however, does not fail in this respect. As to suggestibility he raises the question as to whether it is a 'trait' with an original 'neuropsychic' basis and thinks the evidence on the whole is negative [3]. But he goes on to say: 'To be sure, a few individuals seem chronically to accept any and every suggestion offered them, lacking *the power to resist* proposals which are discordant with their own self-determined plans of action.'

The reader should note the words I have italicized. What exactly is this 'power to resist'? I suggest that it is precisely the impulse of assertiveness. Contra-suggestibility (or in Allport's terminology 'negativism') he does think a genuine trait in some individuals who always go 'contrary'. These I suggest are just those with a strong tendency to self-assertion. We may recall the rebellious period (described in Chapter 4) common during the third and fourth years when the child begins to realize its capacity for asserting itself and to enjoy playing with this new-found power. The game of contradicting I have described earlier was a case of contra-suggestibility in embryo.

As the child grows older the dominant leaders among his companions begin to acquire a prestige which, while very different from that of the parent, may begin to rival it in influence within a limited circle of action. Consequently the child's behaviour may sometimes seem, and indeed be, very different in the home from what it is in the playground or the classroom.

During adolescence (and indeed often before), as we shall see in a later chapter, the dominance of the parents often decreases (even if the child's affection for them does not) and teachers or individual friends, or even relative strangers, may be supreme in suggestive influence. Even before adolescence the gang or group may be powerful in its influence. To this we shall refer in the next chapter.

CHAPTER II

Social Development at School

IN our earlier chapters we have been mainly concerned with behaviour, emotions, and innate tendencies or drives, as they appear in early infancy. In this chapter we shall discuss some important aspects of social development, chiefly at school in the period after early infancy. First, however, we may summarize the most important facts about social behaviour in infancy.

The pre-school child. In adopting this common label for the child between 2 and 5, I must comment on the fact that investigators, to get evidence on large groups of such children, have usually had to go into nursery schools and kindergartens to find them. There have also been, however, many reports gathered from parents, as we have seen in earlier chapters, and other investigators have visited homes, or observed children at play centres or brought to clinics for the purpose. If we survey the great mass of reports from these various sources, there are of course some apparent inconsistencies, which we should expect from the different circumstances in which the children were observed, from the differences in home training, or in the atmosphere and methods of different nursery schools. Nevertheless, several general points clearly emerge.

1. There are at all these early ages such great *individual differences* that they are greater between different children of the same age than is the difference between the average or usual for the different ages between 2 and 5. These individual differences are hard to explain merely by reference to

earlier training; they appear indeed at much earlier ages than the 2 to 5 years we are considering. Thus Charlotte Bühler, reporting on a group of infants of 0:6 to 0:11, studied in pairs, writes as follows: 'We find even in this early stage marked individual differences among these infants in their social attitudes. There are some who, in spite of their being stronger or more skilful, always seem inhibited in the presence of another child; there are some who, in spite of a superior companion, are always aggressive and overactive. There are some who never seem to become aware of the other child and who seem to be interested only in their toys and their manipulation of materials' [1, 12].

As we shall see directly, little conflicts between children in the nursery school are very common at the ages of 2:0 to 3:0, but tend to decline in number from the age of 4:0 or so. Here again, however, there are extraordinary individual differences. Thus in one inquiry [62], in which the conflicts of children from 2:0 to 5:0 were noted, it was found that 'At one extreme was a child who engaged in 141 conflicts during the course of the observations, while at the other extreme was a child who took part in only seventeen; one child made a personal attack on another (hitting, pushing, throwing things at, holding, threatening gestures, and so forth) eighty-seven times, while there was another child who did not lay hands on another, or threaten to do so, a single time.'

2. A second general mark of the period is the *instability* of the child's traits or tendencies already referred to. He seems to be one thing at one moment and quite different at another. The social impulses are unco-ordinated, and sometimes it is as though experiments were being tried, which are abandoned or become stabilized as the results of experience.

3. A third special mark of the period is the ease with which *regression* takes place – a reversion to an earlier stage of development, sometimes accompanying a highly emotional state or a time of marked frustration. As we saw in

Chapter 2, violent temper tantrums are common in these years and these sometimes represent a regression in a child to behaviour even more characteristic of a child a year or two younger. I may add that regression of this type may appear at times in later childhood and, alas, even in adults. Bearing in mind these three points of great individual differences, instability, and regression, we may now summarize the main findings as to the most common forms of social behaviour for the various ages.

Characteristic social behaviour in school for the years 2 : 0 to 5 : 0.
The 2-year-old. In the nursery school the child usually adjusts himself to the school routine fairly well after a few days or at least weeks. Some may be rather aggressive to other children at first, until they learn wisdom by experience. Most children play alone most of the time. The very shy and unaggressive child tends to remain aloof longer than most.

At first the child is greatly dependent on adults: but before the end of this year most children are very anxious to do things for themselves and become more resistant and assertive towards adults – the characteristic rebellious period already described in Chapter 4.

The 3-year-old. The child now tends to play with another child, or at times in a group of three or four. There are often brief conflicts, even with special friends, the conflicts being often about the possession of some toy. Yet most children will sometimes sympathize with and help others. Most children show occasional emotional disturbances, or some nervous habit.

The 4-year-old. The child now usually prefers to play in small groups. Many are 'bossy' and like to show off. Conflicts are fewer, but tend to last longer. Yet most children will often share their toys, and may defend other children. With adults most children are more co-operative, but the characteristic rebellious period may still appear with some.

The 5-year-old. By the age of 5 it is exceptional for a child to play regularly alone. On the average more than half the time is spent in playing with others. Individual friendships are stronger. The child enjoys independence of adults and may go to school alone if it is near home.

So far we have been considering those children who have been sent to some nursery school or kindergarten. We turn now to the whole group of children who at 5 : 0 are going to school.

The child in the infant school or first grade. The most obvious new factor in the majority of cases is entrance to school. For many children this will be the first introduction to large groups of children. Naturally the more secluded the infant's life has been at home, the bigger the change. One may expect a considerable difference in the effects of the first entry to the infant school at 5 : 0 if the child has already been for a year or two at a nursery school : but an interesting and important question is, Can the child who has not been to school before 5 catch up soon with the others in social development, or is he apt to suffer permanently?

The influence of the nursery school on early years in the primary school. There are many studies of social development within the nursery school or kindergarten, and everyone would agree that decided changes in behaviour take place as the result of a year or even six months of such experience. But precise and conclusive evidence is exceedingly hard to obtain, for so long as schooling before 5 : 0 or 6 : 0 is optional we cannot be sure whether the children sent to school before then are fairly representative of the whole age group. Some mothers will place a child in a nursery school because the father's wages need supplementing by the mother's earnings. On the other hand, some comfortably-off mothers may send their children to kindergarten because they are rather a nuisance at home, the mothers being not very interested in children. Some specially nervous or difficult children may be kept back because over-protective mothers want to have their children entirely in their own care as long as possible. In view of this uncertainty as to the reasons why children are sent to some school before the age at which it is compulsory, it is unsafe to compare the behaviour, in the infant school (or first grade), of children who have been to no school before, with the behaviour of those who have been to a nursery school or kindergarten.

The comparative evidence as to the behaviour in the nursery school itself of those who entered at 3:0 or 3:6 with those who entered at 2:0 is slight, but so far as it goes it suggests that the late entrants soon catch up with the others in social adaptation – like the infants in the maturation experiments, who started learning skills later than others.

As, in Great Britain, at least the great majority of children do not go to any school before the age of 5, the standards of normal social development are set by them. We simply do not know how much some might have been affected by previous schooling if they had had it.

Late entry to school. It so happens that four of my five children were much older at their first going to school than is usual, the earliest age being 6:6, the latest 8:6. Now reports on a few children in one or two families are of no use for generalization; yet as I argued in Chapter 2, one or two cases can at least demonstrate possibilities, so I give some records for my own five children.

Our eldest boy did not go to any school until he was 8:0, partly because there was no appropriate school near, partly because of the very rapid progress he made in reading at 4: and 5:, and in arithmetic at 6 and 7, with only some ten minutes a day of instruction in arithmetic. When he did go to school, he was well ahead of boys of his age. As regards social training he had had a neighbour's boy as a friend, and at 7:0 had a brother of 5:0 and a sister of 3:0, and he was a happy child with many interests.

My records do show that the first two days at school

were a big strain, more particularly because his friend joined the other boys in teasing him, calling him 'Vaseline'. But even on the first day, after afternoon school, he came home and said, 'I've got a friend'; and he was soon adjusted to the life, and later was very sociable and popular at high school and the university, perhaps rather more so than was good for his work; and later in the war he was quite at home in the officers' mess of the Grenadier Guards, so I think we may take it that even very late entry to school did not spoil social development. Of the two girls who went to school only after 7:0, one became head girl of a large co-educational school, the other, when in the A.T.S., was promoted to the rank of Junior Commander. The child who went earliest to school (at about 6:6) was, even in the later school years, much shyer than the others, though greatly liked by some of his schoolmates; and at about 10:0 was highly commended as one of the ten boys who were 'keenest' in the school. Certainly on the whole our own experience suggests that late entry to school *need* not result in unsatisfactory social development. On the other hand, of course, under some home conditions, and especially for an only child, or one with no friends of similar ages, early entry to school seems on general grounds desirable, though we have no decisive evidence on the matter.

Some writers who have been educated privately at home have deplored it, including Bertrand Russell [89]. He attributes to it his inclination to suicide at adolescence, clearly ignorant of the fact that about one-third of adolescent boys have that inclination, as we shall see in a later chapter. Russell also says that, when he began to associate with contemporaries, he found himself 'an angular prig'. Clearly he did not remain so. Strangely enough he thinks there are a 'certain number of boys and girls who ought not to go to school', especially boys 'with abnormal mental powers and poor physique and great nervousness'.

We do know of some cases in which children of unusual ability have been unhappy at school (e.g. Anthony Trollope and Winston Churchill, who writes of his years at school as 'the only barren and unhappy period of my life'); but we have no evidence that they would have been better in the long run for staying at home. We are brought back to the plain fact that we have no conclusive evidence that social development is permanently injured by absence of schooling before 5:0 or 6:0 or probably even a somewhat older age, but that so much is gained from association with others, that it seems very probable that social development will be hindered in the great majority if schooling be delayed much longer.

Reports on immediate effects of entrance to the primary school. One useful inquiry made in the U.S.A. may be referred to, based on mothers' reports on children before entering school and two months later [96]. A sample of schools was chosen and a sample of about 250 parents were enlisted. About half the parents were labelled 'middle class', while most of the rest were 'lower class'. The following were the main findings.

Most parents (197) said the child was looking forward to going to school; only fifteen said he was not. Of the 170 parents who reported some change in behaviour, 78 per cent recorded improvements, such as taking more responsibility, helping more at home, being less irritable and more controlled. The remaining 22 per cent reported deterioration, such as 'acting smart alecky', increased aggressiveness with siblings, or more irritability.

One special question put to the mothers was whether the teacher was held up as a higher authority than the mother. Some 58 per cent reported no change, but the rest thought there was a change. Individual differences were marked. Thus one mother reported: 'He thinks the teacher is perfect and that I don't know anything. He corrects me all the time'; another said, 'The child always holds *me* up to the teacher, but I tell her, "Well, honey, the teacher's the boss there".'

While 92 per cent of the mothers reported that the child liked the school and the teacher, nevertheless 39 per cent said there had been days when the child did not want to go to school. Probably these times of antipathy were due to occasional difficulties with other children (e.g. being teased or ignored) which were reported by over 60 per cent of the mothers.

As pointed out before, inquiries based on the reports of parents are liable to involve different standards as to behaviour, adopted by different parents: also the attitudes of the different mothers to the child's going to school would vary and would influence the child. It is clear, however, that on the whole these mothers thought their children were gaining in social development, as judged by home behaviour even in so short a time as two months.

Some types of teachers. With all types of children, from the most well-adjusted and friendly or 'sociable' to the ill-adjusted and morose or aggressive, the attitude to the teachers varies, of course, greatly, according to the nature of the particular teacher. There are some teachers who are popular with practically all their pupils, while some are unpopular with all or nearly all. To say this I have no need to go beyond my own experience first as a pupil, then as a teacher in four very different schools, and later as the recipient of the frank comments of our five children on their teachers in some half-dozen different schools.

Equally valuable have I found the discussions in my lectures over a period of some thirty years with large groups of practising teachers, of a wide range of ages up to 50 and from every type of school. Even if not always frank about their own behaviour in class, they usually were about colleagues – anonymously of course. Finally, I have discussed over the same period, with well over 2,000 graduate students in teaching, the desirable attitude of teachers to pupils and the traits that make them liked or disliked, and they have often drawn freely on their own experience of all types.

I mention these various sources of information because I think that one can get through such media a clearer view on a topic of this kind, than one can from inquiries based on questionnaires given to children or students as to desirable or undesirable traits; because so often we find a teacher in whom two or three greatly admired traits quite overwhelm several other traits usually disliked: while another, who may seem most of the time a model of what a teacher should be, ruins his influence and popularity in his class by one deplorable weakness, for example, violent anger at mere ignorance or intellectual dullness in a pupil, as I have known in my own experience. This can be brought out in discussion better than a questionnaire.

One of the simple questions I have put to many large groups of teachers and students in training was this: Which of you, in schools where you have taught or been pupils, have known at least one teacher who at times shouted so angrily at pupils that they have been heard in an adjoining room? I regret to say that the vast majority had had that experience.

We have to bear in mind that, as stated in Chapter 1, in recent investigations in this country it has been found that about a quarter of the general public suffer from some trait which may be regarded as at least mildly neurotic. Careful selection of students for the teaching profession may well reduce the proportion there, and among those who are mildly neurotic some particular symptoms may cause no harm in the teacher's work. Indeed, one of the finest schoolmasters I ever came across was definitely neurotic and eventually committed suicide. Nevertheless there are some neurotic traits which are likely to produce in a teacher irrational and extreme reactions to relatively minor childish offences. The truth of this assertion is supported by an investigation in the U.S.A. [26]. Two hundred teachers selected at random from twenty-eight elementary schools were tested for personality traits suggestive of mental health or ill-health; e.g. depression, nervousness, co-operativeness, inferiority feelings. They also indicated their views as to the seriousness of over 100 items of 'objectionable pupil behaviour'. There was found a tendency for the more mentally healthy teachers to be less annoyed than the others by certain forms of behaviour, e.g. inattentiveness, dirty clothes, chewing gum, nose picking; but the more mentally healthy teachers were more resentful of behaviour items, most of which do seem to reveal more serious weaknesses of character and especially disregard of others, e.g. disturbing other pupils, bullying other children, especially younger ones, being a 'tattle-tale', and even coughing without covering the face.

In a recent inquiry in England it was found that among 124 maladjusted children whose maladjustment seemed to be caused by some school circumstance, especially a teacher, transfer to a new school was followed by a complete improvement in 73 per cent of the cases [22].

Let us now consider some reports of children on their teachers.

Children's attitudes to teachers. A good number of inquiries have been made, especially in the U.S.A., as to what children liked or disliked most in teachers. The answers of very young children are not very trustworthy and even older ones may be afraid to give reasons for disliking teachers, even when their reports are anonymous. More reliable are the reports of adults based on their memories of school life. The main results are pretty much what one would expect. Friendliness and kindness, fairness in discipline, and a sense of humour are very prominent as reasons for liking. Important also are good temper, and with older pupils and especially girls, even appearance. The comments I have heard by some senior high-school girls on the slovenliness of some of their mistresses would have surprised some of the latter.

Firmness of discipline is not widely resented by pupils, provided it is just and consistent. We may recall the judge-

ment of the boy on the Head of a famous public school –
'He's a beast, but he's a just beast'. Pupils, especially boys,
may seem to be having a good time with a master who fails
to keep them in control, but inwardly they are apt to
despise him.

The respect for strictness among boys up to the age of 12
appears clearly in an extensive inquiry by one of my research students, Major K.D. Hopkins [57]. It was planned
mainly to obtain the ideas of pupils as to punishments in
schools, but in one section of the questionnaire given, the
pupils were asked about the most important qualities they
thought a teacher should have. Ten qualities were arranged
in pairs and the children were asked to underline the
quality they thought more important. Each quality was
paired in turn with each of the others, making forty-five
choices in all. The following table shows the results. The
children numbered over 2,600, the great majority being
between 10+ and 15+. The schools included three
grammar schools and one junior technical school; the seven
elementary schools were in districts which varied from
'good' to 'very poor'.

Teachers' qualities ranked by children

	Boys		Girls	
	Adolescent	*Pre-adolescent*	*Adolescent*	*Pre-adolescent*
1.	Fairness	Manners	Fairness	Manners
2.	Cleverness	Cleverness	Manners	Cleverness
3.	Enthusiasm	Strictness	Sympathy	Fairness
4.	Manners	Good at sport	Cleverness	Sense of humour
5.	Sense of humour	Sense of humour	Sense of humour	Sympathy
6.	Sympathy	Sympathy	Enthusiasm	Good at sport
7.	Appearance	Fairness	Appearance	Appearance
8.	Good at sport	Appearance	Good at sport	Enthusiasm
9.	Strictness	Enthusiasm	Dignity	Strictness
10.	Dignity	Dignity	Strictness	Dignity

I may have seemed to dwell rather long on the teachers,
though our topic is the child. That, I think, is justified
because the teachers are so varied in personalities that one
cannot judge the 'normality' of the child's behaviour in, or

of his attitude to, school, unless one constantly bears in mind these possible variations of type among the teachers.

It is no proof that a child is 'abnormal' in a bad sense if he comes into conflict with one or two teachers in the course of his school life; on the other hand, if a child gets on with none of his teachers there is likely to be something seriously wrong. It may be, of course, that his intelligence has been overestimated and that he is incapable of doing the work assigned him, however hard he tries, so that he is declared to be lazy by a whole series of teachers. I have known this happen even with borderline mental defectives who, never having been given intelligence tests, were assumed to be normal and were pushed up the school according to their age, and thought to be slackers. More frequently, however, if a child has serious difficulties with nearly all teachers through his bad behaviour, that does suggest strongly that the cause is in the child himself, though some fond mothers are apt to assume that everyone is 'against him'. A relatively specific trait in a given teacher may clash with specific traits in a given pupil; or specific traits in another teacher may be the salvation of some pupils who threaten to become 'problem' children.

I may give one example to illustrate how a particular teacher may cause trouble even with a highly conscientious pupil, and one example to illustrate how one right kind of teacher can get good results out of a child condemned by the rest of the teachers. When I was a boy at a well-known grammar school one of the masters persuaded some half-dozen of us in the upper fifth to enrol as students in one of his evening classes in mechanics, which was not taught in the school. (The classes were supported by government grants, if they did not fall below a certain number.) He taught us very well (better than he did in school), but one night, when the master was writing on the blackboard, some of our group were repeatedly noisy. He could not apply penalties in the evening school, but next day at the grammar school he gave us all 500 lines. Some of us, including myself, had taken no part in the disturbance, but he would not take our word for it. The rest did their lines, but I refused. I was working very hard for an examination and I grudged the time wasted on writing lines; but the ground on which I based my refusal was that he had no right to apply a punishment to us, as grammar-school pupils, for what was done in quite a different institution. That was a sound legal point, it still seems to me; but *en revanche* the master proceeded to ignore me in his mathematics class, so that none of my work was corrected. This went on some time and my progress would certainly have suffered. Then one day the headmaster (a very fine man) summoned me to his room, and asked me as a personal favour to himself to do the lines. He gave me the impression that he thought my view was justified, though he was careful not to say that the teacher had no right to impose the imposition. My respect and, indeed, affection for the Head was such that I yielded to his appeal.

Now for an example at the other extreme of another type, namely, of a teacher who can deal with a most unpromising pupil. In a primary school there was a little boy of 9 who was stunted in growth to the extent of being peculiar in appearance, Though no tests were applied, I was satisfied by various reports that he was decidedly below average intelligence and especially slow in response to questions. The teachers in whose classes he had been regarded him as a nuisance and almost ignored him. Then he came under Miss X, a teacher who at once felt a keen sympathy with him. She would wait patiently for his answers, though they were often futile. She was friendly to him out of class, and finally won his deep affection. It was not enough, of course, to counteract his innate lack of intelligence, and at the end of the year, he, with one other, failed to get his remove. And was his old inferiority complex re-established? Far from it. He vigorously jeered at the others because they would have to leave the beloved Miss X, while he was privileged to remain with her! The testimony of the mother made it clear that Miss X now had a great influence on the boy through suggestion, coming from so admired a teacher.

During the present century teachers in day schools have taken more and more active a share in the life of children outside the classroom – in games, camp life, and various school societies, and this has greatly helped in the establishment of pleasant relations between teacher and pupil and towards a fuller understanding of the child's whole personality by the teacher. I well remember when I was a master in a school (St Olave's Grammar School, London) which was a pioneer in organizing summer camps for boys and masters, how a week of camp life quite changed my judgement of one boy in my class. His work had been far from satisfactory and I thought it due to lack of effort, but at camp I found him the most co-operative and friendly of all my boys. I came to the conclusion that I had overestimated his intellectual abilities and our camp life together quite altered my attitude; and greater patience and understanding led to much happier times for both of us later on in school.

As children grow older the special interest taken in some specific subjects naturally affects their relations to the teachers concerned. There is some tendency for children to like a subject which is taught by a teacher they like very much; and some tendency to like a teacher who takes a subject in which the pupil is keenly interested and successful. But among abler pupils the nature of the subject itself may be the more influential. Thus in an inquiry in English grammar schools, the following questions were asked of 974 of the pupils [87].

(1) Have you put down as your *best*-liked subject a subject which is taught by the teacher you like best?

(2) Have you put down as your *least*-liked subject a subject which is taught by the teacher you like least?

The results were as follows:

Best-liked subject taught by best-liked teacher, reported by 249 pupils.

Best-liked subject not taught by best-liked teacher, reported by 714 pupils.

Least-liked subject taught by least-liked teacher, reported by 146 pupils.

Least-liked subject not taught by least-liked teacher, reported by 288 pupils.

The investigator concluded that his evidence was against the view that the popularity of the teacher is the main influence in such preferences; but we must bear in mind that in many cases a subject might have been much lower in the list but for the pupils' liking for the teacher of that subject.

An inquiry in the U.S.A. among nearly 1,000 pupils mostly between the ages of 16 and 18, was aimed at finding out the relative importance of various factors in contributing to 'classroom' enjoyment [80]. The teacher's method of teaching came first, and the teacher's personality second; then confidence in the teacher's knowledge of the subject. 'Both boys and girls decidedly preferred teachers who frequently participate in extracurricular affairs of the school, even though they are not brilliant in the classroom, to teachers who rarely participate in the extracurricular affairs of the school, even though they are outstanding in the classroom.'

This section, however, should not conclude with a record of averages. At all stages, whether the pupil likes a particular teacher depends not only on those qualities which are generally liked by pupils, but what the pupil's own special characteristics are. Knowledge and academic distinction are likely to win the admiration of pupils who are themselves ambitious in that direction; athletic prowess will win the adoration of the keen athletes of the school – and many more; idealism and fineness of character will draw the devotion at least of the discerning few and that at younger ages than many may suspect.

The child and his fellow-pupils. For the sake of continuity we have followed the study of the child's relation to the teachers up to adolescence. We must now consider his social behaviour towards his school-fellows, and, in doing so, go back to the first school years. Here we have no definite norms of behaviour for different years. Individual differences surpass averages for adjoining years even more than they did in earlier years. Some children at 8:0 resemble the majority at 6:0 more than those of their own age; others at 8:0 seem as mature as most at 10:0 or over. Gesell [43], who did such magnificent pioneer work on the first 5 years, has indeed, in the book referred to, tried to describe typical behaviour for each of the years 5 to 10. Fifty children were examined for each age up to 9, all, we must note, being above average intelligence. The authors are fully aware of the wide range of individual differences. Indeed, they refer to each child's 'unique pattern of growth'. Yet they seek to establish special characteristics of the 6-year-old as compared with the 5- or 7-year-old, and so on. 'Percentage frequencies were noted', we are told, 'but were not made the sole basis for the final conclusions and are not reported in this volume. Sometimes a single but revealing behaviour led to the identification of a significant developmental trend.' The result is some statements as to development changes which cannot be accepted without much more precise and extensive evidence. Consider, for example, the following, taken from the summary of changes in affective attitudes and suggesting a marked change of equilibrium in each year, with a reversal of that change in the next year:

'Five years. Serious and businesslike, well equilibrated, poised, but may be resistant.

'Six years. Highly emotional; marked disequilibrium between children and others.

'Seven years. Gets on better with others, though disequilibrium within own feelings.

'Eight years. Tendency to disequilibrium between self and others.

'Nine years. Better equilibrium.'

What seems to have happened is that merely chance variations in the samples for each age (only about twenty-five boys and twenty-five girls) have not been equally typical of the whole age group; and so some genuine average age differences have been swamped by individual differences even more than they should have been. Let me add, however, that one welcomes this further testimony by the authors to the supreme importance in the development of the child of the maturing of innate tendencies and the dominance of development by internal principles of growth. Here is a counterblast to the extreme Behaviourist's emphasis on the omnipotence of environmental influences, though the label 'Behaviourist' is not even mentioned in their index.

While, however, we cannot enumerate the various traits or social behaviour which distinguish each age group from the one a year younger or older, we can recognize certain trends, on which reports by a considerable number of different observers in different countries substantially agree, and which cover a wider range of types of children than does Gesell's report, and far greater numbers.

Group play. Here there is usually marked development in children from the age of about 7 or 8 up to 12 or more. Many observers endorse Gesell's report that at 8:0 there is more co-operation in group play. The number of different play activities declines after 9:0, because of the influence of conventions as to games, and the impulse to join a group, and to compete. Thus the mere kicking of a ball about becomes now the joining in a group for a competitive game, in which the younger child may be enlisted to make up a team. Yet even now the group bond is not always very strong. It is interesting to watch, as I have often done on a public recreation ground, a cricket match in which boys of varied ages are involved. The 14- and 15-year-olds have got the team idea and are co-operating well, but youngsters of 9 or 10 when fielding will often be seen momentarily having a game of their own with a spare ball, till a yell from their captain calls their attention to a ball which they should be fielding.

A child of 8 or 9 who almost invariably plays by himself is unusual. It may be that he is excessively timid and shy; or that he is so selfish or rough that children of his own age avoid him, though children of this type often turn to children younger than themselves and boss them about. The rough and boisterous games which boys of this age usually love may be especially distasteful to the timid boy who has been over-protected by his mother, and this may rule him out of the main groups of his immediate circle.

Occasionally loneliness is due to the child being much above the intelligence of the children in his class or play group. The child much more intelligent than his class fellows, with a wider vocabulary than theirs and more intellectual interests, is apt to be thought to be 'putting on airs' and avoided. Promotion to a class more of his own intellectual level may cause a big change.

Sometimes, on the other hand, a change to the grammar school puts a strain on the child's equilibrium. The *average* social rank of parents of grammar-school children is somewhat higher than the average in the primary schools; and all the pupils are picked, so that a child may be one of the least clever of his class after being used to coming at the top of his class in the junior school. In some cases this transfer has been followed by immediate maladjustment [22].

Clubs and gangs. The tendency to join in groups at this period is also shown in the many 'clubs' and 'gangs' that are formed. Of course, these often serve the purpose of making some particular game or sport more possible. But sometimes the sheer love of coming together in a friendly group seems to be the main factor. One of my boys at the age of about 9 helped to found a club which met secretly in the loft of our old stable. It was called 'The society for the abolition of ladies'. What they meant to do with the ladies when they were 'abolished' I never found out, but I learned that the boys' mothers were exempt from this abolition. One of our girls at about this same age was President of a 'Society for kindness to animals'. The first notice she sent round the members said 'Anyone who can think of a good rule for the club should send it to the secretary'. Often no doubt such clubs have quite innocent aims, in spite of their secret procedure so frequently adopted. Yet the frequency of some mischievous, or even illegal, behaviour is indicated by a report as to gangs which had been joined when they were children, by students in a teachers' college in Australia [29].

Of the ninety men and thirty women students four-fifths of the men and two-thirds of the women said they had been gang members between the ages of 9 (boys) or 11 (girls) and 13. Most were single-sex gangs 'strongly antagonistic' to the opposite sex, sometimes with a penalty applied if a boy even talked to a girl! Secret signals and initiation ceremonies were common, but the most surprising fact is that these gangs of boys and girls who were to develop later so satisfactorily that they were selected for the teaching profession, very often indulged in mischievous or illegal activities.

Thus 44 per cent of the boys' gang occupations were labelled 'predatory' – raiding orchards, pulling down fences, birds-nesting. Other 'socially disapproved' actions – smoking, telling sex yarns, and swearing – formed 41 per cent of the activities of the boys. Massing these with the 'predatory', the author found that the boys' gang activities were 90 per cent socially disapproved and only 10 per cent approved, the girls' activities being 36 per cent disapproved and 64 per cent approved.

In view of the later satisfactory development of these children, we clearly cannot say that to be a member of a mischievous gang at these ages means the sign of a future delinquent (as some have said), or indeed is in any bad sense 'abnormal'. They were, it would seem, just playing at revolt against adult domination, and enjoying some assertiveness with the added delight of close companionship.

Sex grouping. There is little of this at the nursery-school stage, but after about 7:0 or 8:0, especially as group games become more popular, there is a natural tendency for the sexes to separate. The rougher games such as football, or those involving hard knocks, e.g. cricket, are more popular with boys; less aggressive games, such as hopscotch and skipping, with the girls.

Games then themselves become one dominant factor in determining groups, and even in individual friendships the sexes from about 8:0 or 9:0 tend to separate. It will be recalled that in the report on the Australian 'gangs' mentioned above, sex antagonism appeared in both the boys' and girls' gangs, though there were six gangs with a good number of boys and girls and six boys' gangs each included one tom-boy girl!

Friendships and popularity. These topics have been studied by several different techniques. First there is direct observation. A small group of children in a free play time may be watched and the approaches of one child to any other noted for say a quarter of an hour. From the notes may then be recorded as to the boy John:

1. The number of times he has made a friendly social approach to Fred, Tom, etc.

2. The number of times he has made an aggressive approach to Fred, Tom, etc.

3. The number of times he has received a friendly approach from Fred, Tom, etc.

4. The number of times he has received an aggressive approach from Fred, Tom, etc.

From such notes a table may be drawn up as follows:

		Approaches Made		Approaches Received	
		Friendly	Aggressive	Friendly	Aggressive
John to or from	Fred	12	5	2	2
	Tom	8	6	9	1
	Bill	6	9	3	9
Total		26	20	14	12
Fred to or from	John	2	2	12	5
	Tom	1	0	5	0
	Bill	3	2	4	6
Total		6	4	21	11
Tom to or from	John	9	1	8	6
	Fred	5	0	1	0
	Bill	4	3	4	8
Total		18	4	13	14
Bill to or from	John	3	9	6	9
	Fred	4	6	3	2
	Tom	4	8	4	3
Total		11	23	13	14

Four rather extreme types are represented above.

John is generally sociable in the sense that he makes many advances – friendly and aggressive. We may recall that in the study of pre-school children there was found some tendency for friendly and aggressive approaches to go with one another. The more contacts a child has the more scraps are likely to arise, though most may be merely playful.

Fred is the reverse. He is reserved, or shy, or timid; he makes few advances even to John, whose favourite he seems to be. Tom makes rather fewer friendly advances than John, but far fewer aggressive ones. Bill is aggressive – the only one whose aggressive approaches are more numerous than the friendly; but only the active John pays him back in his own coin. The contrasts have, of course, been made marked on purpose. The majority of children show more mixed figures.

This method of studying the social relations between school-fellows has obvious difficulties; unless the group observed is very small many contacts are apt to be missed, and some children may attract too exclusively the attention of the observer, though these errors can be avoided by the observer watching each child in turn for a given period.

The behaviour of some children, especially bullies, may also be greatly affected by the presence of an observer, if he is visible, but in some research centres one-way screens have been installed which allow the children to be seen but not the observer by the children. We turn now to a different type of approach to the study of friendships and groups.

Sociometric studies. The method of approach described here is relatively new, and the looseness of some inquiries has been severely criticized. I give some space to it chiefly as an interesting example of method which with further refinements may produce useful results.

To a class of children of about 9 years or over papers are distributed with several questions on them, such as the following:

1. Whom would you most like to sit next to in class?
2. Whom would you choose as your best friend if you could have only one?
3. Whom would you choose first to play with after school?

In addition, a series of qualities are listed with their opposites, e.g. very talkative – very quiet; very friendly – very unfriendly, and so on. The children are asked to guess who is being described in each case. The method is known as the 'Guess Who' technique, and is used to give a clue to the qualities in a fellow-pupil which cause him to be chosen as a friend. By such means we can get further estimates as to the popularity of individuals and an indication of groups. The results may be shown in a diagram such as the one below. The lines indicate that a choice in one of the groups has been made by one boy of the other boy to whom the arrow points.

Sociogram

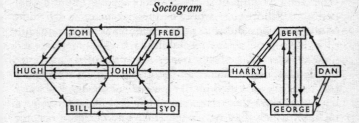

The figure has been restricted to a few boys and to first choice for simplicity. From the number of lines it will be seen

1. that John is very popular – he receives eight choices;
2. poor Dan receives not a single choice. He would be labelled an 'isolate';
3. two clearly distinguishable groups appear: one (A) to the left of the sociogram, centred round John, who receives at least one choice from each member of that group and who gives all his own choices to some member of the group. A second group (B) appears almost independent, except that Harry gives one choice to John.

The 'sociometric' technique is flexible. The children can be asked to give second choices and third choices and they can be asked or allowed to name 'rejections' – one they would dislike sitting next to, or would not choose as a friend. The method, however, is by no means perfect. Thus each child who fills up a form will know that his choice will be seen by the investigator and perhaps by his teacher; and a boy may hesitate to give a girl his choices, or *vice versa*, or to give a choice to a boy whom he knows will give him none; in the sociogram above it would perhaps take the boy Harry some courage to give one to the popular John.

In the study of children possibly the most instructive results refer to the finding of marked groups or cliques of children with common ideals of sport or work, and sometimes rival groups with different ideals or values, and sometimes the revealing of 'isolates' more lonely than a master might realize in class work, or the esteem in which some 'stars' are held. But so far, few generalizations about children have been soundly established by this method and some devotees of the techniques seem apt to over-emphasize the determining influence of the group and underestimate the influence of individuality and of innate tendencies. I have described the technique chiefly for its interest as a method, which may with experience and criticism become increasingly useful.

Most of the studies by the sociometric technique have been made in the U.S.A., especially by J.L.Moreno; but I should like to refer to one interesting report made in England by Mr H. J. Hallworth [50]. It dealt with children in a grammar school between the ages of 11:0 and 16:0, so that most would be adolescents. One special value of this inquiry is that the technique was applied to each class several times: first in September 1947, then in January 1948, April 1948, and July 1948. The 'Guess Who' test was also given in July 1948. As the experimenter was the teacher of this class, he could also make written observations on general behaviour. The school was a mixed one and the groups which emerged showed an almost complete cleavage throughout the year between the sexes, so boys' and girls' results were treated separately.

Another general finding was the 'tendency to make progressively larger and better integrated groups'. Not surprisingly, among the new entrants to school no groups appeared in the first test (September 1947), though among the girls one popular star already appeared; but an extra test two months later (November) showed groups already appearing, and among the boys one poor 'isolate' and a large number of 'rejections' were concentrated on two boys. By April the boys showed two stars and two isolates; also there was a triangle of boys separated from the larger group. The 'Guess Who' test in July revealed that the popular traits (or 'values' as Mr Hallworth labels them) were 'friendliness, ability to get on well with older boys and with adults, a sense of humour and ability to take a joke, a happy and smiling disposition, good looks and attractiveness, and a general restless activity. Negative values were listlessness, lack of a sense of humour and inability to take a joke, extreme personal untidiness, and physical aggressiveness towards other boys.'

The girls in this class never developed one large group. They lacked a leader with a small group of devotees, which seemed essential in all classes if a big stable group was to be formed. The one girl who 'could have acted as a centre' apparently was more interested in friends outside the school.

Among the older children the groups tended to be more closely knit near the end of their year together. Thus in a class of boys of 14 or 15 years of age there was a nuclear group of four with numerous reciprocated choices, one of the four being a special star. The ten other boys gave many choices to these but not so many to one another. The star in the 'Guess Who?' test was shown to be popular because of his ability in games, pleasantness, enthusiasm, and because he never tried to attract attention to himself.

It is easy to see, in the light of our chapter on Imitation and Suggestion, how much influence such a nuclear group of admired and liked boys might have on the others. The suggestion prestige of the main leader would be increased by the homage paid to him by the minor leaders, themselves liked and admired by the other boys. We get an approach to mass suggestion; probably there would be not only the adoption of ideas through suggestion (intentional or not) but imitation, both deliberate, and non-deliberate or primary, so that manners, ways of speech, observance (or disobedience) of such rules would be imitated.

Where there is a smaller rival group, it is likely to consist, it would seem, of pupils who are so antagonistic to the ideal or 'values', to use Mr Hallworth's term, of the main leaders in the class that suggestion does not succeed, or the smaller group includes one or two who are so self-assertive that they want to be leaders and yet cannot get acceptance by the main group, and must be content to dominate, or at least be pals with the smaller group. In other words, we get the familiar 'cliques' forming.

It is illuminating to consider the case of one 'isolate' in one of Mr Hallworth's classes, the boy labelled 'Lyon'. The 'Guess Who' test showed that others considered him as 'always trying to attract attention to himself, sure of himself, but unable to sit still in class, constantly talking, causing or taking part in fights, being childish in outlook, daring, unkempt, and always trying to boss others.'

The pupils were told not to put their own names down in the 'Guess Who' test, but Lyon did. He revealed that 'he considered himself grown-up in attitude, neat and tidy, and good-looking and attractive, but apparently had some insight into his own personality in that he realized he was bossy.'

The girls in this same form (in age about 14 or 15) were also split into two groups early in the school year. Three girls formed a separate triangle, with mutual choices, but none receiving any from the other seven girls. By May every girl in the larger group expressed a positive rejection of each of the other three. By the end of the year each of these three was an 'isolate'. 'It appeared that each girl was trying to improve her own rank by associating with those of superior rank, whilst herself rejecting those of inferior rank.' The four main leaders of the big group were the only ones listed as being 'friendly' and as 'happy and always smiling'. Good looks and attractiveness were also clearly of weight with these girls, sports much less so than with the boys.

Limitations of group influences. Having exemplified the power of group influences we must point out its limitations. So far as a child's behaviour is dependent on imitation of his leaders and on their immediate suggestive influence, he may act differently in other circumstances; there is, indeed, ample evidence that a child may behave rather differently at school and at home, or indeed in a class group as compared with his behaviour in a different games group or a club (e.g. Boy Scouts) outside the school range. We must emphasize again that it is only as he develops permanent sentiments or attitudes not only to individuals, but towards general principles or ideals of conduct that his character becomes integrated and stabilized; and stabilization or integration may tend in some cases to a 'bad on the whole' rather than to a good. In many more, such integrations take place only incompletely.

In all this we must also guard against the impression that the group or other environmental influence is the sole factor in personality and character development. True, in trying to understand the social behaviour of children (or adults) we must take into consideration the total 'field' of the moment, to use a popular term in recent psychology. But some psychologists seem to slip so easily into acting or speaking as though the environmental circumstances were the sole and determining 'field'. Yet one of the leading pioneers and exponents of 'field' psychology, K. Lewin, has himself emphasized that the child himself with his individual 'needs' and 'goals' is part of the total field, and that behaviour is determined by the person *and* the environment and not by the person or the environment alone [70].

Lewin rightly emphasizes too that the environment to be considered must be the environment *as perceived by the child*, including thoughts of future changes in that environment. A mere description of the environment as it appears to the adult may be quite inadequate.

Lewin made great use of diagrams in which were represented the various forces at work in the field – the child's attraction towards one thing or end and repulsion from another, blockings and 'barriers' of his aims or needs, and so on. Such diagrams may help some to analyse the situation more thoroughly and see it more clearly, but they do not enable us to solve the problems by geometrical calculations, as may be done in the study of mechanical forces.

The significance of the individual's own particular personality for the permanent consistency of behaviour is well brought out by an inquiry by Professor Vernon Jones [67]. He found that 'improvement in measurable character made under the conditions of good group morale is largely dependent for its permanence upon the maintenance of the group intact.'

In eight classes of children about the ages of 12 to 14, to whom he gave instruction for a school year in character and citizenship, he found that the class with the best group morale made the greatest gain. Then followed a few months in which the pupils were rearranged in different classes. When they were brought together again for testing it was 'found that the original gains were maintained most poorly by the students of the class which had developed the best group morale, and they were maintained best by those students who improved in spite of the weakest group morale.'

I have given considerable space to this sociometric study partly because of its interest as a method of child study; but the results I have given also illustrate further a point especially stressed in this book, namely, that of individual differences. It may also have some bearing on another point of special interest, namely, the detecting of something undesirably abnormal. There is surely something undesirable in the existence of an 'isolate', at least after children have been in the same class for weeks or months. We have, however, to bear in mind the possibility in some classes of a not too pleasant type of child obtaining an exclusive influence over a group which may become large and dominant, and of a body of really superior character and personality being isolated, because he is strong enough to resist the general drift.

Our warning about the possible great variations in the

general type of personality within the dominant group of different classes, owing to the small numbers involved, is confirmed by the fact that in one American sociometric inquiry it was found that rejections in the class correlated highly (0·7) with the ratings of 'poor adjustment' by the California Test of Personality, whereas another investigation found a very low correlation (0·2) between rejection and bad adjustment (see our p. 230 for explanation of correlation).

The relation between popularity and personality traits. The factors determining popularity have been estimated by quite a different method from those we have so far discussed. Some twenty years ago Professor Cyril Burt arranged some inquiries, the results of which he has kindly handed over to me, and which have not been published. Burt himself does not attach much importance to the differences in different types of schools, as there was only one boys' public school and one girls'. Accordingly, I shall only give some of the more striking results.

Pupils were asked to rate their fellow-pupils on a five-point scale (A, B, C, D, E,), showing how much they liked them. In addition, ratings were obtained, on a five-point scale, from two teachers (or one teacher and a senior pupil) of all these pupils in reference to such characteristics as sociability, good temper, good looks, etc. The correlations between popularity and the various traits were then reckoned, and finally an order drawn up showing the degree of close connexion between each characteristic and popularity. There were thirty characteristics in the list. I give below some main findings for the different types of schools among whom the inquiry was made and for a group of delinquent boys.

Among the elementary school pupils (all about 11 years of age), sociability, good temper, cheerfulness, and a sense of humour were all very clearly associated with popularity; so they were in the girls' public school, but with the public school boys candour (not being deceitful or secretive) was more important than sociability. Talkativeness was very attractive to the elementary school girls, but the opposite to the public school boys! Assurance and leadership was very high among the boys, but not quite so high with girls. A marked tendency to 'self-display' was noted in very popular boys in the group of delinquents. It was decidedly associated with unpopularity in all the other groups.

CHAPTER 12

Moral Behaviour and Children's Ideals

Moral habits. It has long been recognized by psychologists that popular ideas about 'habits' and training in good habits are inadequate. Such phrases as 'cultivating habits of truth-fulness or honesty' are too vague and to some extent misleading. In the child, and indeed in many adults, habits are often highly specific. A woman neat in her person and clothes may have a very untidy dressing table, a man whose books are precisely arranged may have ruffled hair and a sagging necktie; a youth who would not dream of stealing the money of a friend may seize the chance of escaping the payment of his bus fare. Every experienced schoolmaster knows that some boys who would scorn to cheat in school games would not hesitate to do so in school work.

From the earliest years a little child may acquire some definite habits, such as proper table manners, e.g. not grabbing food, and saying 'please' when asking for things, as the result of parental reproof or approval, of small penalties or rewards, or by the imitation of an older brother or sister, or through the suggestions of a loved parent.

Of course, when there is some strong conflicting personal motive – the sight of a specially liked titbit on the table – even a very regular habit of good table manners may be broken. Furthermore, suggestions from the parent are more likely to be adopted if they also appeal to some strong personal tendency; for example, one of the earliest effective appeals one can make to a child of 2 or 3 is to say that '*big* boys (or girls) don't do that'.

Now suppose some particular habit, say speaking politely to a rather stern father, has become well established; it by no means follows that the child has developed a general habit of politeness even in speech. He may be very rude in speech to his nurse. The habit is tied to a particular person or situation. For a wider application of politeness the child must be trained to it also in various other types of situations – visitors to the house, shopkeepers he meets in visits to shops with mother, and so on. Later, and ideally, he should come to formulate a general ideal of politeness, to see a reason for it and to care about it, a stage which it is to be feared many adults never reach, and which, as we shall see, we can hardly expect in children much before adolescence; though there are intermediate stages in which the total impression of a new situation is sufficiently like the one in which a specific response was learned, that there is some spread of the habit without the conscious formulation of a general ideal.

Objective tests of honesty and cheating. A number of inquiries and experiments have been made on this question of general or specific habits and ideals of conduct. In one extensive research, supervised by H. Hartshorne and M. May [52], over 10,000 school children in the U.S.A. were given tests in which they had an opportunity of cheating. The tests were so devised that they revealed whenever the child had cheated. The tests were also very varied and concerned not only with classroom work, but with school work done at home, with games and with athletics. In other tests there were opportunities to give false replies to questions about their personal conduct, and in yet others there were chances to steal coins, when it appeared quite safe to the child. In addition to the special tests, real-life situations were planned and the children's behaviour noticed; e.g. parties with games were arranged, at which it was possible to cheat; the children were sent on errands and wrong change noted; opportunities were arranged for being unselfish or generous.

The tests were by no means infallible, as we shall see later, and as, indeed, the authors very frankly admit, but they do show one thing clearly which is of main interest for our present purpose, namely, that there was little evidence of any *general* habits of invariable honesty (or dishonesty), or of truthfulness (or lying).

There was, it is true, a decided tendency for cheating in arithmetic to go with cheating in a vocabulary test, and such difference as there was might well be due to a child being better at one than the other and so not needing to cheat so much to score well. But cheating in school and cheating in athletic contests proved to be rarely conjoined – as we hinted above. (The correlation was only about 0·2. For the meaning of correlation see p. 230.) There was even less connexion between the tests of stealing and those of lying. In other words, there was little tendency for the child to be honest or straightforward *in general*. The habits of lying or cheating were largely specific, though small resemblances between the scores in the different tests ('positive correlations') do give evidence of some slight general tendency towards the good or the bad already revealing itself in the children tested. We shall discuss these experiments more fully later in this chapter, but one other main fact may be added here. In the scores on the honesty tests and in others as to 'helpfulness', it was not found that pupils could be divided into two clearly differentiated groups – one very honest and one dishonest (or one very helpful and one unhelpful). On the contrary, there was a wide scatter of scores, with many near the centre of average, and then a gradual falling off on the one hand, and a gradual improvement on the other, with only a few pupils at either extreme. When graphs were plotted they were very much the same as that which indicates the scatter of intelligence, listed on our page 237. Furthermore, it was quite clear that cheating or deceit was no abnormality in the sense of unusualness. On the contrary, massing two typical groups, one especially honest, the other specially dishonest, the authors found that only 6 per cent did not cheat at all – at home or school.

The heroes and ideals of children. We need hardly point out the great difference between (*a*) choosing a fine person as your ideal and (*b*) trying to live up to his standard; yet few I think would assert that ideals make no difference to conduct, and even the cynic would agree that having poor ideals would limit the upward range of conduct.

Again, knowledge about what is usually regarded as right or wrong certainly does not ensure right conduct. Yet to some extent the two do 'go together'. Thus in the elaborate research by Hartshorne and May, referred to above, a measure was finally obtained of the extent of 'integration' or consistency of the various forms of honesty, that is, the extent to which the various forms of honesty went together, or 'correlated'. In addition, tests of 'moral knowledge' were given (including judgements as to rightness of actions), and it was found that there was a substantial though not a large correlation between 'integration' and moral knowledge, even when differences of intelligence were allowed for. (The correlations were round about 0·4 [53].)

Even apart from their possible influence on conduct, the choice of personal ideals by young children is of great interest, and reports on them give us some clue as to where for the time being the children's ambitions lie. Various studies of the ideals or heroes named by children agree at least in one thing: when children are asked, 'Who would you choose to be if not yourself?', 'Whom do you admire most?', or 'Whom would you most wish to be like of all the people you have known, or heard of, or read about?'

The very young children of 6 or 7 almost invariably choose some member of the family or someone in their small circle of acquaintances. This is to be expected, as they have heard or read of relatively few outside, From one inquiry in the U.S.A. about a third of the children of about 7:0 chose father or mother as the ideal; by 10:0 the proportion is more like one-tenth. As age increases and experience widens, the persons chosen as ideals are found to be increasingly someone read or heard of in history, in fiction, or in the Bible, or some prominent public personality.

I may give fuller details of an inquiry made by one of my former research students, Miss Eve Macaulay [73]. The inquiry was made in three types of elementary schools: (A) in a slum district of a city; (B) in a semi-slum district; (C) in a good artisan district, and in (D) two grammar schools, one a boys' and one a girls'. About half the children were in A or B schools, and, of course, the influence of environment reveals itself. The children were asked:

1. What person whom you have ever known, or of whom you have ever heard or read, would you most wish to be like?

2. Give a list of reasons which make you choose this person.

The children were asked to give their ages but not their names. There were 1,600 children dealt with, nearly all between the ages of 7 and 16. The following are the results of greatest interest:

Percentage choosing some acquaintance as the ideal

Boys and girls combined

Age	7	8	9	10	11	12	13
Per cent	65	59	40	32	24	17	8

Girls chose an acquaintance more frequently than did boys, and after the age of 15 there was a tendency for the choice of acquaintances to increase again, though the numbers were too small to be worth giving.

There was a decidedly greater tendency for girls to choose a man as an ideal than for boys to choose a woman: e.g. of the girls at 9:0, 20 per cent chose a man, after 9:0 there was a drop, but at 13:0 it was 26 per cent. Practically no boy over 10:0 chose a woman, those of 7, 8, and 9 averaging 7 per cent choices of a woman. As will be seen from examples given below, the persons chosen were more frequently 'heroes' or people in occupations which the child himself would like, rather than moral ideals.

Adventurous characters were frequently selected by the boys, with a peak of nearly 40 per cent at the age of 11 : 0. They were much less frequently chosen by girls, the highest percentage, viz. 20 per cent, being at the age of 10 : 0, after which the numbers fell rapidly.

Monarchs were chosen surprisingly often, the peak of the frequency graph being, for boys 23 per cent at 10 : 0, then about 13 per cent up to 13 : 0. For girls the peak was 18 per cent at 9 : 0, with a slight decline after that.

In a later paper [74], Miss Macaulay (with a collaborator) reported on larger numbers of elder children and on 180 training-college students, and the percentage choosing acquaintances shows a rise again after 13. Thus:

Ages	13	14	15	16	17	18	19
Per cent	8	11	11	19	21	38	31

The reasons given for choices reveal that these later choices of acquaintances are on very different bases from those of the earliest ages. Thus from 10 to 13 the acquaintance is, in the majority of instances, an adult engaged in some occupation which the child admires and holding a dominant position therein; e.g.: Boy (10): 'Mrs —, because she keeps a sweet shop, and she can make money and do what she likes.' Boy (12): 'Mr —, a painter. He has a good easy job, and bosses the men. On Saturday he stops at 12 and he can go to football matches.' At these early ages the teacher is often chosen, his power over others often appearing prominently, e.g.: Boy (10): 'Mr —, because I would teach and write on the board and learn them everything, and I would make them mind me, and I would give them the cane.' Girl (11): 'Miss —. I should have pretty clothes. I should teach the girls and correct their sums, and tell them if they were wrong. I would take them for nature walks and take them across the roads.'

After 14:0 or 15:0 acquaintances are chosen usually because of qualities possessed. Thus: Boy (14): 'Mr — (a master). He is tall and strong and played for Oxford in football. He is a sport and very straight, anyone would be proud to be like him.'

Girl (15): 'Mrs —. She is gentle and truthful, and always sympathetic. Also she has a lovely figure and dresses perfectly. She is very ladylike.'

The reasons for the choice of monarchs reveal that for the younger children it is because of their possessions or their power over others: 'having lovely clothes', 'anything they like to eat', 'servants to wait on them', and 'nothing to do'!

Occasionally the local M.P. was selected, and up to the oldest groups he was described as having 'an easy job', 'good pay', and very little to do!

Probably most children would assume that the choice of Jesus or God was ruled out; but 'religious characters' (almost invariably Jesus) were chosen, in the earlier inquiry, by about 5 per cent of the girls up to the age of 13, but by less than half that proportion of boys. The great increase in the choice of Jesus among the girls of 14 and 15 was attributed largely, but not entirely, to the strong religious attitude in the girls' grammar school which supplied all the 15-year-old girls.

In general, these inquiries revealed the rarity of any concern about, or even any grasp of, general moral qualities before adolescence at about 12 or 13. When general qualities do appear earlier it is difficult to be sure they are not merely quotations of things heard, without a real understanding of their important value as general principles. We shall refer to this again as it appeared in another inquiry to be discussed later.

We may recall again that over half the children lived in very poor districts and were probably therefore as a group below average intelligence. We shall counterbalance this later in the chapter by reporting an inquiry among specially gifted children, coming mostly from homes above the average socio-economic level. Before, however, we examine more carefully the development of ideals and general ideas about conduct, let us consider some further findings of the inquiry about moral habits and behaviour in middle childhood, already referred to near the beginning of this chapter.

Is there no advance in moral behaviour in middle childhood? As to the various tests on cheating, lying, stealing, and on unselfish co-operation, carried out by Hartshorne and May among 10,000 children in the U.S.A., the authors in their earlier volume make the surprising report that they found little evidence of any marked improvement on the average in desirable behaviour during the years from about 10 to 15. Even if we agree that in the majority of their children there is little evidence of the formation of high, general ideals of conduct before the age of adolescence, Hartshorne and May's results seem to go beyond the consequences we should expect from that; and furthermore, their findings seem to apply to a good many children (though by no means all) who were in age groups in which adolescence has usually been reached, e.g. 14 and 15.

These results are at first very disconcerting. Is there really no improvement in moral conduct, even in specific habits or in the following of general moral rules or principles even in these later years of childhood? Few experienced teachers or thoughtful parents would, I imagine, be willing to agree to this; and on further reflection and on consideration of the tests we can find several things which largely dissipate the apparent contradiction.

1. First there is substantial evidence here and in other investigations that the important trait of *persistence* shows a steady increase during the years of childhood up to 13 or 14.

In the second place, the very point we made at the beginning of this chapter about the specific nature of habits of conduct applies here. The fact that in such matters as specific forms of cheating in tests or of lying there is little or no improvement during these years, does not rule out the acquiring of other specific good habits, or the possibility of considerable improvement in other ways and in broader matters of equal or greater importance; for example, consideration for parents, or refraining from bullying younger children, or conscientiousness about working well at school.

In the third place, I must point out what seem to me certain defects in some of the character tests of Hartshorne and May, highly ingenious as they are; and let me add that the authors themselves are wisely cautious in their conclusions and constantly emphasize the fact that any inferences as to the moral behaviour of children only apply to these particular tests given under their own particular conditions.

Consider first the tests of cheating. These were presented by outside examiners, the teachers being excluded at least from the first testing. Now it is probable that many of the pupils might have their own ideas as to the purpose of the tests. The older pupils might quite likely think that, even in the individual competition tests, the school standard or a well-liked teacher was on trial. (Even teachers are often hard to convince that when an intelligence test is being given to their class it is not a means of assessing the *teacher's* efficiency!) Any greater loyalty of the older pupils to the teacher or school might very well result in more cheating. This would be still more pronounced in the tests in which the children were told that their school grade was to be compared with others.

I may also mention another variation in the attitude towards cheating shown in my own experience as a boy. In junior classes we were rather selfish. Most boys would keenly guard their own answers to a test, lest others should copy. But later, among boys of 15 or so, there was much more co-operation, and even in the annual examinations there was a lot of open mutual help when a master was absent. I do not think any of us regarded it as wicked or morally wrong. We were rather like one big group of friends pitting our wits against the masters. Our attitude towards the visiting Frenchman, who taught the fifth-form composition and conversation, had an additional element in it. We liked him, but we thought him an 'awful ass'. He was, as I can see now, a very bad teacher; and we knew we could often divert him from the lesson proper by asking him questions about Napoleon, or even making pointed remarks about Waterloo. Consequently when he set our weekly composition, we collaborated with each other generously, and the boys known to be best in French had their efforts freely copied by others. That the master did not detect this added to our contempt.

On the other hand, when I was myself a schoolmaster I found that even a difficult and lazy class would co-operate with me finely when an inspector or other outsider appeared. They were then on the side of the master and the school against a possible critic.

In some of the Hartshorne and May tests of cheating the pupils were allowed to correct their own answers and give in the score, or even had solutions at hand when doing the tests. My school-fellows and I would certainly have regarded such a test as highly peculiar, and the examiner we should, I think, have labelled 'dotty'!

Fourthly, it is to be noted that the various tests of cheating and lying were so arranged that the child had no idea that its cheating or lying could be detected. Now admittedly the ideal thing is that a child should act from attachment to a general principle, a love of truth or honesty for its own sake. But how many adults are quite uninfluenced by the thought that others will know what they do? And, indeed, for the children the motives of pleasing mother and living up to the teacher's expectation are worthy motives; and personally I should think it better that a child should act well in their presence, or when he is aware that they will know, even if he acts otherwise when he thinks they will not know, rather than that he should be quite indifferent to their feelings. He is at least some way on the path towards a moral ideal. My fifth comment is on the fact that little or no increase was observed during childhood in *the tendency to help others*. This fits in well with the contention earlier in this book that helpfulness in early childhood is dependent first on an *innate* tendency which appears very early. Modification of this may, of course, take place as the result first of parental or other home influences, and later those of school and friends, etc., and such modification may mean an increase or a decrease in what we called active sympathy. Here we find ourselves in agreement with Hartshorne and May when they write: 'On the whole, children do not become more helpful merely by growing older. They may become either less helpful or more according as the experience gained in their particular environment discourages or encourages co-operation and charity.'

Finally, the most important comment on the generalization that there is little improvement with increasing age in honest behaviour, at least in middle childhood, is provided by Hartshorne, May, and Shuttleworth themselves in the third volume of the series [53]. Here they reveal the great difference between results obtained with children mainly from homes in the higher economic levels (population Y) and those obtained from children in homes of the lower levels (population Z). Not only are the scores in all the tests higher in Y than in Z, but a remarkable fact emerges when changes with increasing age are noted. In the more favoured homes the children (on the average) do become more and more honest as they get older and move up from the lowest to the highest grades in the schools, whereas in the poorer homes the children become less honest with increasing age. These differences with age would, of course, be obscured in the massing of all results from different types of homes.

At the same time, it was found that 'integration' (or consistency) increased decidedly with age in the favoured population Y, but only much more slowly in population Z. In addition, integration was found to be correlated with 'moral knowledge'. There was the substantial evidence of the influence of home and school (more especially of particular school classes) on the honesty and helpfulness of the children. But to me the most interesting cases are those of individual triumph over bad environment. I quote one case [52], a girl from an exceedingly poor home. 'The father is dishonest and a rather vicious personality. The parental relations are unhappy. The parents' attitude toward the child is unsympathetic or hostile, and their discipline does everything to her except spoil her. They live in the worst part of the community, and the general level of the home background is almost as low as there is. One parent is German and the other Italian, and they report themselves as Catholic. The child herself is of less than average intelligence, but is somewhat ahead in her school grade; 60 per cent or more of her classmates cheated on the test taken in school. This would seem to be an almost perfect picture of a child who has the handicaps leading most frequently to deception. Yet this child did not cheat at all.'

In a previous chapter we have stressed the influence of a loved parent or an admired teacher through example or the suggestion of particular action; but improvement in external behaviour may take place in two other ways:

First, experience may lead to calculated individual acts of helpfulness based on really selfish motives because children see that it wins approval or praise; and second, some general principle or ideal of action may be adopted, either for selfish reasons or as the result of the suggestive influence of an admired or loved person, e.g. parent or teacher. The grasp of a generalized principle, however, is not likely to appear in a child much before the period of adolescence, unless he is of exceptional intelligence, so that by, say, 10 years of age he is up to the average mental ability of the 13- or 14-year-olds, as we shall see in our next chapter is possible, Hartshorne and May, indeed, found no evidence that what they call 'integration' could be attributed to general ideals in the children they studied. Here then it may be well to consider the findings of some other estimates and tests of character on precociously intelligent children.

Tests of character among gifted children. An important report by Terman and his colleagues [100] dealt with children who were, in intellectual ability, several years ahead of average children of their age. They had intelligence quotients of 130 or over (see our page 236 for an explanation of 'intelligence quotient'). Terman used various 'character tests', e.g. 'social preference' (i.e. types of friends preferred), over-statement (as to books read in a list containing a good number of invented titles) and activity preferences. The results of these tests on over 500 gifted children were compared with the results given by a large 'control' group of children of average intelligence in the same schools.

In addition, Terman obtained estimates of character traits by teachers and parents on both the gifted and the average groups. Terman's report contains a great number of interesting findings, but we have only room here for a brief summary of the results that bear most directly on our present topic of character development. They are as follows, actual quotations from Terman being in inverted commas: 'Considering total score on the seven character tests used, one can say that the gifted child of 9 or 10 years has reached a stage of moral development which is not attained by the average child until the age of 13 or 14. Approximately 85 per cent of the gifted surpass the average of unselected children. The test results on this point are confirmed by the testimony of special class teachers of gifted children. The tests in question are measures of untrustworthiness, of dishonesty of report, of tendency to overstatement, of objectionable social-moral attitudes, and of interest in questionable books and questionable companions.'

We must point out, however, that we cannot assume that the earlier appearance in the gifted of good response to tests of moral traits is due entirely, or even largely, to greater intelligence. There is a strong tendency for the ablest child to be found in higher economic and social grades, and Terman himself admits that 'the majority of our children have had the advantage of superior cultural advantages in the home.'

In addition, it is possible and, I think, highly probable that the gifted children inherited not only intellectual abilities above average, but also above-average personality traits or innate tendencies, some of which are surely useful in climbing the socio-economic ladder.

2. According to the teachers' ratings, the following were the traits in which on the average (A) the gifted children greatly surpass the control group, and (B) the traits in which the difference was not great. (I omit some very intellectual traits, e.g. originality, common sense.)

Percentages of gifted children surpassing the average
of the control group

A	Boys Per cent	Girls Per cent
Prudence and forethought	79	83
Self-confidence	81	82
Will and perseverance	83	86
Sense of humour	72	77
Desire to excel	81	88
Conscientiousness	71	74
Truthfulness	72	70
B		
Fondness for large groups	48	55
Popularity	53	59
Sensitiveness to approval	58	56
Sympathy and tenderness	59	58
Generosity and unselfishness	55	55

The differences between the traits in A and B are worth remarking. The biggest differences are in 'will and perseverance', 'self-confidence', and the 'desire to excel', none of which need involve much unselfishness. On the other hand, there was little difference between the groups in sympathy or in generosity. It is notable that the correlation between intelligence and 'helpfulness' or 'co-operation' was also found to be very low by Hartshorne and May and by Vernon Jones, referred to above, the latter dealing with children of about 13 or 14.

Individual and sex differences in character among gifted children. In view of the stress I have laid throughout this book on the wide range of individual differences between children, some findings by Terman even among his highly selected group of clever children, are very relevant. Terman himself stresses this and writes: 'It should be emphasized that one could find in the gifted group numerous exceptions to the general rule with respect to character, personality, and emotional stability. The gifted are not free from faults, and at least one out of five has more of them than the average child of the general population. Perhaps one out of twenty presents a more or less serious problem in one or another respect.' The evidence, indeed, suggests that there were greater individual differences in character traits among the gifted than among the average children.

As to sex differences, some superiority of the girls appeared in certain tests and superiority of the boys in others; but in both there was a marked improvement about the age which is generally regarded as the beginning of adolescence, and this improvement started in girls about a year earlier than in boys, both among the gifted and among the control group. In our chapter on adolescence we shall see that the earlier maturing of girls reveals itself not only in sex development, but in several other ways, and that the girls are usually advanced by 1 or even 2 years.

The growth of general ideas of right and wrong. We have indicated that progress in a little child's behaviour (or moral conduct) takes the form chiefly of the acquiring of specific habits or, if you prefer it, specific reactions to specific situations. To advance beyond this we clearly need either more good specific habits or a widening of the situations which stimulate them. Sometimes there seems to be a kind of implicit grasp of a general rule which functions without explicit conscious formulation of the principle. For full maturity, however, we need a conscious realization of a general idea.

Now it has long been recognized by psychologists that such abstract terms as kindness, justice, and charity, indicating moral qualities, are not clearly grasped by children, on the average, before the age of 13:0 or 14:0. Burt, for example, assigns the definition of those terms to the age of 14:0, and even so allows the following definitions by children to pass: 'kindness' – 'being polite to others'; 'justice' – 'when you punish wicked people'; 'charity' – 'when you give poor people some money'.

As we shall see in our next chapter, many precocious children of 10:0 (such as Terman's 'gifted' children) are already up to the average intelligence of 13- or 14-year-olds, and such general ideas are within their grasp. So far, then, as more general moral ideas are needed for moral development the gifted children may be equipped for it at an earlier age, provided they are in a suitable environment.

All this, of course, does not mean that no general ideas covering conduct can be grasped even much earlier; but they are apt to be very distorted. For example, once when his younger brother said that something I did was 'naughty', I asked my boy B (at 4:4) what he (B) meant when he said I was naughty. B replied, 'When you do something I don't like, that's naughty'. So what B had gathered from our frequent use of the term 'naughty' in our dealings with him for two or more years, was that we called a thing naughty which we did not like, and he had adopted our usage. (I should add that intelligence tests showed that at 4:4 B would have about the intelligence of the average child of 6:6.)

That, indeed, is typical of the first ideals of little children about what is right and what is wrong. 'Right' is what is approved by parents and other superiors around them; the 'wrongs' consist of offences against parents and other superiors. These facts are well illustrated in the inquiry already referred to by my former research student, Miss E. Macaulay and her collaborator [74]. They report as follows about the replies of the children as to what they thought was 'wicked' or 'naughty': '(1) The first stage, which extends to about nine years, is that in which the child lives in a small world of immediate personal relationships. Informed by no general moral principles, he merely states as crimes those small personal acts which he has been taught to consider wrong by the categorical prohibitions of his parents or teachers. At this age, therefore he does not write down "stealing", "assault" or "disobedience", but gives a list of objects that may not be stolen, injuries he must not inflict, and rules he must not disobey.'

Typical of such attitudes are the following: 'steal apples', 'bite', 'spit' (boy 7:0), 'be rude to mother', 'not say your prayers' (boy 8:0), 'throw paper on the lawn', 'disturb mother' (girl 8:0).

'From seven to eight years of age "mother" is the predominating individual in the child's life, and the crime is "being naughty to" or "disobeying mother". After nine years "teacher" comes to the fore, a sign that the school influence is superseding that of the home, and that the child is issuing forth into a wider world. Mentions of "mother" fall to 6 per cent, and "teacher" rises from 2 per cent to 16 per cent.'

This attitude of most children up to the age of 8 or 9, implying that things are right or wrong merely because of the edict of some parent or other adult, was confirmed later by the findings of J. Piaget in his observations on children in Geneva [85]. He also stressed the fact that at these early ages the child's judgement of the naughtiness of an act is determined by the objective facts and not by the motive;

so that an accidental breaking of ten glasses may appear naughtier than an intentional, defiant breaking of one.

During these early years such rules of conduct as are grasped are apt to be interpreted very rigidly. As we have seen, motives are apt to be ignored, nor can there be any extenuating circumstances; if a lie is wicked it is always wicked, and so on. Matters are comparable to the rules of children's games, which, as Piaget showed, are at these early ages regarded as rigidly fixed. We may indeed look back still further and find that Sully emphasized the rigidity of even the child under 5 as regards the rules and customs of his daily routine – unless, of course, there was a strong personal dislike of some of them! [99].

First general concepts of right and wrong. About the age of 9 or 10 a few general concepts as to right and wrong do appear. Macaulay and Watkins found that such general terms as 'stealing' or 'murder' tended now to take the place of descriptions of particular acts of the type likely to occur in the child's own immediate experience. Often, however, these general terms seem adopted from hearsay, sometimes clearly from the Ten Commandments. 'This stage,' they wrote, 'is characterized by an extremely conventional conception of moral offence, not the individualistic conventionality, however, of the first stage quoted, for the child now names the generally accepted forms of wrongdoing. But his outlook is, as yet, uncritical; he never, for instance, adds any mention of possible mitigating circumstances as older children frequently do.'

Occasionally, however, the wording suggests a judgement on a definite specification. Thus while some children of this age refer to 'adultery' (or 'dudilty' or 'douldery'), one little girl of 9 gives in her list 'A man going in a room to a girl in the night'.

Of course, we again find great individual differences. Some general concepts as to moral conduct can be grasped and used correctly earlier by the more intelligent children;

and variations in the age of functioning will occur according to the influence of the home and school environment. Probably each of these factors is partly responsible for the differences which appear between the answers of children over 12, (*a*) who were in the schools in the poor areas, and (*b*) who were in the better-class elementary schools and grammar schools. Only among the latter were found mentioned such things as 'selfishness' and 'not helping others'.

To some extent, however, it seems that some marked differences between the judgements as to the wrongness of actions given by children from slum districts as contrasted with the better districts is due to over-familiarity with some misdemeanour. 'Drunkenness', for example, is mentioned by the following percentages in the different types of schools:

Slum	Semi-slum	Good-class artisan	Grammar schools
5 per cent	11 per cent	20 per cent	34 per cent

It is tempting to quote from a large number of papers written by the children in response to these requests for a list of 'The most wicked things anyone could do'. These throw a lurid light on the conditions under which some of the poor children had to live. They also reveal a quaint classing together of deeds which the mature adult would regard as poles apart. I must, however, be content with a few by girls of 9 : 0.

'When we are told to put out the tea cups and we won't. When little boys are rude to their mothers and other ladies. People goes and haves beer and whiskey and are took up to the police station, and are put in a dark cell and are tied up with thick ropes. When ladies fights with babies in their arms and the babies cries out loud, and the people do not stop. Men goes in pubs, and they gets drunk and comes home and hits things off the table. Little boys are sent to school and they do not go.'

The transition at adolescence. To follow up this topic beyond 12 or 13 would bring us into the period of adolescence, which we deal with in a later chapter; but for the sake of continuity and because some children precocious in intelligence and in personality development show adolescent traits as early as 11 or 12, I give some findings which appear about the ages of 13 or 14. One is the appearance of signs of a sense of responsibility to their fellows: e.g. the listing among 'wicked' things of 'leading others astray', 'setting a bad example to younger children', 'not trying to help others'; another is the recognition of exceptions to general laws, e.g. telling lies, except when it is for a good purpose, such as 'a doctor not telling a patient how ill he is'. Yet another is the more frequent reference again to parents, as though their claims are now beginning to be recognized; e.g. 'not being grateful to your parents' and 'despising your parents'. Finally, references to sex relations now begin to appear in a way which is more personal, and these increase till late in adolescence.

Children's ideas as to punishment. Once more may I recall that in this book I can only aim at description and explanation. Not only have we no room for a fuller discussion of the development of character or practical methods of training in behaviour, but I have dealt with these topics elsewhere and must avoid repeating myself. If now I give more space to the ideas of children about punishment than to their ideas about rewards, it is merely because there are more useful reports about punishment than about rewards. I trust therefore that the reader will not imagine that I regard the reward and encouragement of good conduct as less important than the punishment of wrong. On the contrary, I think the *ideal* to aim at in home and school, is to dispense with punishment. On the other hand, some very loose thinking has been indulged in by some writers about child discipline, at times with wild assumptions and inferences from experiments on animals, some of which have shown that severe punishment may not be the best way of teaching rats to learn a maze!

The extensive inquiry referred to above as to children's ideas about punishment, carried out by my former student, Major K. D. Hopkins, dealt with over 2,600 children mostly between the ages of 10 and 16 [57]. Before dealing with the findings about punishments, I may mention a preliminary and minor part of the inquiry, which supplements the facts given earlier about children's ideas of right and wrong. The following appeared in the questionnaire given to the children – on which they were told not to write their names so that they could feel quite free.

'Below is a list of six things for which boys and girls frequently get punished in school. Write down opposite to each one what punishment you would give for each. If you think no punishment should be given for some of them, write "none". 1. Inattention; 2. Disobedience; 3. Bad work; 4. Forgetfulness; 5. Telling lies; 6. Bullying.'

Hopkins found that the children clearly indicated the degrees of seriousness of the punishments assigned and so of the offence. From this he inferred the following as the children's ideas of the order of seriousness of the offences, massing all ages together:

1. Bullying	4. Bad work
2. Telling lies	5. Inattention
3. Disobedience	6. Forgetfulness

The result is surely a testimony to the good judgement of the children as a whole, but we must mention that over half the children were between the ages of 13 and 17.

For *bullying*, the usual punishment prescribed was corporal punishment; so it was for *lying*, but '30 per cent of the boys and 70 per cent of the girls, aged 15 and 16, suggested a confidential talk with the liar because "caning is not the proper punishment" and "to find out why he or she was telling lies"'. *Forgetfulness* was rarely punished, and one third of the children gave no punishment for *Inattention*, chiefly on the ground that the teacher should have made the lesson more interesting.

The effectiveness of different forms of punishment. The main questionnaire referred to three supposed boys, Dick, Harry, and Tom, in different schools who were caught cheating. Dick's teacher talked to him, saying it was dishonest and he would never do well at his work if he cheated. Harry's teacher scolded him in front of the class and said what a mean thing he had done. Tom's teacher gave him a good caning.

A few days later one of these boys was found cheating again. Now the children were asked 'Which boy do you think it was, and why?' They were also asked how each boy felt after his punishment, and which teacher they would like to teach them.

The private talk was judged the least effective except by the older children – ages 14 to 16. The figures were:

Percentage failures of Private Talk method

Ages	16	15	14	13	12	11	10	9
Boys	28	23	27	40	47	59	60	61
Girls	14	19	16	37	47	55	69	66

Note the big drop in failures after 13 especially among the girls. *Corporal punishment* was thought to be most effective by children under 12, and was selected as the type which failed by only 51 per cent of the boys even at age 15.

In a supplementary questionnaire 300 children were asked to choose which punishment they would prefer of these three: (1) Two strokes with the cane, (2) 500 lines to be done at home, or (3) one half-day's detention in school. Of the boys 90 per cent chose the cane and so did 37 per cent of the girls, but it was noted that 'no girls above the age of 15 chose the cane nor, except in a few cases for bullying, did they recommend caning as a punishment'.

The National Foundation research on rewards and punishments. The report of this widespread inquiry [83] deals mainly with customs in the schools and with the ideas of teachers, but it does include a summary of the views as to punishments and rewards expressed by nearly 3,000 boys and over 4,300 girls, ages 11 to 15, in different parts of England and Wales, and in all types of schools. About one-third of the boys and rather more than a third of the girls were in grammar schools. The pupils were asked which of fifteen punishments they 'disliked most' and which least. They were asked to number them in the order in which they were disliked. The median orders found for the various punishments for (*a*) all the boys and (*b*) all the girls were as in this table. The punishment most disliked by boys (or girls) comes at the top of the table, that least disliked at the bottom. Readers unfamiliar with the term 'median' may take it as meaning the middle rank of all the ranks given for a particular item.

	Median Ranks	
Punishment or Deterrent	Boys	Girls
An unfavourable report for home	3	3
Deprived of games or some favourite lesson	4	6
Being regarded as a person to be closely watched by the staff	5	5
Given cane or strap	6	4
Sent to Head for misbehaviour	6	6
Made to look foolish in class sarcastically	8	7
Made to look foolish in class jokingly	8	10
Made to report daily to Head because of poor work or behaviour	8	5
Given detention after school	9	11
Given extra work to do to make up for unsatisfactory work	9	11
Given a good talking to in private	10	10
Given a cuff or a slap by the teacher in passing	10	8
Sent from the room for misbehaviour	11	11
Suspected of slacking and urged to make an effort	11	11
Threatened with punishment	12	12

The most notable differences between the boys and the girls are that the girls dislike (1) being reported to the Head daily, and (2) corporal punishment more than the boys do. Estimates of averages are, of course, not the whole picture, and it is worth adding that 25 per cent of the boys dislike corporal punishment most, while 25 per cent of them gave it a rank below 11.

In the same schools the Heads and Assistants were given the same list of penalties and asked to number them in order to show which they thought 'most essential for preserving a good balance between discipline and freedom' in the school. Here very different lists appeared from those of the pupils. All four groups of staffs – Headmasters, Headmistresses, Assistant Masters, and Assistant Mistresses, put first 'Given good talking to in private'. Second came 'Given extra work to do', except for the Headmistresses, who put 'Suspected of slacking and urged to make an effort' just before it. It may, however, be true that these are more effective in the long run than what the pupils dislike most. We may recall that in the inquiry by Hopkins, while the children under 12 thought little of the effectiveness of a private talk by the teacher, after 12 the opinion of its value improved, especially among children over 13.

Opinions as to rewards. The same pupils were also given a list of rewards or incentives and asked to number them in order, showing which they would like most to happen to them, and which they would care about least. The median orders were as follows:

| | Median Ranks | |
Incentives	Boys	Girls
Favourable report for home	3	2
Success in a test	4	4
Score success for team or house in sports	4	5
Given marks for team or house in class work	6	6
Given a prize	6	7
Good marks for written work	6	6
Quiet appreciation from teacher	7	6
Going with form on some outing	7	7
Election to position of leadership by fellow-pupils	7	7
Election to position of authority by teacher	8	7
Temporary leadership in games	9	9
Public praise	11	11

The supreme influence of the home report comes out again; and merely doing well in a test comes second. I am not at all surprised at 'public praise' coming bottom for both boys and girls. It would be a sure way of incurring unpopularity.

The same list of incentives was also given to the staffs to number in order of effectiveness. The results are most illuminating, and suggest a grave misunderstanding of the mass of pupils.

Ranking of incentives by staffs

Incentives	Head-masters	Assīnt Masters	Head-mistresses	Asstnt Mistresses
Quiet appreciation	4	4	3	4
Elected by staff to position of authority	3	5	4	5
Public praise	5	5	$7\frac{1}{2}$	4
Good marks for written work	7	5	6	5
Election to leadership by fellow-pupils	4	6	4	6
Favourable report for home	6	6	6	6
Marks for team or house in class work	6	6	5	6
Success for team or house in sports	6	7	6	$6\frac{1}{2}$
Temporary leadership in games	7	8	8	8
Success in test	8	8	8	7
Given prize	9	9	10	10
Go with form on an outing as a reward	11	10	10	10

If we take the estimates of the pupils as a reliable indication of the effectiveness of these incentives then the staffs greatly underestimate the effectiveness of (1) mere success in a test, (2) a good report to home, and they greatly overestimate the value of (1) being selected to a position of authority by staff, and especially of (2) public praise.

CHAPTER 13

General Intelligence – Normal, Sub-normal and Super-normal

OUR consideration, in earlier chapters, of emotional traits and types of behaviour showed how difficult it is to draw a definite line between the usual and the unusual, even in reference to some particular traits, and especially how wrong it is to label a child abnormal because he reveals one or two emotional reactions or nervous habits to an unusual degree. Our earlier chapters have also demonstrated the marvellous range of individual differences in temperament and behaviour which can appear among children who should not be labelled abnormal, maladjusted, or neurotic.

In any study of the normal child, however, general intelligence and the various special abilities must of course loom large; in addition, our immediate topic, the estimating of intelligence, is one which will best enable the novice in psychology to realize the great range of individual differences between children, and to form an ideal of method or procedure in estimating what is normal, and of the meaning of 'normal' in a statistical sense. For with all the weaknesses of intelligence tests, no competent psychologist would deny that by means of them we can make far more accurate measurements of intelligence, or, if that term is too vague, of general and special abilities, than we can of the strength of emotional tendencies and innate impulses or drives.

Popular misconceptions as to intelligence tests. Before proceeding to deal with estimates of intelligence, we must get rid of some misconceptions about intelligence tests which may be in the minds of those whose opinions about them have been based largely on comments and letters in the press. It is amazing to find the violent antagonism roused in some people against intelligence tests. It might be understandable in parents whose children have failed to gain admittance into a grammar school, if that were based entirely on the results of an intelligence test, but that is rarely, if ever, the case in Great Britain. Then why do not the disappointed parents rail equally against the tests in English and Arithmetic which are almost invariably included? No doubt because these strange intelligence tests are easier to make fun of, at least in the presence of those really ignorant of the matter. When intelligence tests were first introduced in Birmingham into the general examination for pupils trying for admission into the local grammar schools, an irate father wrote to the local press complaining that one of the questions was impossibly difficult for children of 11. The question was as follows: 'A guard on an express train going at fifty miles an hour, walked from the back end of the back van to the front end of the front van. He then turned round and walked back again to the back of the back van. On which occasion did he walk the further?' 'Now,' wrote the father, 'I put this question to a friend of mine who had been a guard on the railway for twenty-five years and even he couldn't tell me!'

It would have surprised that father to learn that a very large number of the brighter children of 11 solved that problem quickly enough. The particular test quoted is not a very good specimen of intelligence tests, but the story illustrates the main misconception I wish to stress. The father concerned clearly thought that experience and knowledge were the important things if an intelligence test was to be done well; whereas those are precisely the things of which good intelligence tests are largely independent. In such tests psychologists try to estimate the *inborn* ability, even of children who have had a poor home environment and little schooling. That the tests do so fairly successfully is shown by the plain fact that a great many children from very poor homes, and even from slum areas, do much better in intelligence tests than do some of the children from well-to-do homes or very bookish homes.

It was precisely because children from semi-illiterate homes, or whose parents could not afford to have them specially coached for the examinations in English and Arithmetic, were far less at a disadvantage in intelligence tests, that these tests were first introduced for the selection of pupils for grammar schools in England. I know that was the main object in one of the first cities to introduce tests, namely, Birmingham, as I happened to be chairman of the committee in charge of the examinations. We were very concerned with the fact that many parents were arranging for special coaching in English and Arithmetic for their children, and so some children were just scraping into the grammar schools, though with inferior ability to some failing to get in. The concentration on English and Arithmetic was also causing undue early pressure in the junior and even in the infant schools. The introduction of intelligence tests at least lessens, though it does not entirely remove, these evils; yet we now have loud protests from people who proclaim their concern about 'equality of opportunity' when they find that the tests do help to keep out many from poorer homes – as well as from more well-to-do. Such critics are usually ignorant of the fact that there is abundant evidence that intelligence tests given to children of about 11 years of age provide as good a prophecy of how they will do three or four years later in the grammar schools, as do the combined examinations in English and Arithmetic, in spite of the fact that these latter are to some extent also evidence as to conscientious work, and persistence, which are of course very important.

One final misconception about intelligence tests must be mentioned. The fact that a child's performance in an intelligence test can be improved by coaching in similar tests has been widely publicized of late in England. Some

critics have written that now psychologists have themselves
shown that the tests are of no use because their results can
be affected by coaching. In fact this has been known for at
least twenty-five years. What the critics usually ignore is
the fact which recent researches have established, that the
maximum improvement through coaching (usually up to
about 6 per cent or 8 per cent) can be obtained in about
one and a half or two hours' coaching. Any coaching beyond
that is waste of time, and it is a simple matter for any local
education authority to arrange that *all* the children in its
schools, who are entering for the admission examination
for grammar schools, shall be given two hours' coaching in
the schools, so that any advantage gained by children whose
parents arrange coaching for them is nullified.

General intelligence and general ability. The reader may have
been surprised at my referring, early in this chapter, to the
term intelligence as vague. Yet in fact psychologists have
been criticized for failing to agree on a definition of the
term; some have regarded it as the capacity to grasp relations between things or ideas; others as the ability to apply
what has already been learned or understood in certain
circumstances to new circumstances or conditions – which
latter indeed would itself require the grasp of some relations; others again define general intelligence as all-round
intellectual ability, and so on.

Some forty years ago the present writer, in an early book,
suggested that a strictly scientific psychology would not be
content with such a vague term; and, in fact, though for
practical purposes we find it convenient to speak of, and to
devise tests of 'general intelligence', psychologists tend now
to speak more precisely of general ability and special abilities or primary mental abilities.

The reader may doubtless wonder how, if the psychologists do not agree as to the term intelligence, they set about
estimating either intelligence or those general and special
abilities. Let us tackle this problem forthwith. Suppose we

start with the assumption that reasoning is a process involving mental ability, and that good reasoning ability would be one sign at least of intelligence.

Now consider one or two reasoning tests which have been used with children. I take them from the series prepared by Cyril Burt [15], the first psychologist to devise a complete set of reasoning tests suitable for children from the ages of 6 to 15, though some items in the famous Binet tests involved a kind of reasoning.

The first that we select can be solved by about half the children of the age of 10½. I have ventured to simplify the words in one or two places:

'The Doctor thinks Violet has caught some illness.

'If she has spots, it is probably chicken-pox, measles, or scarlet fever.

'If she has been having a cold or cough, she may have whooping-cough, measles, or mumps.

'She has been sneezing and coughing for some days, and now spots are coming on her face and arms.

'What do you think is the matter with Violet?'

The next test is suitable for children of 14; half of the children of 14½ solve the problem correctly.

'John said, "I heard my clock strike yesterday, ten minutes before the first gun fired. I did not count the strokes, but I am sure it struck more than once, and I think it struck an odd number." John was out all the morning from the earliest hours; and his clock stopped at five to five the same afternoon.

'When do you think the first gun fired?'

Readers may find that some of their adult friends do not get the answer right the first time. As we shall see later, innate general ability in the average child does not grow much after the age of about 15.

One such test, of course, settles nothing. We should require a score or two score of varied reasoning tests to make a fairly reliable test of reasoning ability. Suppose then we give fifty such tests, already found suitable for the age of, say, 10 years, to 100 boys all aged 10. On the results we can draw up an order of merit in reasoning ability among these boys.

Now let us take another test which clearly requires some mental ability – the Analogies Test, which involves the grasping of relations.

We first explain the test by saying to the boys:

Night is to Day as Black is to White

Sailor is to Soldier as Navy is to Army

Good is to Bad as Long is to Short

Then we require a series of fifty such analogies to be completed, e.g.:

Heat is to Cold as Summer is to ... what?

Tuesday is to Wednesday as Wednesday is to ... what? The words involved should be simple, such as are sure to be understood by these boys of 10 years of age, but it is the grasping and applying of the relation that is the real point of value. On the basis of these fifty analogies we can now get another order of merit among the 100 boys, and we find by merely inspecting the two orders (in reasoning and analogies) that they seem to resemble one another. (We must not, however, rely on mere inspection and shortly we shall see how a precise calculation of their resemblance can be made.)

'Yes,' the critic may say, 'but these two tests both involve language, and perhaps it is just those who have a special facility in language who do well in each.' Very well; let us take some quite different tests not concerned with words.

Non-verbal tests

a. *Number series.* We show the boys these figures:

1, 2, 3, 4, 5

and say, 'Now you can go on with that set of figures, can't you? What about these?

1, 3, 5, 7

What will the next figure be?'

Having explained the idea we now give, say, six series of such figures, gradually getting harder, asking for the next figure to be added in each row, thus:

1, 4, 7, 10 . . . .?
1, 2, 4, 8 . . . .?
1, 3, 3, 5, 5, 5 . . . .?
1, 3, 9 . . . .?
1, 3, 7, 15 . . . .?

Very little arithmetic is involved here; the difficulty lies in detecting the *relations* between the successive numbers.

We may give one mark for getting the first right, and one for the second; then two each for the third and fourth, and three each for the fifth and sixth; but that gives us only twelve marks as a maximum. Now we proceed to another non-verbal test.

b. *Diagrams test.* The boys are shown the following shapes:

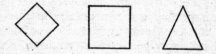

and told: 'These figures are alike because they are all made up of straight lines. So if you are shown these other shapes and told to underline the one that does not belong to the same set, you should underline the one shown:

Now look at the rows of shapes on the sheet given you. The first three are the same in some way, and so are the three on the other side of the middle line, except for one. Underline the one that does not belong to the set:

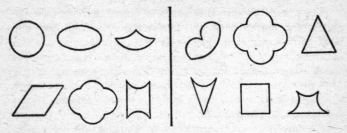

We may easily devise a series of ten of these, gradually getting harder, and giving one mark for each of the first two, two marks for each of the next four, and three each for the last four, making a maximum of twenty-two.

c. *Patterns test.* We show the boys the first pattern with one piece left out:

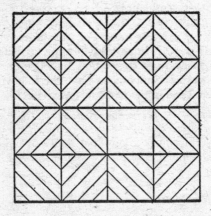

Then we show these four squares and ask which is the one to fit into the blank square in the big pattern.

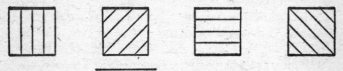

The correct square is the second, so we underline it. We can prepare a series of, say, twelve patterns, each with one section left out and gradually getting more and more complicated, and the boys are required to choose the right piece to be inserted from a group of four, as shown. Scoring one mark for each of the first four patterns, then two each for the next four, and three each for the last four gives us a maximum of twenty-four.

We now have a maximum of sixty marks on the three non-verbal tests, and we can draw up an order of merit on these non-verbal tests.

If we compare this new order of merit with the other orders previously obtained on the Reasoning and Analogies Tests, again we are likely to be struck by a resemblance; but we must now discuss a method of finding the precise degree of such resemblances.

The correlation of orders or scores. For the student of modern psychology it is most important to know at least what is meant by a measure of correlation, and the essentials are really quite simple. Suppose we have the following orders of merit of ten boys in the two subjects given:

Boys	Arithmetic	Algebra	Difference
A	1	2	1
B	2	1	1
C	3	5	2
D	4	4	0
E	5	3	2
F	6	7	1
G	7	6	1
H	8	10	2
I	9	8	1
J	10	9	1
		Total	12

The differences between the two orders add up to twelve.

Obviously the closer the two orders resemble one another the less the total differences will be. If the orders were exactly alike the differences would be nought.

Now suppose the orders for Arithmetic and French are as follows:

Boys	Arithmetic	French	Difference
A	1	3	2
B	2	2	0
C	3	5	2
D	4	8	4
E	5	1	4
F	6	4	2
G	7	10	3
H	8	9	1
I	9	6	3
J	10	7	3
		Total	24

Here the differences come to twenty-four – twice as much as those between Arithmetic and Algebra. We can certainly say that there is more resemblance between the orders for Arithmetic and Algebra than there is between those for Arithmetic and French; or, as we say, there is a higher *correlation* between Arithmetic and Algebra than between Arithmetic and French. Of course, I have only used small numbers of boys to make the illustration simple. To establish the general statement we should have to test hundreds of boys in many different schools.

We have, however, not got far in our estimate of the degrees of correlation; but the statisticians have devised methods of calculating these degrees quite precisely. We need not trouble the reader with the methods or formulas, but he should be familiar with the term given to the figure indicating the amount of correlation, viz. the coefficient of correlation. If two orders are precisely alike the correlation is perfect and the coefficient works out at 1. This figure 1 is rarely or never obtained between two tests or between examinations unless there happen to be very few persons involved.

If there is no more resemblance between two orders than would be got by picking numbers alternately out of two bags, each containing discs numbered 1 to 1,000 and thoroughly shaken up; in other words, no more resemblance than given by mere chance, then the correlation works out at approximately 0.

We may give a few examples of correlations which have actually been calculated. I should add that usually correlations are reckoned from the marks themselves rather than the orders of merit. I have used the latter for my illustrations as I think the principle is easier to grasp. Different formulas are, of course, used for marks and for orders, but it is not necessary to know these in order to understand the significance of various degrees of correlation.

The correlation between height and weight among men has been found to be about 0·6; that between the length of an arm and the length of a leg of the same person about 0·87. The orders of merit in History drawn up by the teachers of sixth-form pupils and based on several class tests have been found to correlate with the performance of those same pupils in a public examination in History, only to the extent of about 0·65; and the same is true for English; for Mathematics it is about 0·75. The order of merit in Handwork has been found to correlate with that in Drawing to the extent of about 0·5 in a group of schools.

The correlation of different tests of abilities. Even with this elementary knowledge about correlations, we are now much better able to deal with our samples of tests in reasoning, analogies, and the number series. We need not be content with saying that the second order of merit (Algebra) looks very like the first (Arithmetic), or with guessing that the third (French) is not quite so like the first. We can reckon the resemblance precisely. As a result of repeated tests we can report that very high correlations have been found between reasoning and analogies tests. They reveal a 'common factor' or factors. The actual degree of correlation will vary with the excellence and thoroughness of the particular test and with the range of ability in the group of persons tested; but we may take 0·8 as a fair estimate of the correlation between these two. The most reasonable explanation of this great resemblance is that the two tests involve to a considerable extent the same ability or abilities.

If now we pass on to consider the number series test, we find still a high correlation between this and each of the other tests; it may be as high as 0·7, though we have now eliminated any special facility in dealing with words. The problems all, however, involve the grasping of relations, and this gives us at least a clue to what is important in any general ability which is the basis of these correlations.

Still more remarkable, when we pass on to diagrams and patterns tests, we find here again substantial correlations with each other and with the earlier verbal tests. Success in these new tests is not then entirely due to quite specific abilities involved in the diagrams and patterns tests and not in the reasoning and analogies tests.

The evidence of a general ability. In view of an immense amount of evidence of the kind given above, psychologists have concluded that there is such a thing as 'general ability' which is very important in such tests in varying degrees, but that there is also some special ability (or abilities) involved in each test, e.g. a specific verbal ability, ability for dealing with numbers, spatial ability, and so on.

This 'general ability' is often symbolized by the letter 'g'. It is not essential for us to understand precisely the nature of this general ability; as to that there is considerable difference of opinion, though there is substantial agreement that it does reveal itself especially in the apprehension of *relations* between things or ideas.

One more remarkable thing the statisticians have done;

they have found out how to estimate the extent to which performance in the various tests depends upon this general ability and how much it depends on other abilities. So they speak of the degree of a test's 'saturation' with 'g'. Hence if we want to estimate the relative amounts of general ability possessed by a group of children, we can use for our purpose just those tests success in which has been found to depend chiefly on 'g'. Reasoning tests are pre-eminent here. Success in them seems to depend almost entirely on general ability, and ordinary school training and experience are surprisingly unimportant. For example, in some very difficult reasoning tests I devised recently, in which university graduates with first-class honours rarely gained more than 70 per cent of the marks, a group of forty-five high-school boys (aged about 18) who had won open scholarships at Oxford or Cambridge, actually gained an average score as high as that of the university graduates with First Class Honours, and much higher than those with Second Class Honours, though the graduates were some 4 or 5 or more years older and had had all the further training in reasoning provided by university studies and discussions [106A].

Though no test seems to involve merely general ability, there are means of avoiding or neutralizing the influence of any one special ability, which we shall discuss later in this chapter. Here I want to show what happens if we apply a series of good tests of general ability of the types exemplified above to, say, 1,000 children from homes of the various social and economic grades, so that they are fairly representative of the population as a whole.

Individual differences in general ability. First we find an enormous range of performance; some of the 10-year-old children do as well on the tests as do the average children of 14 or 15 years of age; others of the 10-year-olds do so badly that they do not equal some of the youngest children who can be given the tests (because of vocabulary difficulties), say, at ages of 7 or 8.

Second, we do not find that we can divide the children clearly into three separate groups – average, very superior, and very dull. We find a very gradual transition; in fact, some such scatter of marks as is represented in the table below. Only round numbers are given as being roughly representative and the gradations are artificially neat. The precise numbers would, of course, vary greatly according to the difficulty of the tests applied.

Number of children in representative 1,000 *gaining the scores specified*

Scores	Children
91–100	10
81– 90	40
71– 80	80
61– 70	170
51– 60	200
41– 50	200
31– 40	170
21– 30	80
11– 20	40
0– 10	10

Such a scatter of marks reveals a big group of children – just two-fifths of the thousand – within the marks 41 to 60, too big a range to be described as 'average'. Above those are groups we might describe as good, very good, and excellent, with groups below gradually getting poorer, the lowest groups describable as subnormal. Such general terms are too vague, however, for the psychologist; and one method he adopts for indicating more precisely where a child stands among his fellows is to find his place on a proportional percentage scale; so that a child could be described as coming, in these tests, say, within the top 5 per cent of all the children of age 10; or exactly at the 50 per cent level, and so on.

The statistician has still other methods of dealing with the scores, a description of which would be out of place in a book like the present. But we must describe one other method of great practical value and easily understood.

Mental age. On the basis of a wide range of tests like those given earlier, each involving chiefly general ability, and with suitable modifications when applied to 9- and 8-year-olds, or to 12-, 13-, and 14-year-olds, we can find the average score of children of 8, of 9, and so on. Now if a child aged 10 gains about the average score of all the 10-year-olds, he is said to have a mental age of 10; but if he only performs as well as the average child of 9 he is said to have a mental age of 9. By this method we can bring home, even to those with an antipathy to statistics, the enormous range of individual abilities among children. Thus a very few of the 10-year-olds will reveal a mental age of 14 or 15; a few others will have to be rated at the mental age of 7 or less.

Here then is more than a rough and ready way of indicating the degree of variation from normality, and this concept of the mental age of a child – which so stated is always taken as referring to his general intelligence – has also been used in reference to attainments, in, for example, Reading or Arithmetic, so that we read of a 10-year-old boy's 'Reading Attainment Age' as being only 9, and his 'Arithmetic age' as being 8. The idea has also been sometimes applied to emotional development or behaviour; so that we may read of a child of 10 having the 'Social Maturity Age' of only 8.

Intelligence quotient. This is the last technical term we must refer to in this chapter. It is one now generally familiar, though there are frequent misconceptions about it. Suppose a child of 10 reveals on the basis of a set of intelligence tests a mental age of 12, then we say his intelligence quotient or mental ratio is $\frac{12}{10}$, i.e. 1·2, or as a percentage 120 – which is his I.Q. If his mental age is only 8, his I.Q. is $\frac{8}{10}$, or as a percentage 80.

Now if we apply a good series of intelligence tests we find a similar wide range and scatter of intelligence quotients to what we found in the test scores. The following tables gives a representative distribution. The I.Q. of 100 is, of course, the average; but we may take the range of 95–104 as indicating the average. Within this range there are likely to be about 25 per cent of the whole mass of children. The others would be grouped somewhat as follows. Again, however, we must emphasize that the range and the particular figures would vary according to the particular series of tests applied, and the scale is made unduly neat and balanced.

Distribution of intelligence quotients in the whole population of children

I.Q.s	Percentage of children
145–154 or over	1
135–144	2
125–134	5
115–124	10
105–114	20
95–104	24
85– 94	20
75– 84	10
65– 74	5
55– 64	2
54 or below	1

How wide a group can we regard as 'average' or 'normal'? Suppose we are considering the 10-year-olds, then, 100 being the precise average, an I.Q. of 110 would represent a child of mental age of 11, and an I.Q. of about 90 would represent a child with a mental age of about 9. Now the range of mental age 9 to 11 is surely rather wide to call all the group within that range average or normal; yet even this wide range would only give us about 45 per cent of the whole child population as 'normal', with some 27 per cent subnormal and 27 per cent super-normal. The group of normal would be flanked on one side first by a big group which may be labelled dull, and a very small group of feeble-minded or mentally defective. On the other side of the normal group we should have a large group, which we might label 'bright', and a very small group 'very bright'.

Incidentally we may note that even with a narrower range for the application of the term normal or average, those labels would not indicate that a child was fitted to enter a grammar school. It is generally agreed that, with the present organization of curriculum and present standards of work in our grammar schools, an I.Q. of 115 or at least 110 is required. We see then how inadequate are the terms 'normal' or 'average' in reference to intelligence for anything more than very rough classification.

I may add here, that while the I.Q. is a very useful means of indicating approximately the general ability of a child compared with others of his age, for strictly scientific purposes a superior method is to state the position of a child on a percentile scale of performances on the test concerned, or by other statistical devices beyond the scope of this book.

The need of more than one testing. We must not overstress the precision of estimates of the mental age or intelligence quotient. Some immature enthusiasts are apt to talk as though there were a decided difference between (*a*) a child who has gained on one test a score which gives him an I.Q. of say 100, and (*b*) another child whose I.Q. works out at 95 or 96; whereas many reports show that even when a second alternative form of the same test (shown by applications to thousands of children to be of the same difficulty on the average) is given to a group of children who have already done the first form, most of the children get a different score from what they got in the first form. Let me illustrate by some results in a town where I have been for some years chief examiner responsible for the intelligence tests. The tests used were the famous Moray House Tests, the most widely used in this country for the selection of children of 11 + for the grammar schools. In this town all the pupils had first an hour's practice and coaching with an old set of the Moray House Tests. A week or two later they were given a new Moray House Test, and then a week or so later, a second Moray House Test – of the same form and difficulty, but with all the hundred or so individual items different.

Let us consider the results for the boys tested in the year 1953; the girls' results were very similar, and so were the results for 1954.

Total of number of boys tested	1093
Number gaining precisely the same I.Q. in second test	172
Number with increase of 1, 2, or 3 in second test	220
Number with decrease of 1, 2, or 3 in second test	161
Greatest individual increase	23
Greatest individual decrease	10

Taking the group as a whole, the *average* fluctuation was only 4; but 540 children fluctuated by 4 points or more, and it will be seen that one boy's I.Q. was 23 higher in the second test, while another boy's was 10 lower. It seems likely that one boy was in poor form in the first test, the other boy in the second test. In 1954 the average fluctuation was 5·14 for boys and 5·5 for girls. The greatest increase was 26 for one boy, and the greatest decrease 12 for one girl. It will be seen that it is quite unsafe to rely on one testing with a group test for an estimate of a child's I.Q.

Group and individual tests. The tests we have been referring to are 'group' tests; that is, they can be given to large numbers at the same time. They consist of printed booklets with many small items, which can usually be answered by writing one word or number or underlining a word.

The differences between I.Q.s formed by the use of quite

different group tests are sometimes considerable, and if a child's I.Q. is reported, the name of the particular test should always be stated.

Individual tests are given to one child at a time, the answers being noted by the tester. With individual tests in which there are two alternative forms or series of items of equal difficulty, the fluctuations of I.Q. are not usually so great as with the group tests. But they may be just as great and even greater, if the child is very ill at ease and nervous at first with the tester, or is unco-operative. This difficulty occurs especially with the very young children and with some types of maladjusted children. With them so much depends on the appeal of the personality of the tester to the child and the way of approach. That is almost certainly the explanation of some great divergences of estimates of the I.Q. of the same child by different testers, even with the same type of test. Thus one of my former students, then a psychologist in a Child Guidance Clinic, told me he had recently had referred to him a child reported as very dull on the basis of a psychiatrist's testing. My student re-tested the child after only a few weeks' interval with similar tests, and found his I.Q. some 20 points higher.

Special precautions and techniques are needed with very young children, but these would take us beyond the scope of this book and I have dealt with them elsewhere [105].

The constancy of the intelligence quotient at different ages. Broadly speaking, if we can once get a really reliable estimate of the innate intelligence of a child, even as early as the age of about 7 or 8, we may take it that in most cases the estimate will remain substantially true for him for four or five years, and to a less extent even seven or eight years later. In other words, the boy whose true I.Q. of 130 or 140 marks him out at 8:0 as exceptionally intelligent among his fellows of that age, will also be exceptionally intelligent among his fellows at 10 and at least well above the average at 15.

The extreme dullard with a *true* I.Q. of 80 will reveal

low innate ability also at 10 to 15, though careful training may help partly to conceal his shortcomings in everyday life. There is substantial evidence in favour of this view, but of course it is easy to see how what, at first sight, looks like sound evidence, can be brought against it. Sometimes cases have been quoted of children having an I.Q. of, say, only 80 at the age of 6:0, but of 100 or higher at 10:0 or later; or an order in intelligence test performance of a group of children at, say, 9:0 is compared with the order of the same children on an intelligence test at 12 or 14 and many changes found. But, as we have seen, many slight changes and a few very large ones may occur in the I.Q.s gained by children in a second test of the same type and standard if given even only a week or two later.

It is for that reason I have emphasized that the approximate constancy claimed only applies to a *true* measure of the innate ability. It may be that we can never get an absolutely reliable estimate of this, because of some influences of environmental training, but certainly we cannot rely on one testing for any age; still less can we be content with quoting I.Q.s gained by different tests at, say, 7 (or 8) and much later, say, 14 (or 15) without ensuring that each of the two different tests (*a*) really tests mainly general ability; (*b*) is of approximately the same degree of difficulty; (*c*) involves the same special abilities so far as such are involved; and (*d*) gives a similar scatter of I.Q.s for the two age groups.

Let us consider the findings of research most frequently quoted by opponents of the view that the I.Q. remains substantially constant from 7 or 8 to 15 or so. Dearborn and Rothney [34] report follow-up studies of several hundred children from the age of about 7 to 16 or later; and they do give examples of individuals whose intelligence quotients based on different tests do vary greatly and in a few cases go steadily down or up as the years pass. Some writers have seized on these, but fail to report the following general summaries given by Dearborn and Rothney: 'In general, children tend to remain throughout the period of their mental growth (to age 16) in the same classification as they were at age 8.' By the same classification they mean apparently within the same group within a range of 10 on a scale of 100.

Some further comments on Dearborn and Rothney's report must be made:

1. They admit that the group tests they used differed widely in their results from one another and from the highly standardized individual test (Stanford-Binet) when that was given; and though they took various measures to counteract such differences (and the effects of practice), they only claim that they were partially met by these measures.

2. They used group tests even for the age range 6:5 to 7:5. Now group tests at such an early age and even at 7:5 to 8:5 are notoriously unreliable, and performance, especially in the age group 6:5 to 7:5, might be very largely affected by the extent to which the children had learned to read. It is not surprising, therefore, to find some examples of big sudden changes in scores taking place in the year 7 to 8, and the scores remaining fairly steady after that. Dearborn and Rothney, indeed, say that the non-verbal tests tend more to place individuals constantly in the same position, over the nine-year period.

3. Dearborn and Rothney emphasize (as we have done above) the unreliability of one testing at a given period; and add 'Many of our diagnoses based on a single test may be faulty, since at one year we have the individual when he is at the crest of the wave while at the testing period a year later we may have him far below that crest.'

4. They also add that the tests they used were less satisfactory than present-day tests. In fact, they concluded that the different tests were 'not always measuring the same thing in the same sense.' Indeed, when a few tests differ greatly in assessing a child at the various ages from the majority of the tests given him they say: 'In most such rare cases we are

forced to assume that the excessive variability is a function of the test or the testing situation rather than due to the extreme variability of the individual.'

5. The various tests were given by a considerable number of different individuals, and in some cases, in spite of some previous training, the individual method of approach might have had considerable effect.

I will conclude this section with some results given me by Sir Cyril Burt, which he gathered with an individual test (the London Revision of the Stanford-Binet Scale) given to as many as 527 children in London, and by himself in every case, so that the comparisons are unusually reliable. At the first testing the children were all between 7½ and 8½ years of age; at the second testing they were about 12 years of age. The majority of the children had I.Q.s between 90 and round about 110; in fact, at each testing 68 per cent of the children were within that range.

If the children are grouped into classes each having a range of one mental year, then it is found that, after the four years' interval

72 per cent of the children remain in the same class
22 per cent of the children change by one class
and only 6 per cent of the children change by two classes.

Here, again, performance on the Stanford Revision of the Binet Tests was by no means free from the differential influences of training, as Burt himself pointed out, so that the general stability of the estimates of the I.Q. is all the more remarkable.

Finally, I would warn the reader against an idea sometimes expressed by immature psychologists who seem to study only researches published in the last decade or two. They think apparently that the discovery that I.Q.s are not 100 per cent reliable and stable over many years is a new one – just as they suppose that it has only recently been shown that intelligence test scores can be affected by coaching. The truth is that as long ago as 1921, Burt, in the first edition of his *Mental and Scholastic Tests*, reported that, in a few cases, marked changes can occur in the I.Q. within a few years among children of school age, and that 'deficiency as well as normality may wait until a later age to declare itself.'

Estimates of intelligence before the age of 5. There are grave doubts as to the validity of some of the tests for children up to 4 or 5 years of age. Thus the correlation between I.Q. scores on the Merrill Palmer Tests with the scores on the Minnesota Tests at the ages of 3 or 4 were found lower than the correlation of the I.Q.s on the Minnesota Tests at 3:0 with the Stanford-Binet tests at 9:6 – an interval of 6½ years [47 and 105].

As to the very early years of two or three it is highly probable that we have not yet discovered the right types of tests to give a reliable prophecy of general ability at, say, 10 or 15. Nevertheless, we do know that some forms of mental deficiency can be detected even before 2:0 and that some children reveal at 2:0 signs of the high 'g', which is clearly present in later childhood. On the other hand, in a relatively few cases the usual rate of growth seems checked and early promise is not fulfilled, or the rate is accelerated in later years. In many of such cases there seems to be an unusual physiological cause at work.

By about 5:0 we can find reliable tests, which not only give higher correlations with results at 10 or 14, but also give a fairly reliable prophecy as to educational performance in school. Thus one Headmaster compared the scores of forty-four children, of the age of 5, on my own *Intelligence Tests for Children*, with their educational attainment at 8:0 in Reading, Arithmetic, and Spelling, and he found a correlation as high as 0·81 [109].

I may conclude this section by suggesting that, though there are apparently individual differences in the rate of growth even among children who eventually reach about the same level of general ability, in the great majority of cases the pupils who are described as 'late developers' are not examples of delayed maturing of innate 'g', but children whose persistence and steady work gradually brings them up to the level in school work of fellow-pupils with higher 'g' but less persistence.

The maturing of innate general ability by adolescence. Keeping strictly to a consideration of *innate* general ability, we may say that this seems to mature almost completely for the great majority of children by the age of about 15 or 16. Thus, so far as innate elements are concerned, even children of 15 or 16 may have more general ability than their parents or teachers. A slight increase seems to occur after even 16, more especially in the ablest children. To him that hath is given still more. On the other hand, in very dull children the innate ability seems to cease increasing before 15 or even 14.

The influence of general ability on school work. There is ample evidence that those pupils in a school who do best on good intelligence tests tend on the whole to do better than those who do badly on the tests. There are, of course, exceptions, for reasons which we shall discuss in the next chapter; but, apart even from the results of intelligence tests, we know that a 'general factor' pervades the results of pupils in very different subjects, not only such as need careful thought and reasoning, e.g. Arithmetic problems, and Science, or History and Composition, but even Handicraft, though to a less extent. This is shown most in the early years, up to about 10 or 11. The boys with a high degree of 'g' *tend on the average* to be above those with low 'g', even in Handicraft. There are many apparent exceptions, partly because the very clever boys may take much more interest in other studies and not bother much about Handicraft. There are other reasons for some striking exceptions which we shall discuss in the next chapter, but these striking exceptions have given rise to the erroneous impression that children with inferior ability for so-called academic subjects, such as English or History or Mathematics, tend to be compensated by being given exceptionally good abilities for Handicraft and other more 'practical' subjects. This idea is, however, unfortunately contrary to the evidence.

*

Since the last reprinting of this book I have come across a remarkable case, which exemplifies still further the independence of performance in the 'reasoning tests for higher levels of intelligence' of education and training, already exemplified on p. 234. It is that of a boy of 12:2 who gained, on these tests, a score well above the average score of First Class Honours graduates, who had had about 10 or more years' further education and training in reasoning.

This boy had obtained an I.Q. of about 190 on the basis of my *Intelligence Tests for Children*, at the ages of 3:8 to 5:8. At my advice the boy was given different tests at the age of 10:0 and the National Institute of Industrial Psychology reported his I.Q. as about 190–200, based on two different tests.

That my Reasoning Tests are a good measure of general ability is shown by the fact that they show differences between the scores of First Class and the scores of Second Class Honours graduates and again between Second and Third Class Honours graduates, differences which have a high degree of statistical significance.

CHAPTER 14

Special Abilities and Interests

SOME readers of the last chapter may be thinking: 'But surely we often find children who are excellent at English and History but "no good" at Mathematics; and clever mathematicians who are very weak in French. So good general ability cannot be the main thing needed for success in these different subjects.' These observations as to the facts are often substantially correct; let us try to find some explanations.

First, such statements are usually made about pupils in the upper forms of grammar schools and high schools. Now we know that grammar-school pupils are, as regards general intelligence, a highly selected group, few having an I.Q. below 115. By the time the sixth form is reached and specialization begun or intensified, the weaker pupils have usually dropped behind or left the school. Hence the upper sixth are all likely to have I.Q.s of about 120 or over and will not differ greatly in general ability. Hence the differences in their respective excellences or weaknesses in various school subjects will depend largely upon their special abilities and interests. The boy A may have remarkable special ability for mathematics in addition to his good general ability, whereas B with equally good general ability may be exceedingly weak in the special abilities needed for success in mathematics at this higher stage; though B may have the special abilities needed for success in Latin or French to a high degree, while A is weak in these. Thus the teachers and parents of these children are apt to think that success in these subjects depends almost entirely on the special abilities; whereas it depends just as much on good general ability as a precondition of success. Indeed, at the earlier age of 10 or 11 we find that pupils who are high up in, say, their English studies, tend also to be better than the average in Arithmetic or Mathematics.

The influence of interests. This is the second thing to be stressed in connexion with the large differences between performance in different subjects in the top forms of the grammar school. The fact that a boy is much more interested in one subject X, rather than in Y and Z, means that more and more he advances in that subject X. He learns more easily because of his interest and he is also likely to give more time to the subject X, and at least when he is allowed to specialize a little, to neglect Y and Z. Thus the initial differences between the boys A and B become greater and greater.

I should, however, like to guard against the common assumption that interest and ability always coincide. No doubt the fact that a pupil finds he *can* do well in a certain subject usually increases his interest in it; and an initial interest stimulates work and so improves performance. This conjunction of interest and ability shows itself especially in Arithmetic and Algebra, but less in English and History, in which there may be many items which interest even the dull pupils who make slow progress in them. In other words, where the subject has 'content' value, it may appeal to pupils with little ability for it. Thus one boy wrote that he liked chemistry because 'It is exciting; you never know what is going to happen next!' Another wrote that History was like a 'long true story', and one even said, 'History makes me forget more or less about school' – a near relative apparently of the old woman in London who actually said she rather liked air-raids because they took her mind off the war!

Where, on the other hand, a subject such as mathematics or Latin composition consists in carrying out difficult mental operations, interest depends chiefly on success. Lack of ability to make progress may be the main factor in causing an intense distaste for the subject, this revealing itself especially in Arithmetic, Mathematics, and Latin and to a less extent in French. These facts about interest have been shown in wide inquiries, both in reference to unselected school children of the ages of 10 to 13 and grammar school children aged 12 to 16, by two former research students of mine, and they also brought out the great influence of the pupil's idea of the utility of a subject as a basis for being interested in it, more particularly in the year or two just before the child was expecting to leave school and enter some occupation [92].

In the grammar schools it was clear that many pupils, especially boys, loved the mere mental activity involved in Arithmetic and Algebra, just as many people enjoy working out a difficult crossword puzzle. The pupils refer to Arithmetic as a 'pleasant pastime' or as having a 'curious fascination'. 'It keeps my brain working all the time,' 'I like a subject in which there is hard working,' 'I like puzzling out sums,' 'I never give up trying till I find out the right answer,' 'It is exciting when working out a sum and the answer is a great surprise.' Similar things were written by some about Algebra, though it came near the bottom of all subjects in the average order of popularity. Some say, 'It is more like an exciting game than work.' 'It is interesting to work out dreadful lines of figures and find out how small the answer is, also you can make it look so neat' [87].

Alas! for many those answers rarely came out, and where there is little success there is no delight. The reasons given against Arithmetic and Algebra are nearly always based on a feeling of incapacity. Arithmetic is 'muddling', 'it is all hard thinking', 'it is boring to keep on adding up'; as to Algebra, 'I can't understand it however much I grope'.

From the primary schools came two of those remarks which sometimes cheer the investigator wading through hundreds of papers. 'I don't like Composition or Arithmetic,' wrote one boy, 'because I can't do them, although I know I shall be a *washouse* without them', while a little girl pathetically wrote, 'I don't like singing because it makes my legs ache'!

The influence of specific factors. There is ample evidence that general ability is the most important factor for success in ordinary school work at least up to the age of about 12, provided, of course, that the child works steadily [16 and 17]. Yet the statistical analysis of school test results shows also that even at 10 or 12 other factors are of considerable importance. First there is, of course, the great influence of persistence and conscientious work. Some have estimated that for success in examinations at the end of a grammar-school career this is almost as important a factor as good general ability – granted, of course, the possession of at least the minimum intelligence needed to gain entrance to a grammar school. The plain fact is that both ability and conscientious work are essential, and to say that one is more important than the other is like saying that one blade of a pair of scissors is more important than the other.

Persistence and hard work are, however, dependent on temperament or character traits and are not mental abilities in the sense we are now considering. In our calculations we can avoid the effects of character or temperament largely by considering, instead of school examinations, the results of a wide range of very different kinds of mental ability tests; and these reveal clearly not only the influence of general ability in all or nearly all kinds of tests, but the presence of a large number of special abilities. Psychologists do not profess to have labelled or even to have discovered all of these as yet; but there is general agreement that the following are of special importance and are independent of one another:

Verbal ability, involved in the learning of words and in understanding and using them.

A special ability involved in dealing with numbers.

Special Abilities and Interests

A special ability involved in apprehending and dealing with space relations.

Mechanical ability entering into constructive processes and to a less extent in some more routine manual process.

Retentivity, involved in all learning.

More specialized rote-memory abilities – separate ones in learning and in recalling (a) things seen; (b) things heard; and in (c) memory of movements.

Musical abilities – including several which seem independent of one another, viz, discrimination of pitch and apprehension of rhythm.

These abilities listed above must not be taken as single or unitary special abilities; most if not all of them may be split up into independent and more specific elementary functions; e.g. the term verbal ability, as Burt has shown, covers two or three partially independent functions: (a) understanding isolated words, and (b) facility in dealing with verbal patterns. (I may add that each of the abilities mentioned in the above list enters into such a wide range of activities that they had been labelled 'group abilities'.)

Now we have no reason to suppose that special abilities tend to 'go together'. A child may have a high degree of, say, verbal ability, but a low degree of spatial ability; or all his specific rote-memory abilities (e.g. of words seen or words heard) may be low, yet his special ability for dealing with numbers may be high, and so on. Still more important, though his general ability may be high, he may have a very low degree of some or even most special abilities, that is, so far as the innate element is concerned [113]. This may be partly concealed in his school work, because so often good 'g' can compensate for low specific abilities. Thus in Latin a very low specific verbal memory may mean that the rote learning of parts of verbs takes a boy longer than it does most boys; but his high 'g' helps him to understand the syntax more quickly and to grasp the meaning of complex passages, even when he has to guess the meaning of some of the words.

Independence of general and special abilities. The popular idea that the child who can learn foreign vocabularies or dates quickly by heart is 'clever' is largely illusory, at least if we take cleverness to mean possessing a high degree of general ability. Pupils who come very high in rote-memory tests (as purely rote as they can be made) sometimes come very low in the recall of passages of prose containing interconnected series of ideas.

If, as I have indicated, these special abilities, so far as they are inborn, vary independently of general ability and of one another (though all probably largely determined by inheritance), then we may expect to find, as indeed we do, examples of 'normal' children of average (or good) general ability, with an abnormally small degree of one or more special abilities. Indeed, I was such an example myself. That I was up to the average of general ability even in a grammar school is shown, I think, by my being runner-up for my form prize at the age of 11 and gaining the form prize at the age of 13, and still more by my progress in mathematics when I went to a new school at 14. At first I found myself right behind the pupils in my form in Mathematics, but in a year and a term I finished the first four books of Euclid and passed in the Higher Mathematics paper of the Cambridge Junior Examination – a mathematics course which was supposed to cover two or three years. Yet against this I had extreme difficulty in learning by heart, at least when mere rote-memory was involved, as in Latin and French vocabularies, the Latin declensions, and the parts of irregular verbs, and this weakness pursued me even to the university. Over and over again did I find myself staring at a word in a Greek play and thinking 'surely I have seen that before', but being quite unable to guess the meaning. Then I would look it up in the dictionary, write it out in my vocabulary, only to find later on that it had already been written out ten minutes earlier on a previous page!

In later years this weakness appeared in my marked

inability to remember names. I would usually forget the name of a student a few minutes after I had been told it and even after several repetitions. Here, then, was one of my own abnormalities. If more precise experimental evidence is needed I may report that on one occasion I myself took the tests with the class. I came bottom of the list in the rote-memory tests; modesty forbids me to say at which end I came in the logical memory tests! Another of my own abnormalities, however, was of the other type: my excellent remembrance of faces has been often commented on by persons whom I have detected as among my former students some five, ten, fifteen, or more years after they had left the university, and that among some 2,500 who had passed through my classes in the course of over thirty years.

How frequently a specific ability may be found to be very weak, irrespective of the general ability of the children, is shown by the results gained by Burt, with a control group of 200 children, who were not backward in their school work. In the tests of speed of word associations, he found that of his control group about 19 per cent of the boys scored less than the average of children having less than 85 per cent of their mental age; and so with 9·6 per cent of the girls [13].

We will now consider very briefly some of the most important special abilities, mainly to illustrate the possibility of extremes of these (very high or very low) being found among children.

Imagery – visual and auditory. A specific ability which varies greatly among persons of similar general ability is that of visual imagery. Thus I have found many students who could picture mentally a face or countryside they had seen, with intense vividness, and some who could get a visual image of an imagined scene with similar intensity; others, however, reported that the visual imagery was extremely vague. Some eminent philosophers have, indeed, reported that they had no visual imagery.

Students with little visual imagery, on the other hand, often report that they have intensely vivid auditory imagery, and again I can cite myself as a marked example of this. As to children, it is no doubt harder to obtain precise reports from them than it is from adults. Nevertheless, I agree with Burt and others that, with the proper approach and careful questioning, fairly reliable information can be gathered from children about 9 or 10 about their imagery. Burt found that, among children of that age or over, the correlation between vivid visual imagery and vivid auditory imagery was only 0·27. Another investigator with children of ages 7 to 14, who found a slightly higher correlation between the two forms of imagery, found practically no correlation between either form of imagery and general intelligence [24], another piece of evidence as to the highly specific nature of the abilities to form visual and auditory images. As to the relative independence of other forms of imagery, again there is ample evidence. I have known numerous students report that they could get very vivid images of the smell of a rose – as vivid as their visual image, yet others (including myself) who can get no smell images whatever.

Musical abilities. Perhaps no other special abilities reveal themselves so markedly or so early as do those involved in music. These include the capacities (*a*) to discriminate different pitches; (*b*) to apprehend rhythms: and (*c*) to apprehend melodic patterns. Experiments have shown that these capacities involve highly specific elements which are largely independent of one another and of general ability. Another important ability involved in the general aptitude for music is the memory for musical notes and phrases; still other factors also seem to be involved in the reproduction of tunes by the voice. Of course, some intelligence is required for the mere understanding of the tests of special musical abilities, so that for very young children especially the results of the tests do correlate somewhat with tests of general ability. But this can be allowed for and estimates made of the pure special abilities.

That high general ability is no guarantee of the possession of such special musical abilities is indeed shown, not only by experimental tests, but by everyday observation of young children. In my own family, for example, of five children all with I.Q.s of about 130 to 150, not one at the age of 7 or 8 could sing reliably even a simple tune often heard, and only one of them could do so even when adolescent; yet all the children heard a great deal of music in the home, as well as in church and school. On the other hand, I have come across examples of infants under 3 who could sing accurately a considerable number of simple tunes. Gesell records that one girl he tested could at 3:2 sing about seventy-five little tunes and sang one carol correctly after hearing it only twice. Terman, indeed, reports as to one of his 'gifted' children that she hummed a simple tune correctly at 1:3.

The most remarkable examples of the early maturing of musical abilities are to be found in the biographies of some of the great composers. Thus Mozart at the age of 3 took a keen interest in the music lessons of his older sister and was able to detect a slight variation in the pitch of a violin. At 4 he began his musical studies in earnest and at 5 he was composing 'little pieces', though with many weaknesses. The idea that such precocity is due to early forcing was scouted by friends of Mozart and others. His father found that the difficulty was to get him away from the keyboard at which he played 'as other boys play with soldiers or railway trains' [6]. By the age of 7 Mozart was giving public recitals in London, and he was able to play pieces by Bach and Handel at 8. Handel's own passion for music in early childhood had to meet the opposition of his father, and only the intercession of the Duke of Saxony, who heard the boy play the organ at the age of 7, led to his having more serious lessons on the organ.

As a sample of the many results of tests of musical ability

I would mention the case of a boy aged 10, whose I.Q. was over 150, putting him into the top 1 per cent of all children of his age group in the tests of intelligence. Yet in tests of pitch perception, sound intensity, consonance, and tonal memory he was in the bottom 10 per cent of children of his age [16].

Again, with series of tests for pitch and intensity discrimination and for consonance and tonal memory given to forty-nine children with I.Q.s over 135, it was found that their scores gave the same sort of 'scatter' as those of children of only average ability; indeed the graphs, if amalgamated, gave very much the same scatter as that for intelligence tests given on our page 237 [55].

Drawing. There is again general agreement that a highly specific ability is involved in drawing. Even with the test of 'drawing a man' in which some co-ordination and 'sense of proportion' are involved, the correlations between the test results and estimates of general ability have been found to be low by both Burt [18] and Vernon [108].

Burt found that 'g' was somewhat more involved among girls than among boys, while the specific spatial ability reveals itself earlier in boys. Precocity in this special ability for drawing has not been detected so markedly as in the case of music, but it does appear at times. Thus Gesell cites the example of a little girl of $3\frac{1}{2}$ years who had been given no instruction in drawing, yet was producing drawings well up to the average 7-year-old level, and was apparently maturing rapidly. On the other hand, Gesell also gives examples of highly intelligent children far behind in their drawings the usual level for their mental age. I may add that one of my own little girls at 3 : 5, with a mental age of over 5, was decidedly below the level of the average 3-year-old in Burt's 'drawing a man' series.

In the book referred to above [55], Hollingworth gives a remarkable picture of a rabbit running, a copy of a silhouette made by a mental defective (I.Q. 55) aged 11, who had a marked ability for drawing. The picture is full of life and movement. With it she gives a copy of it drawn by a boy, also aged 11, with an I.Q. of 150. It is quite unrecognizable as a rabbit, or any other animal. Of course, by the age of 11:0 even a mentally defective child, who had initially, in a high degree, the special abilities involved in drawing, might make rapid progress by practice with his one talent.

When we consider more generally artistic creations, the independence of the specific ability becomes if anything clearer, at least in the productions of young children.

Verbal ability. There is ample evidence of a special verbal ability (or more correctly special verbal abilities) independent of 'g', though general ability is of course involved in most if not all forms of mental processes expressed in words. Burt found that verbal ability began to show its effect at the average age of 8 in primary school work and that by the age of 10+ it had about one-quarter the influence of general ability.

So pervasive, indeed, is the influence of verbal ability that some supposed tests of general intelligence are strongly biased in favour of children who have special verbal ability above the average. On the other hand, in good intelligence tests, even chiefly of the verbal type, the influence of the verbal factor is not so great as some people imagine, Thus one investigator tested over 2,000 children in Glasgow and divided the homes into five socio-economic levels [38]. Her results showed one important fact which has been generally overlooked. As might be expected, children from the better homes did better in the Reading Tests than those from poorer homes; but the superiority of the former in the Intelligence Tests was decidedly greater than their superiority in the Reading Tests – another piece of evidence against the view that children from better homes surpass those from poor homes in Intelligence Tests chiefly because of their greater facility in dealing with words.

I

The special aptitude for dealing with words, and especially the range of vocabulary, is, however, greatly affected by environmental influence. Unusual time and trouble taken by the parents to teach the names of things to the mere toddler, to talk to him frequently and to correct his mistakes, have a marked effect. At later ages the type of friends and of schooling also have a great influence.

Nevertheless, it is easy to observe marked differences of response in different infants in the same home to the efforts of parents to encourage their development of speech, even with children who, in other matters, are at similar stages of development. Among my own five children one of the girls (Y) surpassed all the others at all the early stages of acquiring language, from the first responsive babblings to our talking to her, to the first understanding and use of a few words and the first use of two or three words together, only being passed finally by a brother whose general ability was somewhat greater, in the use of complex sentences, the correct use of 'why' and the expression of reasoned thought. The child with a high degree of innate specific verbal ability will show it by incessantly practising with new sounds and new words, and sometimes by a kind of superlative overflow or surplus of words in expressing an idea. Thus Y at $3:1\frac{1}{2}$ said 'I saw a man a long time ago yesterday.' In some cases there will be the invention by the child of a name for something when he does not know the real name.

The acquisition of language develops substantially parallel with the progress in other aspects of child development, e.g. adaptive movements and social behaviour. The co-operation of general ability in all such special lines of development itself makes a link. Nevertheless, in a good many cases there is some delay in speech development even without any apparent anatomical defect, while in other cases language development is ahead of the other aspects, when compared with average standards. In a few cases there are extraordinary individual differences in the first year or two. Perhaps the most remarkable example on

record is that of a little girl tested by Terman. At the age of
2 : 0 she read fluently from a child's primer, which would
suggest a mental age of 6 : 5 or 7 : 0, i.e. an I.Q. of over 300,
whereas the estimates of the greatest geniuses put them only
about 200.

As to wider surveys, Gesell reports that a few children
he tested have used as many as 150 different words by the
age of 1 : 3, whereas the average number at 1 : 6 is only
about 15 to 25, according to different investigators. On the
other hand, Gesell reports that among normal children
cases in which only one or two words have been spoken by
1 : 6 are not rare. He sums up as follows: 'When a child has
not begun to use words by the age of 18 to 24 months, and
even a little above the latter age, caution must be used in
estimating the significance of this fact. If the child gives
other evidence of normal potentialities, and is not hampered
by deafness, the outlook is favourable, and it may be stated
with confidence that the child will eventually talk. It is
necessary to inquire into circumstances in the home and
past history, to determine whether there is likelihood of
suppression on an emotional basis, a history of severe illness at about the usual age of starting to talk, or a home
situation which fails to supply normal encouragement of
talking.'

Sometimes a child with quite adequate verbal ability will
be content to express himself in very feeble imitations of
the words he hears, and if the mother continues to interpret
these and adapt herself to them, proper language may be
long deferred. Or, again, a child's specially forceful and
independent personality may result in language substantially of the child's own invention. A notable example of
this was the child of the famous German psychologist, Carl
Stumpf, who said that his boy's speech in the third year
gave the impression of a foreign language. Then at the age
of about 3 : 3 the boy suddenly began to speak good German,
as though, his father writes, 'the Holy Ghost had descended
upon him.'

The innate basis of specific verbal ability. In the most comprehensive survey of the vast field of research on language development, that by Professor Dorothea McCarthy [72], the author reports that there is general agreement that, in the first few years at least, girls on the average slightly surpass boys in all types of tests of language development. As, judging from most forms of tests, the general intelligence of boys and girls seems to be approximately the same at least during infancy and early childhood, this superiority of girls in language is in itself one item of evidence that varied verbal abilities in different individuals have some innate basis. As to this innate basis, Burt concludes [19]: 'The superior verbal fluency of the feminine sex, the marked verbal deficiencies of certain families and stocks, the appearance of both verbal abilities and verbal disabilities at an early age, the fact that in orphanages and similar institutions, children showing exceptional verbal ability often prove to have had at least one parent who was verbally gifted, and finally the positive correlation between factor-measurements for members (especially remote members) of the same family – all these facts taken together lend strong support to the hypothesis that verbal aptitude is to a large extent inborn.'

Vocabularies at various ages. The range of vocabularies of children at any given age varies enormously, and, of course, as already indicated, their variations depend greatly upon the efforts of parents and the influence of companions and teachers.

The number of words understood always exceeds the number of words spoken by the children. In estimating the active vocabulary of the child (i.e. words spoken) inquiries have usually relied on the reports of mothers, as the child must be observed over a period of days or weeks, to be sure that all words spoken are included. The standard of precision set by the various mothers would be apt to vary considerably; even so, that could hardly account for the enormous range reported by Gesell among forty children from middle-class homes, at the age of 2:0. Of twenty-eight of these the mothers said the vocabulary was so extensive that they could not estimate them, whereas others reported only ten, nine, six, and even five words.

By means of tests with pictures and by questions the correct answers to which depended on the understanding of some word included in the question, one investigator tested 268 American children, ages 0:8 to 6:0, to find the number of words spoken or understood [72]. The average number of words understood at the early ages were as follows:

2:0 272   3:0 896   4:0 1,540   5:0 2,072

(The I.Q.s of the children from 3:0 upwards averaged about 108.)

With these averages we may contrast the number of words actually spoken and used correctly by the son of one of my former students. At 2:0 the boy *used* 566 words, including eight pronouns and eleven prepositions. At 3:0 he used 1,020 words. At both ages it will be seen the number was far beyond the average given above for words either spoken or only understood. (I have given full details from age 1:0 elsewhere [102].) I may add that, like one or two of my own children with marked verbal ability, he would play with the use of words he could not understand. Thus at 2:0 he might suddenly in the middle of a meal, and *a propos* of nothing at all, exclaim 'Absolutely, Daddy!'

Finally, I add another extreme example of a precocious vocabulary together with the I.Q. at different ages. It is that of a child whom I will label W, the daughter of a friend who is a professional psychologist, and very experienced in applying intelligence and other tests. The I.Q. estimates were as follows:

Age	Test	I.Q.
2:10	Valentine	144
3:4	Terman and Merrill	160
4:5	Valentine	143
6:3	Terman and Merrill	147

This was an only child who spent most of the time with her mother. Her (active) vocabulary scores (words *used*) were as follows:

Age 1:6, 50   1:9, 305   2:0, 730

Now my boy B's I.Q. scores were extremely similar to those of W given above – i.e. about 145–150. As the eldest child he also spent nearly all his time during the first few years with his mother or myself. Yet my estimate of his vocabulary (spoken) at 1:8 was about 21 with perhaps half a dozen more. Yet W at 1:6 had 50, at 1:9 she used 305; and her father's criterion was strict, for a word was not scored until it had been used correctly at least twice, without the child being able to mimic an adult who had just used it. The girl W, I may add, at 6:3 passed the Terman and Merrill Vocabulary Test at the 10+ level easily and was approximating to the 14-year-old level.

Verbalism and fluency. We have already seen that general ability is intimately mingled with the acquisition of language, but special verbal abilities sometimes overwhelm the influence of 'g'. Thus one often comes across persons with extremely weak capacity for reasoning who have a remarkably extensive vocabulary, even if many of the words are used very vaguely and incorrectly. Their thinking often seems to be dominated by hackneyed phrases and simple proverbs, such as 'Live and let live', or 'There's no smoke without fire'. In addition, such persons may have another quality – 'fluency'. Words pour out in a torrent. Fluency is sometimes helped by 'g', but it seems to be largely a temperamental trait – a kind of emotionality or lack of inhibition [101 and 108]. High verbal ability combined with fluency often give at first a false impression of intelligence in an adult or a child and only longer experience of dealing with the individual, or careful intelligence tests, reveals the truth.

Number ability and mathematics. There is ample evidence for the existence of a special ability involved in the manipulation of numbers. Undoubtedly 'g' is important for most forms of arithmetical work and for mathematics. Indeed, up to the standard of work done by the average pupil of 14 or 15 years of age, 'g' seems more important for mathematics than all the other specific factors involved.

In the more mechanical number operations, however, such as adding and subtracting, the specific number ability reveals itself at an early age. Here again great individual differences reveal themselves, as they do in other operations with numbers. Thus in one Binet test, assigned to 8-year-olds, the child is required to count from twenty backwards. Burt found that already at 5 years of age 5·7 per cent of the children could do this, while as late as 10 years of age 4 per cent could not. He also found that the test was a harder one for girls than for boys. Now it is undoubtedly impossible to rule out the possible influence of special training in such tests; but, as with verbal ability, the individual differences are so enormous that the results do suggest great individual differences in innate ability as well. So do the sex differences.

Still more striking are Burt's findings with the test of repeating seven numbers read out to the children in haphazard order. This test was assigned to the age of 11, but Burt found that 2·5 per cent of the 6-year-olds and 5·8 per cent of the 7-year-olds could do it, while about 20 per cent of the 13-year-olds could not, and even 7·7 per cent of the 14-year-olds could not. Now on performance in this test, practice seems to have very little further effect after a short time. Thus one American inquiry showed that the average memory span for digits remained at six for ages 10 to 16, and was less than seven on the average for the ages 17, 18, and 19 combined.

Mathematical geniuses. Where the abilities, both general and special, are sufficiently great and the interest in numbers or in mathematics intense, it may even be possible to dispense with training. Thus Blaise Pascal, the celebrated French philosopher and mathematician, was told by his father that, until he was 12, he must study Latin and Greek before mathematics, and the father put away all mathematical books.

This roused the child's curiosity and he begged his father to teach him mathematics, but his father still refused. Blaise asked what geometry was and his father told him it dealt with making accurate figures and finding their relation to one another; but he forbade his son to think or speak of it again. The boy, however, began on his own to draw accurate figures with charcoal, and finally rediscovered for himself several of the propositions of the first book of Euclid, including the proof that the sum of the angles of a triangle is equal to two right angles [8].

Even more remarkable precocity for dealing with numbers was shown by Gauss, aptly described as 'the prince of mathematicians'. 'Gerhard Gauss was making out the weekly pay-roll for the labourers under his charge, unaware that his young son (then under the age of 3) was following the proceedings with critical attention. Coming to the end of his long computations, Gerhard was startled to hear the little boy pipe up, "Father, the reckoning is wrong, it should be . . ." A check of the account showed that the figure named by the boy Gauss was correct.'

At his first school Arithmetic was not studied for the first two years. When Gauss, aged 9, entered the first Arithmetic class the master gave them a long addition sum 'of the following sort, $81297 + 81495 + 81693 + \ldots + 100899$, where the step from one number to the next is the same all along (here 198) and a given number of terms (here 100) are to be added' [8].

The master, knowing the formula to apply, could find the total without adding. The class took an hour to do the sum; but in a minute or two Gauss, spotting the relation between the numbers, spontaneously devised the right formula and found the answer in a few moments; and he was right and all the others wrong.

As a contrast we may mention Emerson, whose high general ability and verbal ability is indicated by the fact that, at the age of 3, his father recorded that he 'did not read very well'. Up to the age of 14 the study of all subjects was 'no hardship to him' except for Mathematics 'in which he was always dull' [28].

Practical ability. As we have already pointed out, it is a popular fallacy that a child who is below average intelligence usually compensates for this by having a high degree of 'practical ability'. Most of the capacities which are regarded as evidence of practical ability involve 'g' to a considerable extent, except such as require merely manual dexterity, and we saw in the last chapter that there is a fairly high correlation between scores in performance tests and verbal tests of intelligence. Indeed, one investigator, who has especially stressed the importance of practical ability and the value of performance tests, found that the special factor involved in performance tests was no more important, even in technical school shop work, than was 'g', and much less important than a character quality involving 'persistence' [2].

Nevertheless, in his early investigations in London, Burt concluded that there was some special factor or factors involved in performance tests, and later he concluded that there were at least two important ones, the spatial factor and the mechanical factor [19]. The spatial factor 'appeared to be concerned essentially with the ability to perceive, interpret, or mentally rearrange objects as spatially related'. The mechanical factor 'appeared to be concerned chiefly with ability to appreciate processes of mechanical causation. It thus involved an understanding of dynamic relations rather than merely static; and manifested itself in tests not only of apprehension and comprehension, but also of construction and performance'.

While Burt and Vernon have emphasized that in older children (11:0 or more) and in adults such factors appear to depend largely on experience and training, Burt points out that there were indications of an innate ability 'leading its possessor to learn more speedily when the appropriate training or experience was supplied'.

Another investigator found evidence of a special spatial ability revealing itself in boys as early as 7:0; and Burt emphasizes that the two practical-ability factors are much more evident among boys than among girls.

In the child of school age special interests and hobbies soon begin to modify differences in practical ability. The child of good intelligence and good verbal capacities is likely to develop an interest in reading which may so grow as to leave him with little time for carpentry or drawing, even if he could have done both very well. On the other hand, the child with poor verbal abilities or rather low 'g' is likely to turn to handicraft and other more practical hobbies and to neglect his reading more and more.

Interests in the school. We have already seen the close relation that may exist between special abilities and interests, particularly in arithmetic, mathematics, and foreign languages. So far as the particular abilities (and the requisite 'g') involved in a particular subject are decidedly strong, so far the interest in the subject is likely to be a stable one. For the majority of pupils, however, other influences may be the main factors – especially that of the particular teacher taking the subject that term. However, it need not be thought abnormal if a child loves history one year and hates it the next. It may not, of course, be merely the personality of the teacher that counts, but the method. A boy with a poor rote-memory for dates may dislike a history lesson which is largely the cramming of facts, but love it when it is a study of the lives of great men.

In some cases there are inevitable changes in the abilities

needed at different stages of the subject. Thus, as a rule, verbal memorizing is largely involved in the earliest years of Latin; in advanced work the intellectual processes involved are much more complicated. Thus a child who fares well at one end may not be so good at the other, and his liking may vary accordingly.

In addition to individual fluctuations from year to year in the interest felt by a child for a particular subject, we find some remarkable changes in the average popularity of some subjects when one age is compared with another, or one period compared with a period ten years or more later. I have already referred to two big researches on this subject and have summarized results of several others elsewhere [101], but I may give one or two of the more striking results here.

Wide inquiries in 1912, 1925, and 1935, made in elementary schools in London and Worcestershire, showed that with boys Handwork consistently came first or second – including classes with average ages of 7, 10, and 13. With boys Grammar and Scripture (after 7:0) come bottom, or very near the bottom. In the last year at school (14:0) one main criterion for liking a subject is whether it is going to be a help in getting a job or keeping it, and one boy wrote, 'Scripture will be no use to me after I am 14'! In general, Scripture fares better with the girls.

Arithmetic tends to be either very high or very low in a child's preference. In yet another inquiry about over 1,000 pupils in primary schools (only about 100 of them boys) Arithmetic was the best-liked subject by 13 per cent but the least liked by 18 per cent. Even the popular Handwork, put first by 35 per cent of the children of 9 years, was put last by 3 per cent of them.

When we consider preferences in the grammar schools, we are dealing partly with older adolescents, past the age of childhood proper; but in Pritchard's research referred to earlier, if we consider only those of the lower ages we find the following results:

The best-liked subject is put at the top, the least-liked are below:

Boys	$12\frac{1}{2}$	13	$13\frac{1}{2}$	14
Best-liked	Chemistry	Chemistry	Chemistry	Chemistry
	History	History	History	English
Least-liked	Algebra	Physics	Geometry	Geometry
	Geometry	Geometry	Latin	Latin

Girls	$12\frac{1}{2}$	13	$13\frac{1}{2}$	14
Best-liked	English	English	English	English
	History	History	History	History
Least-liked	Latin	Geometry	Geometry	Physics
	Geometry	Latin	Latin	Geometry

This inquiry, it should be added, was made in 1934 when Latin was more frequently studied than it is at present. Of course, as we have seen, such averages conceal marked individual differences; but clearly at that time it was no abnormality in a child if his liking for Geometry and Latin was very low, and it does seem as though a child who greatly preferred Geometry or Latin to all other subjects would be something of an 'abnormality' at these ages, and a very promising one.

Interests outside school. These are so varied that we have not room even to mention all. In recent years the cinema, radio, and television have stolen more and more time from individual hobbies; but it is worth noting that in at least one extensive inquiry it was found that many children who said they spent most of their spare time listening to the radio, revealed that there were other things they would rather do if they had the opportunity.

As to reading, it seems that we must accept as normal the reading of 'comics' and bloods. Thus in one inquiry in England among 3,000 pupils (not grammar-school pupils), about 90 per cent of the boys of 11 : 0 read bloods or comics;

about 80 per cent of the girls read comics, but they rarely read the 'bloods'. Naturally there are substantial differences in the reading of the more intelligent children in the grammar schools, even when we confine ourselves to the children under 15. Still more notable differences were found by Terman among highly gifted children, with I.Q.s of over 130. On the average, the gifted child of 7:0 read more books in two months than the average of the control group children right up to the age of 15:0. Also the range of topics was much greater among the gifted children, who read especially far less 'emotional fiction', though the most popular books even with the gifted were fiction.

While we are considering the gifted child I might add some further facts as to the wider play interests of these highly intelligent children.

1. The gifted boys were by no means effeminate in their preferences for types of games; indeed, they slightly exceeded the control group boys in their preference for sports and games and hobbies which were more characteristic of boys in general than of girls.

2. The gifted children tend to prefer play activities which are characteristic of the older rather than the younger control children. The gifted children also tend to prefer games of a quiet type more than do the control children.

3. Rather more gifted children than control are regarded by other children as 'queer' or 'different' in their recreations, though the number of these is small, and a marked preference for reading over games was the the most frequent accusation against the boys.

Special reference may be made to the making of collections, because these sometimes seem so futile that many parents and teachers may consider them very peculiar, if not really abnormal. They may include, for example, such useless and unattractive objects as bus tickets, used match stalks, match boxes, registration numbers of motor cars, names of railway engines. The gem of my own records is 'names of makers of wash-basins' collected by one of my university graduate women students. How common collecting is even among the more intellectual children is shown by the fact that among over 300 university graduates I found that about 98 per cent had collected something at some time, and most had made several different collections. The peak age for frequency of collecting is round about 9 to 11 or 12. Most collections are temporary affairs, but some with general associated intellectual interests, e.g. postage stamps with their geographical, historical, and aesthetic interests, may last a long time. Even here, however, it looks as though there is often some inborn and irrational urge to collect as the basis of collecting, for the genuine collector wants to do the collecting himself, and not simply be presented with a ready-made collection.

In this chapter one of my main purposes has been to bring home to readers (a) that a child may be above average intelligence and yet very weak in one special ability and so hindered in the type of work for which that is important; and (b) that a child of intelligence below average may have some specific abilities to such a high degree that he may excel at least to a limited extent in particular kinds of work. There are many researches, however, on special abilities which I have not had space to discuss. Readers who want to go further may be referred to the appropriate chapters in one of my own books [101], and for much fuller and more detailed accounts of a wide range of researches to a book by Professor Vernon [108] and to the article by Sir Cyril Burt [19].

CHAPTER 15

The Adolescent Child

WITH the adolescent (roughly 'the teenager') we are beginning to get beyond the period covered by the title of this book. By middle or at least late adolescence the individual is a rather curious blend, half-adult and half-child; certainly he usually dislikes being called a child or treated as one. Nevertheless, even if we regard this book as being concerned with children up to 14 or 15 only, we must say something about adolescence, as many children, girls especially, mature sexually by that age. We shall, however, only attempt a brief forward-looking survey, and not try to summarize more than a fraction of the vast amount of research which has been carried out on the period of adolescence.

Some account of the period is also particularly apt for us, as most adolescents betray conduct and traits which to most parents and many teachers seem strange abnormalities, if not actually neurotic symptoms.

The age of puberty. The beginning of adolescence is usually taken as dating from puberty, the time of the maturing of the sex organs. Puberty, however, even among boys or girls of the same race, occurs at very varied ages. Different inquirers have come to different conclusions, but in Great Britain and the U.S.A. about two-thirds of the girls begin menstruation between the ages of about $12\frac{1}{2}$ and $15\frac{1}{2}$. About one-sixth begin before the age of $12\frac{1}{2}$ and one-sixth later than $15\frac{1}{2}$. Even among healthy girls the age varies from 9 : 0 or less to about 20. The onset of puberty among boys is much harder to discover precisely, but there is general agreement that on the average it is somewhat later than that for girls.

The evidence on the whole suggests that some temperamental changes do follow close on the outset of puberty, but the special psychological characteristics of adolescents do not at once reveal themselves in those who reach puberty abnormally early, while some may precede puberty. The characteristic traits of adolescents are instability of emotional moods, marked alternations of feelings of joy and depression, the intensity of some interests and yet their changeability, great stubbornness at times and yet remarkable submission to a chosen leader. Somewhere in adolescence is the peak age both for religious conversions and for juvenile delinquency. We must, however, stress the fact that there is no sudden and marked change which distinguishes the adolescent from the child in middle childhood, any more than there was a marked change from infancy to early childhood. Furthermore, some adolescents seem to betray none of these trends we have mentioned as characteristic; others show some, but only to a mild degree. When such changes do come they are not merely a result of physiological changes, sex or others, though these have a marked influence. The difficulties are partly due to the new problems in the social life of the child – the choice of a future occupation, the readjustment to parents when the adolescent feels he is now a man (or woman) and has a right to independence, and the adjustment of the attitudes of self to the new and often baffling impulses and emotions roused by sex maturity.

The attitude to the opposite sex. In many boys at the beginning of adolescence or shortly before there is apt to be an intensified antagonism, or at least indifference towards girls, and *vice versa.* Already, indeed, in middle childhood the very types of games each sex specially likes tend to separate the sexes. Then during adolescence the opposite sex begins to be rather attractive. Of 220 university graduates (100 men and 120 women) from whom I gathered anonymous reports, 43 per cent of the men and 45 per cent of the women said they had experienced intensified aversion for the opposite sex during adolescence; but an intensified interest in some member of the opposite sex at some time in adolescence (later in the case of those who reported both experiences) was reported by 84 per cent of the men and 61 per cent of the women. Even before the maturing of the sex organs, however, some of the young adolescents and even younger children may experience an intense awareness of the appeal of a member of the opposite sex. I well remember some three years before the onset of puberty, going home in a wonderful glow of feeling after meeting for the first time a certain little girl of my own age at a church bazaar. I had felt nothing like it before. Strong affection continued for some months, but so far was it from a mere physical attraction that the occasional kissing bored me! There are various reports in biographies of similar experiences before puberty (as of Goethe and de Musset), but I know of no estimate of its frequency based on reports for large numbers, except one as early as 1902 made by Sanford Bell [9], who gathered over 2,000 reports and confessions, partly from his own observations, partly from students; but there were no definite statements as to the ages at which puberty was reached. There were, however, so many reports as to great affection before the age of 8, or earlier, for a child of the opposite sex that we may assume that nearly all were at pre-pubertal stages, and many confessions and reports show proof of very intense devotion.

My own contribution to this question can only be based on the question I put first to eighteen men students (ages 19 to 25), whom I recently asked for anonymous reports as to whether they had had a similar *intense affection* and attraction towards a girl, before their own beginning of physical puberty. Of these eighteen men, eleven were confident they had had such an experience, nearly all at a period of two, three, or four years before puberty. Some said they had not, and one was doubtful whether the experience had preceded puberty. One man wrote: 'I was at 12 quite overwhelmed by her prettiness and saw her as quite "angelic".' Another referring to an experience at the age of 10 (puberty 14) wrote: 'It was so intense I wanted to write about it for posterity'!

I put the same question to thirteen women students (ages about 19 to 24), of whom five reported intense affection for a boy about one to three years before puberty; three reported affection but not strong. One wrote of her experience at the age of 10: 'I thought him the epitome of perfection, but he never glanced in my direction and I was plunged into absolute dejection when he so much as sat by another girl in class.'

All these students were coping satisfactorily with their work with the possible exception of one. Small as the numbers are, we can at least conclude that intense affection can be felt for a member of the opposite sex by a boy or a girl long before puberty without that being a sign of abnormality.

Masturbation. There is ample evidence that masturbation is indulged in at some time in adolescence by the great majority of boys and by a great many girls, probably more than half. So that, whatever may be thought of it, masturbation is not statistically an abnormality. Modern views of medical men suggest that, unless carried to excess, it is not physically harmful; but there is general agreement that considerable psychological harm may come from mental conflict between the powerful impulse and the feelings of guilt produced by being told it is wicked, or of fear produced by hearing it may send one mad, or shame and disgust at the abuse of the impulse and its deflection from its natural channel. Such conflicts about the impulse to masturbation are probably one of the main causes of the occasional marked depressions which many adolescents experience.

Emotional experiences and fluctuations. Before dealing with these, I would mention that some recent inquiries indicate that, for the great majority, adolescence taken as a whole is not characteristically an unhappy period [110]. As, however, the period covers some half dozen or so years, general happiness may well be consistent with there being certain times when intensely unhappy experiences come. Thus some of the assertions by earlier writers on adolescence that serious thoughts of suicide are common among adolescents is confirmed by the report by the 220 university graduates in the questionnaire I gave them. Of the men, 38 per cent said they had had '*serious*' thoughts of suicide, and so did 29 per cent of the women. Some 40 per cent of the men had also contemplated running away from home, and so had 33 per cent of the women. No doubt these young people were in reality much further from suicide than they felt themselves to be at the time; and, at any rate, the parent of an adolescent who in a temper dashes out of the room declaring he will drown himself, or go away and live his own life, need not feel that this child is altogether abnormal. On the other hand, actual suicides during adolescence are not so common as sometimes thought; they are more frequent after 20 than before, but public attention is specially called to the suicide of boys and girls.

That an adolescence which is reported as happy on the whole, may include elements of much unhappiness is indeed confirmed by one of the very researches I referred to above as showing that adolescence was not an unhappy period in general. In his inquiry among seventy-two young women in a training college, Dr W. D. Wall found that three-quarters of the group said they were on the whole happy in both childhood and adolescence. Yet of 'the 214 factors mentioned as stimuli to happiness or unhappiness in adolescence, nearly half are stated to have caused unhappiness, whereas of the 195 factors remembered from childhood, only a quarter are mentioned as having been productive of unhappiness.' About a third of this group mention sources of unhappiness being in the home.

Apart from the rarer desperate moods in which suicide or running away are contemplated, of my own graduate students 61 per cent of the men and 76 per cent of the women mention 'moods of intense dejection'. Yet quite different moods of elation were common too, and some glorious 'expectation of future greatness' was reported by 66 per cent of the men and 57 per cent of the women. As to both my own inquiry and Wall's, we must bear in mind that they were highly selected groups as to intellectual ability, though a large proportion would come from 'working-class' homes; but similar marked changes of mood to what I found were reported in another inquiry by Dr Wall among about 200 young wage-earner adolescents, with a rather low average intelligence; the terms used for this inquiry were 'good spirits' and 'downcast' or 'fed-up'.

Other characteristics of adolescence. In view of the fact that many in mid-adolescence are beyond the scope of the title of this book, and those in later adolescence certainly so, I will merely summarize here the most important facts and characteristics, especially as I have dealt with the whole period more fully elsewhere [101].

1. *The spurt in physical growth* which comes just before puberty is no excuse for inferior mental work at the time, as inquiry has shown that children tend to do better at that period than before or after the spurt.

2. The physical development of the breasts in girls, the breaking of the voice in boys, and in both sexes the frequent marked development of hands and nose, all help to increase the *self-consciousness* of adolescents. The development of sex and interest in the opposite sex also tends to increase the concern about personal appearance.

3. An intense affection of an adolescent girl for a senior girl or woman teacher (a 'crush' or 'pash' or G.P.) is very common, more particularly among those in girls' schools

who have little contact with boys or men. Such experiences can be highly emotional. Some of my women students have described how they have cherished a photo of a beloved schoolmistress, or a book of hers, or have walked past her lighted window at night and gazed at it like a fond lover. My own records were enough to show that such an affection is quite consistent with the girl becoming normal later on in her relation to men, and with great success in the intellectual and social life of a university.

In the case of boys there is sometimes an intense affection of an older boy for a younger, an affection quite unaccompanied by any objectionable physical homosexuality. Such affections (both of boys and girls) are much rarer in co-educational schools.

4. Marked changes in the *attitude to parents* are common, but very varied. As we saw in Chapter 12, in early adolescence the child may first realize his responsibility to his parents, but later the feeling of 'growing up' and the intensification of individual friendship and of group interests often lead to a lessening of the influence of the parents, though affection may remain as great or even increase. There is often for a time much contradicting and stubbornness and contra-suggestibility. Some adolescents rise to high levels of idealism, sometimes impracticable ones; and this may lead to a critical attitude towards a parent who is more realistic.

5. A high degree of *intelligence*, on the whole, helps adjustment to difficulties; but when an adolescent is definitely superior in intelligence to his parents that may accentuate some conflicts. On the other hand, dullness (I.Q.s about 80 to 90) may accentuate difficulties at home if parents expect too much, and cause frustration at school through the child being unable to keep up with most of his own age.

6. The *variability* and fluctuations of the adolescent are often shown in his interests and hobbies. He is apt to take up one thing with excessive enthusiasm and then drop it in a month or two and turn to something quite different.

Are neurotic symptoms normal in adolescents? The frequent extremes of emotion, the sudden changes in adolescence, and the irrationality of many impulsive actions, may well give the impression of temporary neuroticism. There were ample signs of such emotional disturbances in many of the confidential essays on adolescence written for me by university graduates, the great majority of whom were certainly not generally neurotic at that stage. Still more glaring examples are given by Dr W. D. Wall, who states that a quarter of one club group he observed showed behaviour extreme enough to be described at any other period as neurotic – e.g. useless violence with furniture, obstinate silence, the bitter weeping of a girl and locking herself in a room because a friend had deserted her for another, calculated impatience, and so on [110].

We may note here that one inquiry with the Rorschach test (giving interpretations of irregular shapes, such as are made by folding over and pressing an inkblot on paper, but with the shapes coloured) found that the supposed signs of neuroticism were revealed by about one-third of 145 'normal' adolescents [60]. The authors suggest that their findings show the unreliability of some interpretation of scores on the Rorschach test. I hold no brief for the Rorschach test, and indeed am sceptical about its value for discriminating between the temperaments of normal children, as are others much more familiar with the test [107]. But it seems to me that a good many adolescents may at times display emotional reactions which might be classified as neurotic if and when they occur in the mature adult. Happily most adolescents settle down later into a steadier life and experience. We may end this book then on the note sounded in our opening chapters. Many symptoms in the young child and adolescent, which to some appear bad signs of present or coming abnormality, are so common as to be normal. The normal child has his individual, if usually trivial, abnormalities; and many adolescents have, temporarily at least, rather serious ones.

BIBLIOGRAPHY

The following abbreviations are used:

B.J.P.   British Journal of Psychology
B.J.E.P.   British Journal of Educational Psychology
B.J. Stat. P. British Journal of Statistical Psychology
J. Gen. P.   Journal of Genetic Psychology
J. Exp. Ped. Journal of Experimental Pedagogy
J. Ed. Res. Journal of Educational Research
Ch. Devel.   Child Development

The numbers after names of journals refer to volumes

1. ADLER, ALFRED. *Understanding Human Nature*, 1927
2. ALEXANDER, W. P. 'Intelligence Concrete and Abstract,' *B.J.P.*, Monograph Sup. No. 19, 1935
3. ALLPORT, G. W. *Personality: A Psychological Interpretation*, 1938
4. AVELING, F., and HARGREAVES, H. L. 'Suggestibility with and without Prestige', *B.J.P.*, xii, 1921
5. BACH, D. R. 'Father Fantasies in Father-separated Children', *Ch. Devel.*, XVII, 1946
6. BACHARACH, A. L. *Lives of the Great Composers*, Vol. 1 (Pelican Books), 1935
7. BANNISTER, H., and RAVDEN, M. 'The Environment and the Child', *B.J.P.*, XXXV, 1945
8. BELL, E. T. *Men of Mathematics*, Vol. 1 (Pelican Books), 1953
9. BELL, S. *Amer. Jour. of Psych.*, XIII, 1902
9A. BIRCH, L. B. 'The Incidence of Nail Biting among School Children', *B.J.E.P.*, XXV, 1955
10. BLATZ, W. *The Five Sisters*, 1938
11. BRIDGES, K. *Social and Emotional Development of the Pre-School Child*, 1929
12. BÜHLER, CHARLOTTE. 'The Social Behaviour of Children', *Handbook of Child Psychology*, 1933
13. BURT, SIR CYRIL. *The Backward Child*, 1937
14. BURT, SIR CYRIL. Article in *Character and Personality*, VII, 1939
15. BURT, SIR CYRIL. 'The Development of Reasoning in School Children', *J. Exp. Ped.*, V, 1919
16. BURT, SIR CYRIL. *The Distribution and Relation of Educational Abilities*, 1917

17. BURT, SIR CYRIL. 'The Education of the Adolescent', *B.J.E.P.*, XIII, 1943
18. BURT, SIR CYRIL. *Mental and Scholastic Tests*, 1921, 2nd Edit., 1947
19. BURT, SIR CYRIL. 'The Structure of the Mind', *B.J.E.P.*, XIX, 1949
20. BURT, SIR CYRIL. *The Subnormal Mind*, 1935
21. BURT, SIR CYRIL. *The Young Delinquent*, 1925
22. BURT, SIR CYRIL, and HOWARD, M. 'The Nature and Causes of Maladjustment among Children of School Age', *B.J. Stat. P.*, V, 1952
23. BURT, SIR CYRIL, and MOORE, R. C. 'The Mental Differences between the Sexes', *J. Exp. Ped.*, I, 1912
24. CAREY, N. 'Factors in the Mental Processes of School Children', *B.J.P.*, VII, 1915
25. CHANEY, L. B., and MCGRAW, M. B. *Bulletin Neurol. Inst. New York*, II, 1932
26. CLARK, E. J. 'Teachers and their Evaluation of Objectional Pupil Behaviour', *J. Ed. Res.*, 1951
27. CLARKE, R. T. A. *Twelve Delinquent Cases*, M.A. Thesis, Univ. of Nottingham, 1950
28. COX, C. M. *Genetic Studies of Genius*, Vol. II, 1926
29. CRANE, A. R. 'Pre-adolescent Gang', *J. Gen. P.*, VIII, 1952
30. CULPIN, M. *Mental Abnormality*, 1948
31. CUMMINGS, J. D. *B.J.E.P.*, XIV, 1944
32. CUMMINGS, J. D. *B.J.E.P.*, XVI, 1946
33. DEARBORN, G. V. N. *Motor Sensory Development*, 1910
34. DEARBORN, W. F., and ROTHNEY, J. W. M. *Predicting the Child's Development*, 1941
34A. DENNIS, W. 'Infant Development under Conditions of Restricted Practice and of Minimum Social Stimulation', *J. Gen. P.*, LIII, 1938
35. DILLON, M. R. *Ch. Devel.*, V, 1934
36. EYSENCK, H. J. *Uses and Abuses of Psychology* (Pelican Books), 1953
37. EYSENCK, H. J., and PRELL, D. B. 'The Inheritance of Neuroticism', *Jour. of Mental Science*, XCVII, 1951
38. FLEMING, C. M. 'Socio-economic Level and Test Performance', *B.J.E.P.*, XIII, 1943
39. FREUD, SIGMUND. *Introductory Lectures on Psycho-Analysis*, 1922
40. FREUD, SIGMUND. 'Female Sexuality', *Inter. Jour. of Psycho-Analysis*, XIII, 1931
41. GESELL, A. *The First Five Years of Life*, 1941
42. GESELL, A. *The Mental Growth of the Pre-School Child*, 1925
43. GESELL, A., and ILG, F. L. *The Child from Five to Ten*, 1946
44. GESELL, A., and others. *Biographies of Child Development*, 1939
45. GESELL, A., and THOMPSON, H. *Infant Behaviour*, 1934

46. GOODENOUGH, F. *Anger in Young Children*, 1931

47. GOODENOUGH, F. L., and MAURER, K. *The Mental Growth of Children from Two to Fourteen Years*, 1942

48. GORDON, R. G. *The Neurotic Personality*, 1927

49. HALL, E. M. 'A Study of Children's Activity with Plastic Material', *B.J.E.P.*, IX, 1939

50. HALLWORTH, H. J. 'Group Relationship among Grammar School Boys and Girls', *Sociometry*, XVI, 1953

51. HART, B. *The Psychology of Insanity*, 1912

52. HARTSHORNE, H., and MAY, M. *Studies in Deceit*, 1930

53. HARTSHORNE, H., MAY, M., and SHUTTLEWORTH, F. *Studies in the Organization of Character*, 1930

54. HETZER, H. *Zeitschrift für Pädagogische Psych.*, 1929

55. HOLLINGWORTH, L. S. *Gifted Children*, 1929

56. HOLLINGWORTH, L. S. *Special Talents and Defects*, 1923

57. HOPKINS, K. D. 'Punishment in Schools', *B.J.E.P.*, IX, 1939

58. ISAACS, S. 'Neurotic Difficulties in Young Children', *B.J.E.P.*, II, 1932

59. ISAACS, S. *Social Development in Young Children*, 1933

60. IVES, V., GRANT, M. Q., and RANZONI, J. H. 'The "Neurotic" Rorschachs of Normal Adolescents', *J. Gen. P.*, 1953

61. JAMES, W. *Principles of Psychology*, II, 1901

62. JERSILD, A. T. *Child Psychology*, 4th Edit., 1954

63. JERSILD, A. T. Chapter on 'Emotional Development', *Manual of Child Psych.*, 2nd Edit., 1954

64. JERSILD, A. T., and HOLMES, F. B. *Children's Fears*, 1935

65. JERSILD, A. T., GOLDMAN, B., and LOFTUS, J. J. *Jour. of Exper. Education*, IX, 1941

66. JERSILD, A. T., MARKEY, F. V., and JERSILD, C. L. *Children's Fears, Dreams, Wishes, etc.*, 1933

67. JONES, V. Chapter on 'Character Development in Children', *Manual of Child Psych.*, 2nd Edit., 1954

68. KELLOGG, W. N., and L. A. *The Ape and the Child*, 1933

69. KORNER, A. F. *Some Aspects of Hostility in Young Children*, 1949

70. LEWIN, K. Chapter on 'Behaviour and Development as a Function of the Total Situation', *Manual of Child Psych.*, 2nd Edit., 1954

71. LONG, A. 'Parents' Reports of Undesirable Behaviour in Children', *Ch. Devel.*, XII, 1941

72. MCCARTHY, D. Chapter on 'Language Development in Children', *Manual of Child Psych.*, 2nd Edit., 1954

73. MACAULAY, E. 'Social, Age, and Sex Differences in Children's Choice of Ideals', *Forum of Education (English)*, III, 1925

74. MACAULAY, E., and WATKINS, S. H. 'Development of the Moral Conceptions of Children', *Forum of Education*, IV, 1926

75. MCDOUGALL, W. *Introduction to Social Psychology*, 9th Edit., 1915

Bibliography

76. MCFARLAND, M. B. 'Relationships between Young Sisters as Revealed in their Overt Responses', *Ch. Devel. Monographs*, No. 23
77. MACFARLANE, J. W. *Studies in Child Guidance*, I, 1938
78. MCGRAW, M. B. Chapter on 'Maturation of Behaviour', *Manual of Child Psych.*, 1st Edit., 1946
79. MALONE, A. J., and MASSLER, M. *Jour. of Abnormal and Social Psych.*, XLVII, 1952
80. MICHAEL, W. B., HERROLD, E. E., and CRYAN, E. W. 'Survey of Student-Teacher Relationships', *Jour. Ed. Res.*, 1951
81. MOLL, A. *Sexual Life of the Child*, 1912
82. MURPHY, L. B. *Social Behaviour and Child Personality*, 1937
83. NATIONAL FOUNDATION FOR EDUCATIONAL RESEARCH. *A Survey of Rewards and Punishments in Schools*, 1952
84. ORGLER, H. *Alfred Adler*, 1939
85. PIAGET, J. *The Moral Judgment of the Child*, 1932
86. PREYER, W. *The Senses and the Will*
87. PRITCHARD, R. A. 'The Relative Popularity of Secondary School Subjects at Various Ages', *B.J.E.P.*, V, 1935
88. RIVERS, W. H. R. *Instinct and the Unconscious*, 1920
89. RUSSELL, BERTRAND. *On Education*, 1926
90. SEARS, R. R., PINTLER, M. H., and SEARS, P. S. 'Effect of Father Separation on Preschool Children's Doll Play Aggression', *Ch. Devel.*, XVII, Dec. 1946
91. SEWELL, W. H., and MUSSEN, P. H. 'Effects of Feeding, Weaning and Scheduling Procedure on Childhood Adjustment and the Formation of Oral Symptoms', *Ch. Devel.*, XXIII, 1952
92. SHAKESPEARE, J. J. 'An Enquiry into the Relative Popularity of School Subjects in Elementary Schools', *B.J.E.P.*, VI, 1936
93. SHINN, M. W. *Notes on the Development of a Child*, I and II, 1907 and 1909
94. SHIRLEY, M. *The First Two Years*, Vols. I, II, and III, 1931-3
95. SIMPSON, M. *Parent Preferences of Young Children*, 1935
96. STENDLER, C. B., and YOUNG, N. 'Impact of Beginning First Grade upon Socialization as Reported by Mothers', *Ch. Devel.*, XXI, 1950
97. STERN, W. *Psychology of Early Childhood*, 1924
98. STOUT, G. F. *Analytic Psychology*, 1902, and *Manual of Psychology*, 5th Edit., revised by C. A. Mace, 1938
99. SULLY, J. *Studies of Childhood*, 1912
100. TERMAN, L. M. *Genetic Studies of Genius*, Vol. I, 2nd Edit., 1926
101. VALENTINE, C. W. *Psychology and its Bearing on Education*, 1950
102. VALENTINE, C. W. *Psychology of Early Childhood*, 3rd Edit., 1946
103. VALENTINE, C. W. *Parents and Children*, 1953
104. VALENTINE, C. W. *The Difficult Child and the Problem of Discipline*, 5th Edit., 1950 (now out of print)

Bibliography

105. VALENTINE, C. W. *Intelligence Tests for Children*, 5th Edit., 1953

106. VALENTINE, C. W. 'Reflexes in Early Childhood', *Brit. Jour. Medical Psych.*, VII, 1927

106A. VALENTINE, C. W. *Handbook of Instructions* with *Reasoning Tests for Higher Levels of Intelligence*, 1954

107. VERNON, P. E. *Personality Tests and Assessments*, 1953

108. VERNON, P. E. *The Structure of Human Abilities*, 1950

109. WAKELAM, B. B. 'The Application of a New Intelligence Test in an Infants' School and the Prediction of Backwardness', *B. J. E. P.*, XIV, 1944

110. WALL, W. D. *The Adolescent Child*, 1948

111. WALLAS, G. *The Great Society*, 1914

112. WATSON, J. B. *Psychology from the Standpoint of a Behaviorist*, 2nd Edit., 1924

113. WILSON, F. T. 'Some Special Ability Test Scores of Gifted Children', *J. Gen. P.*, LXXXII, 1953

114. WOODWORTH, R. S. *Psychology: A Study of Mental Life*, 12th Edit., 1940

The Experimental Psychology of Beauty by C. W. Valentine, published in 1962 by Methuen, contains many details of children's reactions to colours, shapes, pictures, music, and poetry, and of tests of aesthetic sensibility.

Abilities, group, 251
  independence of general and special, 252
Ability, general, 225, 233
  individual differences in, 234
  influence on school work, 245
  maturing of, 245
Adler, A., 75
Affection, age of maturing of, 98
  disinterested, frequency of, 97
  early, 95
  towards parents, 102
Age and neurotic symptoms, 43
Allport, G. W., 149, 165
Ambivalence, 68
Anthropologists, 72
Anticipatory phenomena, 115
Anxiety, 19, 33
Assertiveness, playing at, 59
Attainment age, 236
Aveling, F., 163

Bain, A., 150
Bed-wetting, or Enuresis, 39, 43
Behaviourists, 67, 72
Bell, Sanford, 273
Biographical studies of children, 44
Birch, L. B., 26
Breast feeding and nervous habits, 27
Bridges, K., 52, 59, 74, 86, 97, 99
Bühler, C., 117, 168

Burt, Cyril, 124, 135, 151, 154, 195, 226, 243, 263, 265, 270

Campbell, H. F., 137
Carmichael, L., 157
Cases
  Anxiety and fear, 19
  Bullying, 20
  Claustrophobia, 18
  Madge (a fine girl in a bad home), 143
  Neurotic mothers and problem children, 16
  Night fears, 30
  Stammering, 17
Castration complex, 113
Character, 155, 193
  in gifted children, 211
Cheating, 199, 205
Churchill, Sir Winston, 173
Collections, 269
Competition, 70
Complexes, 77, 104, 113
Conditioning, 72, 141
Contra-suggestibility, 165
Correlation of orders, 230
Cummings, J. D., 33, 37, 38, 42

Day-dreaming, 33, 35
Dearborn, G. V. N., 82, 95
Dearborn, W. F., and Rothney, J. W. M., 241

Delinquency, juvenile, 124
Differences, individual
  between babies, 71
  in fears, 125
  in innate tendencies, 71, 153
  in sex maturing, 121
  in sympathetic reponses, 89
Dillon, M. R., 114, 118, 121
Dionne Quins, 52
Dissociation, 20
Drawing, specific ability in, 256
Dreams, 137
Drives, 151

Emotional
  disturbances, 33, 34
  experiences in adolescence, 275
  symptoms in infants, 32
Emotionality, general, 153
Enuresis, 39, 43
Environment, 208
Environmental influences, 146, 156
  limitations of, 142
  on language, 258
Erections in infancy, 115
Experiments
  on imitation, 159
  on suggestibility, 163
  with fear, 132

Factors, specific, 250
Father-separated children, 62;
  see also Parents.
Fear, 138
  experiments with, 132
  first innate, 125
  general factor in, 137
  in middle childhood, 135

Fear, of animals, 135
  of pain, 126
  of the dark, 133
  of the sea, 129
  of the uncanny, 127
Field psychology, 193
Fluency, 262
Food faddiness, 33
Freud, Sigmund, 13, 24, 54, 76, 78, 104, 105, 113
Friendships, 186

'g', 233
  saturation with, 234
Gangs, 184
Gauss, Gerhard, 264
Gesell, Arnold, 31, 48, 51, 53, 59, 74, 130, 147, 182, 255, 259, 261
Ghosts, 138
Gifted children, 209
  interests of, 269
Goethe, 273
Goodenough, F., 72
Gordon, R. G., 114
Group influences, limitations of, 192
  morale, 194
  play, 183
Groups, 189
'Guess who' technique, 188, 192

Habits, 160
  moral, 197
Hall, E., 60
Hallworth, H. J., 190
Handel, 255
Hartshorne, H., and May, M., 198, 200, 204, 207, 208, 211

Heredity, 144, 149, 154
Homosexuality, 277
Hopkins, K. D., 177, 217, 220
Hypnosis, 161

Ideals, 200
Imagery, 134, 253
Imaginary companions, 55
Imitation
  deliberate, 158
  primary, 158
Incentives, 220, 221
Inferiority complex, 77
  feeling, 78
Innate differences, illustrations of,
  147
Intelligence, general, 225
Intelligence quotients, 236
  constancy of, at different ages,
    240
  distribution of, 237
Intelligence tests, 226–36; *see also*
  Tests.
  popular misconception as to,
    222
Interests, in the school, 266
  influence of, 248
  outside school, 268
Isaacs, Susan, 42, 111, 114, 120,
  135, 137

James, William, 131, 150
Jealousy, 108
Jersild, A. T., 151
Jones, Vernon, 194, 211

Kellogg, W. N., and L. A., 84

Kissing, as learned sign of affection, 100
Korner, A. F., 63

Langfeld, H. S., 151
Language, 51, 258ff.
Laughter, responsive, 81
Learning, 48ff., 141, 248ff.
Lewin, K., 193
Loneliness, 184
Lying, 33, 199

Macaulay, Eve, 201, 213, 214
McCarthy, D., 260
McDougall, William, 80, 85, 105,
  127, 150
MacFarlane, J. W., 119
Maladjusted children, 176
Maladjustment, frequency in chil-
  dren, 41
Masculinity of games, 65
Masturbation, 117, 119, 274
Mathematical geniuses, 263
Maturation, 50
  and fear of animals, 130
Memory, special abilities, 251
Mental age, 236
Method in psychology, 46
Methods of investigation, 23
Moral behaviour, advance in
  middle childhood, 204
Moreno, J. L., 190
Motivation, trend of opinion on,
  150
Mozart, 255
Murphy, L. B., 86, 89
Musical abilities, 254
Musset, Alfred de, 273
Myers, C. S., 105

Index

Nail-biting, 25, 43
Nervous child, 39, 137
Neurosis, 17
Neurotic symptoms, 15, 24, 25, 42, 43
  in adolescents, 278
Night fears, 30, 137
'Normal' (as average), 21
Number ability, 263
Nursery school, influence of, 170

Obsessions, 24
Oedipus complex, 104

Pain, fear of, 126
Parents, adolescents' attitude to, 277
  child's preferences regarding, 106, 109
  reports on children by, 38
Pascal, 264
Pavlov, 142
Persistence, influence of, 250
Personality, 149
Piaget, J., 213
Play
  dramatic with dolls, 61
  early social, 51
  group, 183
  interpretations of, 60, 62, 114
  make-believe, 52
  meaning of, 47
  of gifted children, 65
  symbolic interpretations of, 53
Popularity, 195
Practical ability, 265
Precocity, in musical abilities, 255
  with numbers, 264
Prejudice in psychology, 145

Pre-school child, 167 ff.
Preyer, W., 84, 101, 129
Pritchard, R. A., 267
Protection, sympathetic, 84
Puberty, age of, 271
Punishment, 219
  children's ideas as to, 216
  corporal, 63, 217

Rebellion, 75
Rebellious period, 73
Reflex, conditioned, 142
  evanescent, 116
Regression, 44, 168
Religious ideals, 203
Rewards, opinions as to, 220
Right and wrong
  concepts of, 214
  general ideas of, 211
Rivers, W. H. R., 17
Russell, Bertrand, 172

School, effects of entrance to, 173
  grammar, selection for, 224
  interests in, 266
  interests outside, 268
  late entry to, 171
School subjects, popularity of, 267
  worries, 139
Self-assertion in infancy, 69
Sex, attitude to the opposite, 272
  curiosity about, 110
  habits, 33
  maturing, individual differences in, 121
Shinn, M. W., 49
Shirley, M., 52, 98, 161
Shuttleworth, 207

Social behaviour, 182
  from two to five, 169
  scale, 87
Sociometric studies, 188
Spencer, Herbert, 47, 150
Stealing, 33, 199
Stern, William, 84, 105, 128, 135,
  160, 161
Stout, G. F., 142
Stumpf, Carl, 259
Suggestibility, experiments on, 163
Suggestion, 132, 161 ff., 191
  as a cause of fear, 138
Suicides, 275
Sully, J., 73, 130
Sympathetic responses in infancy,
  frequency of, 85
Sympathy with distress, 82

Teachers, children's attitude to,
  176
  influence of, on popularity of
    subjects, 180
  types of, 174
Temper tantrums, 39, 69
Temperament, 149
Terman, L. M., 57, 65, 209, 255,
  259, 269
Tests
  analogies, 227

Tests
  group and individual, 239
  Merrill, Palmer, 244
  Minnesota, 244
  Moray House, 238
  non-verbal, 227
  of character, 209
  of honesty and cheating, 198
  patterns, 229
  reasoning, 234
  Rorschach, 278
  scores, fluctuation in, 239
  Stanford Binet, 243
  Terman and Merrill, 261
  Valentine Reasoning, 261
Trollope, Anthony, 172
Twins, 51, 103

Verbal ability, 257
  innate basis of, 260
Verbalism, 262
Vernon, P. E., 266, 270
Vocabulary, at various ages, 260
  precocious, 261

Wall, W. D., 275, 278
Wallas, Graham, 152
Ward, James, 142
Watkins, S. H., 214
Watson, J. B., 125, 132
Woodworth, R. S., 152